through—and He has. The stories in this book are more than just inspiring; they're proof of what God can do through someone fully surrendered.

As you read these pages, you'll get that same front-row view. You'll be stirred, challenged, and deeply encouraged. Buckle up—this is a powerful journey. The work of the ministry we read about in Acts is still happening today, and Dan's story is living proof."

George Commons
Managing Partner, The Barnabas Group Kansas City

"Every so often, a book comes out that is as life-changing and culture-shifting as it is captivating. Fearless Faith *is no doubt that book for this generation. It is not the slightest bit theological, but it will shake your theology. It is not a fiction thriller, but you won't be able to put it down. Reading this book inspires me to put my faith on the line and live fearlessly for the Kingdom!"*

Tiffany Miller Lotz
Director, Threshing Floor Equipping Center

"One of the highest praises I can give about Dan Taylor and his new book is, 'He lived it!' This is no theoretical book; it is written by a man who has walked this out through thick and thin. Dan is someone I find inspiring in his faith. As you read this book, you will be equipped and enlarged in your heart with faith to be a doer. I highly recommend this to all who want to take the adventure."

Jack Little
Church Planter

"Absolutely a must-read! Every page shouts a Holy Spirit-anointed 'Wow!' You will never read a more inspiring and compelling testimony of a lifestyle of fearless faith. From the violent streets of Chicago to the steamy jungles of the Amazon to the towering mountains of the Himalayas, Dan Taylor has carried the transformative love of Christ to places no missionary has ever been. His is an epic adventure. Join him on his remarkable journey."

Dr. Dick Eastman
President Emeritus, Every Home for Christ
President, America's National Prayer Committee

"Riveting from the very first page. I honestly could not put this book down. Vulnerable and raw, these pages burn with the presence of the Holy Spirit, inspiring you to boldly believe God for the impossible. From war zones to remote mountain villages, the stories carry the fire of one who has dared to say yes to God—again and again. Few books mark you forever—this is one of them."

Dr. Hal Sacks
President/CEO, BridgeBuilders International
Author, *Unshakable: How to Prepare for Uncertain Times*

"The day Dan walked into our country church parsonage forty-four years ago, my heart broke with such overwhelming love and compassion for my little brother. A stiff wind could have blown him away. So thin. Cigarettes rolled up in his sleeve, marijuana in his car. He was a mess, filled with anger. I knew he just needed God.

One day, while Dan was out with Tim, I started interceding for him, weeping and crying out to God for his salvation. The minutes turned into hours. I wept so hard for so long; there were no more tears. It was a birthing type of pain. I don't know how many hours I was in the spirit for Dan's soul, but when I was done, I had such peace.

His radical salvation that night was just the beginning. God looked through the years ahead and knew what adventures He had in store for this passionate young man and what a mighty Kingdom warrior Dan would become . . . fearless for Him!

This book will challenge you to a deeper level of intimacy with Jesus, so you can have great faith for the impossible, walk so closely to Him you will truly know His voice, and live in unwavering obedience to Him. I put this book right up there with my favorites, and I know you will, too!"

Tim and Sharon Thomas
Urban Church Planters

"'My brother-in-law just graduated from a Bible School in Kansas City and needs a place to serve. Can you use him?'

In over forty years of leading churches, Dan was the only person I ever asked to serve with me sight unseen. Little did I know the impact he would have on me personally, our family, our church, and some of the toughest neighborhoods in Chicago.

Reading through the pages of his manuscript awakened some gripping memories only God could have orchestrated. Dan's story is a real page-turner that speaks deeply, especially to those who may feel unqualified for ministry and wonder how God could ever use them. Dan has been and continues to be a fearless warrior for the cause of Christ and for establishing His Kingdom on Earth. It's a great honor to call him my friend."

David Robinson
Leadership Coach

"It's been one of the great blessings of my life to know Dan Taylor for over thirty years and to have had a front-row seat to his life and ministry. If I had to sum him up in one word, it would be faithful. *Dan's obedience to God comes from a deep, genuine love for Him—a love that has carried him through some incredibly difficult seasons with unwavering devotion.*

I've watched Dan pour out his life as an offering to the Lord, time and time again. God found in him a willing heart and a life He could work

FEARLESS FAITH

FEARLESS FAITH

What Can Happen When You Relentlessly Seek God . . . and Find Him

DAN TAYLOR

Fearless Faith: What Can Happen When You Relentlessly Seek God . . . and Find Him
First Edition Trade Book, 2026
Copyright © 2026 by Dan Taylor

All rights reserved. No part of this publication may be reproduced, stored in a retrieval system, or transmitted in any form by any means—electronic, mechanical, photocopy, recording, or otherwise—except for brief quotations in critical reviews or articles, without the prior permission of the publisher, except as provided by U.S. copyright law.

Scripture quotations marked MSG taken from THE MESSAGE. Copyright © 1993, 1994, 1995, 1996, 2000, 2001, 2002. Used by permission of NavPress Publishing Group.

Scripture quotations marked NKJV taken from the New King James Version®. Copyright © 1982 by Thomas Nelson. Used by permission. All rights reserved.

Scripture quotations marked NIV taken from The Holy Bible, New International Version®, NIV®. Copyright © 1973, 1978, 1984, 2011 by Biblica, Inc. Used with permission of Zondervan. All rights reserved worldwide. www.zondervan.com

Scripture quotations marked TPT are from The Passion Translation®. Copyright © 2017, 2018, 2020 by Passion & Fire Ministries, Inc. Used by permission. All rights reserved. ThePassionTranslation.com.

To order additional books:
www.amazon.com
www.5riversinternational.org

ISBN: 978-1-952943-65-2

E-book also available

Front cover photo: Dan Taylor
Front cover design: Josh Taylor

Editorial and Book Packaging:
Inspira Literary Solutions, Gig Harbor, WA

Printed in the USA

DEDICATION

I dedicate this book first and foremost to Jesus Christ. Thank You for saving me, redeeming me, and giving me the greatest adventures I could ever imagine.

To my wife, Jan. Thank you for your patience, wisdom, strength, and love that have sustained me throughout the years. Your prayers have saved me more times than I can count. You are forever the love of my life.

To my children, Joshua, Jennifer, and Josiah, and my daughter-in-law, Samantha. I am so proud of each of you. I thank God for the honor of being your dad and for the love we all share. May each of you fulfill God's purpose for your life and have the greatest adventure with Jesus you could ever imagine.

To my siblings, Barbara, Sharon, Bill, Jeanette, John, David, and Garry. I thank God that all of you love Jesus, and by God's grace, you have been redeemed from the pain of the past.

To Momma . . . your prayers are still being answered.

To Daddy . . . thank you for giving me a story to tell.

To the persecuted Church of the world . . . may God give you great faith to live fearless.

"And you will seek Me and find Me, when you search for Me with all your heart."
(Jeremiah 29:13, NKJV)

TABLE OF CONTENTS

Acknowledgments	xv
Foreword by Mark Geppert	xvii
Foreword by Jenni Taylor	xix
Preface	xxi
Introduction	1

PART I: BEGINNINGS

1	Pray for Daddy	7
2	Redheaded Stepchild	16
3	The Violent Take It by Force	22
4	Early Lessons	30

PART II: CHICAGO MINISTRY

5	At the Gates of Hell	41
6	I Believe in You	48
7	Slavery	52
8	The Lord of the Journey	62
9	The Death	68
10	The Resurrection	75
11	The God of Breakthrough	81

PART III: BASEMENT YEARS

12	Lessons in Time	95
13	Forgiveness	100
14	Equipping the Saints	109

TABLE OF CONTENTS

PART IV: SOUTH AMERICA MINISTRY

15	Building Spiritual Foundations	121
16	Interview with a Brujo	128
17	Ancient Inca Strongholds	135
18	He Sets the Captive Free	142

PART V: MINISTRY IN TIBET

19	Go!	155
20	The Roof of the World	159
21	Attack Lambs	168
22	Throne of Shiva	173

PART VI: INDIA YEARS

23	Meeting My Indian Family	187
24	I Am a Little Bit Angry with You	195
25	Focus on Jesus	203
26	No Trespassing	209
27	Chai and a Nap	217
28	Dirty Cups	223
29	Give Him Room	228
30	No One Wants to Come Here	231
31	A Lifesaving Drug	235

PART VII: SOUTHEAST ASIA

32	There Are No Closed Doors	243
33	Prayer That Affects a Nation	254
34	Blood Moon	259

PART VIII: KASHMIR

35	Praying in a War Zone	267
36	The Man of Peace	273
37	The Good Shepherd	280
38	There Is No Explanation for This	286

TABLE OF CONTENTS

PART IX: MATURING MINISTRY

39 Be Fruitful and Multiply   293
40 To Be Found Worthy   299
41 Cliff-Jumping Faith   308

About the Author   315

ACKNOWLEDGMENTS

It is impossible to acknowledge every person who has had a profound impact on my life, but I want to give special thanks to some very special people.

First of all, thank you to Tim and Sharon Thomas, my sister and brother-in-law, who took me in and brought me to salvation. Your prayers literally snatched me from the flames and continue to sustain me.

Thank you to the Arimborgo family in Iquitos, Peru. You have impacted my life and the lives of my family in ways that you can never know.

Thank you to Mark Geppert, who mentored me and laid hands on me, sending me to the nations. Your friendship, wisdom, and spiritual strength have changed my life forever.

Thank you to Tara. Without you, many of these stories would never have happened. Your fingerprints are on my life forever.

Thank you to Jacob and Debra. You will forever be my spiritual heroes.

Thank you to Hal and Cheryl Sacks. Your friendship, wisdom, and partnership in the gospel have deeply impacted my life. I am forever grateful God brought us together to serve Him in Arizona.

And a very special thanks to Arlyn, Chelsea, and the team at Inspira Literary Solutions. You took the sloppy scribblings of a first-time author and turned them into a polished, readable book without losing my spirit and personality. Thank you!

FOREWORD

"It is not about anointing."

With those unforgettable words, Dr. Lester Sumrall welcomed my wife Ellie and me into his study in South Bend, Indiana. He recounted how George Müller had prayed for Smith Wigglesworth, Wigglesworth had prayed for him, and now he was passing on that charge to us: not a mantle of fame, but the weight of responsibility—for orphans, for spiritual warfare, and for a billion souls yet to hear the name of Jesus. That day, he looked us in the eye and asked, "Will you accept this responsibility?"

That holy moment shaped the course of our lives. It reminded us that missions is never about human talent, prestige, or titles. It is about surrender. It is about carrying the gospel into the hardest places, regardless of cost, and trusting God to use broken vessels for His glory.

It is in that same spirit that I introduce to you my brother and fellow laborer in the harvest, Dan Taylor.

From the first time I saw Dan and Jan Taylor, I recognized in them that unmistakable mark of God's calling. At the time, I sensed they were weary in spirit, yet their eyes still shone with hope. And out of that brokenness, God raised up one of the most fearless, faith-filled missionary couples I have ever known.

Dan Taylor is a man who has walked into nations bound in darkness with nothing more than the authority of Jesus Christ and the courage of faith. He has prayer-walked cities, confronted spiritual strongholds, and raised up teams of intercessors and evangelists who now circle the globe. Jan, his faithful partner, has borne the quiet but immense sacrifices of a missionary's life—raising children while Dan traveled, interceding through lonely nights, and standing as a pillar of faith when others might have faltered. Together, they are living testimonies of what it means to "present yourselves unto God, a living sacrifice."

Fearless Faith is more than a memoir. It is a window into the cost of obedience and the joy of seeing God move when His servants step out without fear. Many will tell you of the victories of missions; few will be so honest about the tears, the testing, and the breaking that make those victories possible. Dan does not hide his wounds. He shows how God turns rejection into revelation, defeat into determination, and weakness into strength.

What you will find in these pages is not theory, but testimony. Every chapter bears witness to the grace of God and the power of faith in action. As you read, you will walk with Dan through jungles, villages, and cities. You will feel the weight of his trials, and you will rejoice in the breakthroughs only God could accomplish.

I have prayed with Dan and Jan, and I have seen firsthand the fruit of their labor. They stand in that great line of faith that stretches from Müller to Wigglesworth to Sumrall, ordinary people through whom God does extraordinary things. The Taylors remind us that missions is not about special people—it is about a great God who calls us to trust Him completely.

So, I commend this book to you. Read it slowly. Let it challenge you. Let it draw you deeper into the heart of God for the nations. And above all, may it inspire you to step out in fearless faith, wherever the Lord may send you.

Mark Geppert
Founder, SEAPC—a global Christian community that believes lives and nations are changed through prayer
www.seapc.org

FOREWORD

Dan didn't ask me to write this, but I'm doing it anyway because it's important.

You see, Dan Taylor, the author of this book, is my dad. That means I've had a front-row seat to his character every day of my life and consider myself pretty qualified to tell you if the words he's written have any weight behind them.

And I can assure you they do.

From navigating an extremely difficult childhood to skyrocketing into ministry and having to discern man's way from God's, I have seen my dad consistently and humbly choose Jesus over himself time and time again. There is a purity in my dad's journey that is hard to explain until you read it for yourself. He wants what is true. He wants what is real. He is incredibly honest about the mistakes he has made along the way. His God is alive, verbal, and intimate, and my dad will do whatever it takes to stay in His face. This is the God he will introduce you to in these pages.

This book is full of growth and learning, and none of it has gone to waste. I've never seen a wiser leader on the mission field. There is no ego. My dad is the first one to sit on the floor instead of a chair, to graciously accept yak meat, or to make friends with the gaggle of kids in a small village. He is acutely aware of anything and everything, seeing in the Spirit as he navigates new friendships with people from very different belief systems. He is fearless and trusts God implicitly. And in return, God has shown up with healings, signs, and wonders beyond anyone's wildest expectations.

FOREWORD

It is an honor and a joy to read these stories and know they are not only 100 percent true, but that my dad has endeavored to live these lessons in humility and strength every day of his life. He is exactly as you expect—a man who has been blessed in his brokenness, a man who cries when he says the name of Jesus, a man whose radical obedience has led to the miraculous. And don't worry: I promise he's just as human as the rest of us.

I hope these stories he has written touch your heart, and I hope you all get to meet him in person someday, because a hug from my dad is one of the best things in the world. May you be blessed by his life, as I have been.

Jenni Taylor
Dan's Daughter

PREFACE

This is not a book of theological teaching, a treatise on missions strategies, a thesis on how to be a successful minister, or a guide on how to do strategic prayer and spiritual warfare. While all of those topics are present, this book is simply an account of my personal journey of seeking to know God—and the cost of dying to myself in the process.

I have endeavored to tell it as vulnerably and honestly as I know how—sometimes gritty, sometimes painful, sometimes miraculous. It's a pioneer's journey filled with danger and adventure, pain and passion, failure and success, the journey of a flawed man who refused to stop pursuing the God who first pursued him.

Sometimes I get brutally honest and painfully transparent about the times I wrestled with my own weaknesses and with God—times I cried, doubted, and accused. Times of anger, misunderstanding and brokenness. Times of deep frustration with myself and with God . . . this is your invitation to do the same.

I pray this book will give you hope and challenge you to believe Him for the impossible, that it will encourage you to pursue Him to the end of yourself, and most of all, that it will help bring you into the deepest intimacy with the One who died for you.

In the end, this is His story . . . the story of a God who cannot be contained in any religious structure; who is powerful and delights to do the impossible; who loves, who heals, who delivers, and who redeems everything; who is faithful and has wonderful plans for you

PREFACE

. . . plans that will take you on the greatest adventure you could ever imagine—if you are willing to forfeit your own life for His.

As you read these pages, may you encounter this God face-to-face, and may He give you the desire and courage to live a life of fearless faith.

INTRODUCTION

It was June 14, 2023, a beautiful morning high up in the Himalayas of North India. I was on the back of a motorcycle, and my driver was carefully maneuvering the bike around the twists and turns of a narrow mountain road.

I was told there were thousands of villages in these mountains where the people had never heard the name of Jesus. I was eager to go to this remote region and make Jesus known for the very first time.

My driver was a young man named Ishan. My friends, with whom I had traveled many times, had invited him along, and I agreed he could come. I was looking forward to getting to know him as he would be the one staying behind in these villages to establish house churches after our visit.

There were six of us on the team. Two would travel on the motorcycle, and four would travel by car. It was my turn to be on the motorcycle.

As I rode on the back of the bike, I was full of joy and praise. It felt so good to be back in the mountains, and I was already imagining the many adventures that lay ahead. Every time I came to India, I would return home with miracle stories of what God had done on the prayer journey. I was very excited to see what God was going to do on this one.

Ishan took the twists and turns of the narrow mountain road while I looked out over the beautiful snow-capped mountains and spread my arms wide, saying, "Jesus, thank You so much for allowing me to be here. Thank You for allowing me to partner with You and do what we do!" I could feel the warm summer breeze blowing around us as we made our way around the curves.

As I was enjoying the ride, I suddenly realized Ishan had taken a curve too wide. He was crossing over into the lane of oncoming traffic, where a large dump truck was coming straight toward us. I found myself thinking, *If we avoid that truck, it is going to be a miracle.*

I turned my head away from the oncoming collision and then felt the intense pain of my body slamming against the side of heavy metal. The force of the crash knocked my helmet off, and my body flew through the air, landing with a thud about twenty feet from the point of impact.

Lying in the middle of the road, I managed to turn onto my back. I tried to move my right leg, but it would not obey me. It was twisted in different directions that it was not meant to go, and I knew it was badly broken. I could hear Ishan screaming in pain, but I could not see him. He and the bike were trapped on the other side of the truck out of my view. *Thank God he is still alive,* I thought.

I lay there, propped up on my elbows, looking around again at the beautiful mountains, this time from a much different perspective. As long as I did not move, the pain was not too bad. Slowly, I began to realize I was in perfect peace. I had not yelled or screamed in pain. There had been no adrenaline rush, no surge of fear . . . nothing but perfect peace.

As I looked at my broken leg, I could feel God's Presence all around me. I knew I was not alone. He was there. He had me. He was still in complete control of every detail. Somehow, even though I did not understand, I felt I was in the perfect will of God.

Within moments, the scene became chaotic as cars stopped and people jumped out to help us. Miraculously, at that exact time, a military convoy was passing by and stopped to help. Several Indian soldiers placed a blanket under me to use as a stretcher and carried me to the back of a large cargo truck, where I was placed next to Ishan, whom they had picked up first.

INTRODUCTION

It was then I remembered my phone. Fortunately, it was in the opposite pocket from the leg that had been hit by the truck, so it was not damaged. Before leaving for India, I had formed a group on a social media platform who would pray for us while we were gone. I opened my phone to leave a voice message.

"Hey guys, we had an accident. I was on the back of the motorcycle and we hit a truck. My leg is badly broken. The driver is hurt, but I don't know how bad. It's time to pray!" I was very calm, though there was an edge of pain in my voice.

The military detail knew of a small mountain hospital and took us there for triage. The large, green cargo truck bounced over the rough mountain road, and with each bounce, pain shot through my broken leg. A soldier sat behind me holding me up so I could lean against him and soften the impact of the hard, steel floor. When we reached the hospital, they pulled us out of the truck and placed us on gurneys. Each time they picked me up, the broken bones moved and I groaned loudly from the pain.

A doctor approached and asked me if I could feel or move my foot. The answer was no. He proceeded to take my leg and twist it until the broken bones snapped back into place. I let out a scream as the pain shot through my leg like fire. My hand curled into a fist, ready to punch the doctor in the mouth.

"Can you move it now?" he asked.

Suddenly, I was able to move my foot. I very quickly went from wanting to punch him to thanking God I was not paralyzed.

There was internal bleeding in my leg from the breaks, so they gave me two pints of blood. After coming to India for more than ten years, I had developed a deep love for the Indian people. I did not miss the irony that I now had Indian blood flowing through my veins.

The nurse gave me a separate IV for the pain. I lay back and relaxed, letting the painkillers do their work, and waited for my friends to find an exit plan to get us to a hospital that was equipped to handle our injuries.

FEARLESS FAITH

I looked around the room and could see Ishan being cared for. I still did not know how bad his condition was. I could see my friends discussing what to do to get us out of there, and I felt the doctors and nurses hooking me up to IVs for the blood transfusion. I looked up at the ceiling and thought, *Okay, God, how did I end up here, almost dead, in this remote hospital in the middle of nowhere, in a foreign country?*

Well, as it turns out, that is quite the story. . . .

PART I
BEGINNINGS

Chapter 1

Pray for Daddy

*When you pass through the waters, I will be with you;
And through the rivers, they shall not overflow you.
When you walk through the fire, you shall not be burned,
Nor shall the flame scorch you.*
Isaiah 43:2, NKJV

There were five boys and three girls in our family, and I was number seven out of the eight. It was the early 1960s, and we lived in an old, run-down farmhouse in southern Kansas. We weren't farmers; we just rented the old house that had been abandoned long ago. The house had been painted white at some point in the past, but by the time I came around, most of the paint was gone and the weathered, bare wood was exposed.

We had no running water or indoor plumbing. The only water we had was from a well, hand-pumped and carried into the house in large, metal buckets. We had no indoor toilet, just the outhouse out back, a distance from the house. In the summer it would stink to high heaven, and in the winter your butt would get frostbite. We were considered poor white trash by the people in the nearby town of Whitewater.

My mother was a tall, pretty woman of German heritage, and she loved Jesus with all her heart. Her grandfather had migrated from Russia as part of the Oklahoma Land Rush in 1889. Her parents were originally Mennonite but had received the baptism of the Holy Spirit and were some of the first pioneers of Pentecostalism in Oklahoma during the early 1900s.

Momma would always sing old hymns as she worked around the house, and it seemed she was constantly praying in tongues. She was a woman of great faith, and despite her circumstances, she was quick to laugh and had a great sense of humor. She loved to pray. She had a strong connection with God and constantly brought the fragrance of His Presence into our home. We know it was Momma's prayers that kept us kids alive and eventually brought each one of us to salvation in Jesus.

I remember a time when my brothers and sisters were all at school. I was at home because I was still too young to attend. I had been playing and decided to go look for Momma.

As I walked down the dark, narrow hallway to her bedroom, I could hear the sounds of her crying and praying. The heavy wooden door was slightly ajar, and I could see her kneeling by the bed on the bare wood floor. She was praying intensely, with tears streaming down her face and her hands in the air. I stood there and watched quietly for the longest time. Even as a five-year-old, I knew I was standing on holy ground.

After a long while, I turned and quietly walked away, but that image of Momma on her knees praying, crying out to God, was burned into my spirit. I somehow knew that one day, I wanted to love Jesus as much as she did.

A Life of Fear

While Momma loved Jesus very much, my father was quite different. My earliest memories of him are memories of fear. When I was two or three years old, there were many nights I would run to the bedroom, hide under the bed, and shove my little fingers into my ears to shut out the sounds of the yelling and cursing as my dad, in a drunken rage, beat my mom, and sometimes my brothers and sisters.

My dad was handsome and could be very charming. He was a few inches shorter than Momma and had a barrel chest and strong arms. He played several instruments, and could laugh and be the life of the party. He loved to hunt and fish and enjoyed the outdoors.

But he was also filled with a rage that bubbled just under the surface, waiting for the smallest excuse to manifest into violence, especially when he was drunk, which was pretty much most of the time. Because of his drunkenness and violent temper, our family lived in constant fear, even for our very lives.

He loved guns and was an excellent marksman who loved to show off this skill. That was fine until he came home drunk and wanted to shoot apples off our heads or cigarettes out of our mouths.

"Stand still! Stop moving!" Daddy would yell as he would try to steady himself to take the shot. My sister, Sharon, standing as stiff as she could with an apple on her head, would say, "But Daddy, you're the one moving!"

Sometimes, Daddy would have what we called "war spells." Today, it is called PTSD, but we'd never heard of that term back then. Daddy's mind would snap, and he would think he was back in World War II. He would go into an incoherent rage and point his gun at Momma and us kids, threatening to kill us. Momma would take us all outside to hide in the cornfield until Daddy settled down. Sharon was the bravest one of us kids. Even at twelve years old, she was brave enough to go back into the house and talk to Daddy as calmly as she could and make him coffee until he would finally pass out and we all could go back into the house.

One night, when I was about five years old, Daddy came home drunk and began to torment my oldest brother, Bill, who was about fourteen at the time. For some reason we still don't understand, Daddy had a special hatred for Bill and constantly made his life a living nightmare.

Daddy put him against the wall in our kitchen, yelling at him to stand still as he threw a hunting knife at his head.

"Stand still! If you move, I will kill you! Stand still!" He shouted this again and again as my brother stood against the wall, his arms stiff against his body, trembling in terror.

"Don't kill me, Daddy! Please don't kill me!" he said, his lips quivering and tears running down his face. Daddy was staggering drunk, barely able to stand. Again and again, the knife thudded into the wall, missing his head by inches as Bill begged Daddy not to kill him.

Even now, I remember my five-year-old self standing there in terror, watching Daddy throw the knife and Bill crying. Horrified, sobbing deeply, I cried out, "Don't kill him, Daddy! Please don't kill him!"

Momma was crying and screaming for Daddy to stop as she reached down and grabbed me up in her arms and took me out of the room. She handed me off to my sister, Jeanette, and ran back into the kitchen. She was yelling at Daddy to stop and at the same time praying for God to intervene. Finally, she was able to get Bill out of the room and send him outside to hide in the dark. He hid under the back porch, sobbing, waiting for Daddy to pass out before he could finally come back into the house.

One night, about a year later, Daddy came home drunk again and went on his customary tirade of violence through the house. He then went outside the farmhouse to smoke a cigarette. Bill's bedroom was on the second floor, and he looked out the window and saw Daddy standing in the yard, smoking. By this time, the years of torment and trauma had turned into hopeless despair. Bill felt compelled to do something to make it stop.

He picked up his twelve-gauge shotgun (Daddy had taught the older kids to shoot and hunt), laid its barrel on the windowsill, and pointed it at the back of Daddy's head. His heart raced a thousand miles an hour. His entire body trembled as he began to put pressure on the trigger. In his mind, this was the only way to protect Momma and the rest of us. He had to do something to put a stop to all the pain. The daily life of abuse had finally reached a breaking point. One pull of the trigger and it would all come to an end.

Daddy finished his cigarette and turned to go back into the house. Bill slowly let his finger off the trigger, shaking and crying. He was ashamed he could not take that shot, but later, he was so thankful that God's grace and Momma's prayers had kept him from living with the trauma of murdering his own father. God had better plans for all of us.

On Christmas morning in 1965, all of us kids came running downstairs and into the living room full of excitement, hoping there would be something under the tree for us. We could not believe our eyes. There were presents everywhere! We had never seen anything like this! We excitedly tore through the wrapping to find our treasures, giggling and laughing. It was the best Christmas ever! Daddy sat in a rocking chair, smoking a cigarette, watching us tear open the packages and run off to play with our new toys. He just smiled as we laughed with glee.

Two days later, the authorities came. I remember watching them collect our Christmas presents along with our dad. They put them all in a large, white van and drove away. Daddy had written bad checks for all those presents and would spend some time in jail for doing so. Daddy certainly did give us a Christmas worth remembering. It seemed even his best intentions brought pain.

We had an old, wood-burning potbelly stove that warmed the two-story farmhouse. At night, Momma would gather all of us kids together for family devotions around that stove. She and my sisters would sing and read Scripture. Bill taught me the Lord's Prayer as we knelt down by an old wooden chair.

Momma would tell us, "You all pray for Daddy, now." This was a constant request from Momma night after night. "You all pray for Daddy, now."

Momma prayed for Daddy for twenty-five years without ever seeing anything change. It wasn't until after she was in heaven that God finally did answer her prayers.

Momma's Illness

When I was four years old, Momma was diagnosed with cancer, and for the next three years she suffered, battling that insidious disease. She spent a lot of time in bed and was not able to care for us younger ones or help around the house. My older sister, Jeanette, dropped out of school to care for me and my younger brother Garry, who had been born just prior to Momma's diagnosis.

As Momma's condition worsened, we moved out of that old farmhouse and into a small house in nearby El Dorado so we could be closer to the hospital. I was seven years old, and for the first time in my life, I had access to a flush toilet. Back at the old farmhouse, on cold nights, Momma had put a coffee can in the closet and that would be our bathroom, but we were like rich people now!

Even while Momma was sick and spending most of her days in bed, Daddy continued with his violent tirades. In fact, with Momma unable to get out of bed to protect us, things were worse than ever. One night, while living in El Dorado, Daddy was fighting with my sixteen-year-old brother, Johnny. I remember Daddy knocking Johnny to the floor, sitting on him, pounding his fists into his face and screaming, "Tell me you love me! Tell me you love me!"

"I hate you! I hate you!" Johnny would scream back through the tears as he tried to protect his face from Daddy's punches.

The day after that fight, Johnny came home from school and Daddy was standing at the door of the house with a bag of clothes. "You don't live here anymore," said Daddy. Johnny slowly picked up the bag, looked Daddy in the eyes, and then turned to walk away. Everything he owned was in that bag slung over his shoulder. At sixteen years old, with his mother dying of cancer, my brother was thrown out by his own father. He was totally alone with nowhere to go.

I remember the day the ambulance came to take Momma to the hospital. I had just come home from school, and the EMTs were in her bedroom placing her on a stretcher to take her away. She never came home again. Momma went to be with Jesus one week before my eighth birthday.

Momma was a woman who loved Jesus and believed in prayer. She never gave up hoping, believing, and praying for my daddy.

Momma's Answered Prayer

Now that Momma was gone, there were three of us left living with Daddy: me, my twelve-year-old brother, David, and little Garry, who was four. My three sisters, Barbara, Sharon, and Jeanette, had gotten married and had moved out of the house years earlier. Each of them married at a young age. They found love, but also, by getting married, they found a way to escape Daddy's anger. Bill enlisted in the army and went to Vietnam. He figured war couldn't be any worse than living with Daddy. At least in war, you could shoot back and defend yourself. Johnny had found a pastor and his wife to take him in.

David and I were very close. He became more than a big brother to me; he was the only stability I had left in my life. He was only twelve, but I depended on him heavily. He was the one who made sure we ate, had clean clothes, and went to school every day. He had taken on the responsibility of mother and father to me and Garry.

It was late at night, eight months after my mother died. I walked into our little living room. All the lights were off except for a small lamp near the chair Daddy always sat in. I was completely surprised to see Daddy on his knees in front of that chair, reading the Bible and praying. I had never seen him do anything like that before. I didn't know what to do or say, so I just sat there on an old wooden chair and watched him for a long time. His lips were moving, and his eyes were closed as he prayed. He never knew I was in the room. It wasn't quite like the time with Momma, but somehow, I knew this was a holy moment. Eventually, I quietly got up and went back to my room and went to sleep.

That was the last time I ever saw Daddy alive.

The next morning while I was at school, our principal came into our room. I saw him speaking in a very serious manner with my teacher, Mrs. Brice, and then they both came to my desk.

"Daniel, something has happened with your dad, and we need to take you home."

Feeling confused, I got up and followed them.

The principal drove me to our next-door neighbors' house as I tried to figure out what was going on. A tall policeman approached me and sat me down. With a serious look on his face, he said, "Son, your dad was shoveling snow and had a heart attack. He has passed away." I did not know what that term "passed away" meant. I just thought something bad had happened to him.

"Will he be okay?" I asked.

The policeman paused and looked at me with the saddest expression. "No, son, your dad died this morning. He is gone." I looked across the room and saw my brother, David, sitting in a chair, sobbing. My life had just changed forever.

My daddy was a man with a lot of issues who brought much pain to his family, as well as to many others. He lived a harsh life filled with anger and violence. We found out in later years that he had been with other women and had fathered a number of children outside of his marriage to Momma. We also found out he had spent two years in prison. To this day, we still aren't sure why.

But I believe the night before he died, he got right with God. As he was on his knees reading the Bible and praying, I believe he asked for forgiveness and gave his life to Christ. He did not know he was going to die, but he felt the urgency to get right with God. The next day he was dead. I believe with all my heart I will see Daddy in heaven. Momma's prayers were finally answered.

Chapter 2

Redheaded Stepchild

> *Where can I go from Your Spirit?*
> *Or where can I flee from Your presence?*
> *If I ascend into heaven, You are there;*
> *If I make my bed in hell, behold, You are there.*
> PSALM 139:7–8, NKJV

It was decided that the three remaining boys would be separated to live with different families. I'm not sure who decided that, but it was decided.

Now, within eight months' time, Momma was gone, Daddy was gone, and all my brothers and sisters were gone. I felt scared, completely disoriented, and abandoned.

An uncle from Oklahoma came to pick me up. It had been determined I would go to live with him and my aunt, who was my mother's sister. My uncle put me in the back seat of the car. I had nothing with me except the clothes on my back. No toys, no books, no change of clothes. Nothing.

As we drove away, I asked, "Where's David? Isn't he coming with us?" David had told Garry and me again and again, "No one is going to split us up. We are going to stay together!" Unfortunately, at age twelve, there was nothing he could do. No one wanted, or felt that they were able, to take three orphaned children into their home at a moment's notice.

"No, just you," said my uncle. I sat quietly with my face pressed against the window, looking for my brother one last time, but he wasn't there. The last shred of security had been torn from me. We didn't even get to say goodbye.

As a young boy, I had shaggy red hair and freckles. My hair was such a bright red it seemed it could glow in the dark. Now, I had literally become the proverbial "redheaded stepchild." I was officially an orphan.

Worthless as a Hill of Beans

It was now 1970, and my aunt and uncle were considered middle class at that time. They gave me my own bedroom, and it felt oh so good to have real sheets and blankets to cuddle up under. Within just a few months of being with them, they officially adopted me and my last name was changed to Taylor.

However, while they took good care of me physically, it seemed everything I did reminded my stepmom of my dad. Every time she looked at me, it was as if she was looking at him. She had been present with our family many times when Daddy was being violent. Her heart was filled with hatred for the man who had done so much damage to her sister. She blamed him for her sister's premature death. Momma had been only forty-four when she died.

Nearly every day my stepmother would say, "You are just worthless! You are going to be a bum just like your dad was! You're probably going to be an alcoholic and go to jail just like he did! I wish we never took you! I never wanted you in the first place! You will never amount to a hill of beans!"

I must have heard that line a thousand times: "You will never amount to a hill of beans!"

My stepmother may have been my mom's sister, but she was nothing like her. She never sang and I don't ever remember seeing her pray. She went to church and said she was a Christian, but she sure didn't seem to love Jesus the way Momma had. Instead, she was always angry and never gave me a kind word.

Separated from My Siblings

One of the first things my stepmother did to me was shave my head. In 1970, long hair was the norm, but not for me. I was taken to the barber to receive a 1950s buzz haircut, prompting incessant bullying at school.

During this time, the sadness in me grew darker and darker. All I knew was that I was unwanted and unloved, and there was nothing I could ever do to change that.

When I was nine years old, they let me visit my older brother, David, for one week in Kansas. When I came home, I missed him so much, I went to my stepmother and tearfully asked if I could go live with my brother.

"How dare you be so ungrateful for all we have done for you!" she responded. She did not let me see any of my brothers or sisters for the next four years.

Many nights, I sat up in bed crying, feeling very angry with God. After all, this had to be His fault. This was the beginning of believing God did not love me and did not want me any more than my stepmother did.

"Why did You take my momma and daddy? Why did You have to take them?" I would yell at the ceiling with tears running down my face. I cried myself to sleep a lot of nights in those first years of not having my parents and being separated from my siblings.

When I was twelve, my stepmother forced me to go out and get a job to help earn my keep. My first job was bussing tables at a truck stop near our home in El Reno, Oklahoma. I worked every Saturday and Sunday from seven in the morning to three in the afternoon. I didn't last long, as I was too young to keep up with the work.

By the time I was fourteen, I was driving a tractor and plowing fields during the day, working at a steakhouse doing dishes and cooking at night, and filling in the remaining time with a paper route. Working kept me out of the house and away from my stepmother's disdain. The smallest infraction would bring her wrath, and she would berate me for being worthless and not appreciating them taking me in as an orphan. She was always reminding me she never wanted me in the first place.

As a kid, it was difficult knowing that this woman who should have been a mother figure hated me so intensely. My stepdad was a quiet man and pretty much kept to himself. From time to time, when my stepmother was being especially hateful, he would try to step in and protect me, but that only caused problems in their marriage, so he tended to keep quiet. I looked at my time with her as a prison sentence. I began to count down the years, longing for the day I would graduate from high school and be able to move out.

My stepparents took me and my two stepbrothers to a little church every Sunday morning, Sunday night, and Wednesday night. I did learn the Scriptures, but it was rules with no life and empty religion to me. Besides, how could my stepmother say she loved Jesus and hate me so much?

I do remember something that happened in that little church, though. One night, when I was twelve years old, a guest evangelist came to preach. I was so impressed with how he stood in the pulpit and spoke with authority. Our usual pastor never preached like this! I sat in the front row, totally engrossed, watching this man.

I looked at him and sensed, *I am going to do that someday.* Even then, my spirit knew what my mind did not.

On My Own

I graduated high school when I was seventeen years old. I moved out one week later, after living with my aunt and uncle for nine painful years. The rejection and sadness I experienced all that time had now grown into anger and hatred, and my soul had become a very dark place.

The night I moved out, I loaded my belongings into the back of my Ford Pinto and went back into the house to get the last of my things. My stepdad was in the kitchen. He just nodded at me and said, "Take care of yourself." My stepmom didn't even bother to come out of her room to say goodbye.

I received a drama scholarship to a small university in Chickasha, Oklahoma. My first day there, I realized my roommates were hard-core partiers, consuming copious amounts of drugs and alcohol on a daily basis.

With all the wounds and anger that had been festering in me for so long, it was easy to fall in with them and do what they were doing. I pretty much stayed stoned or drunk every day for the next two years. There were many nights I would sleep passed out, with my arms wrapped around a toilet bowl. When I couldn't make it to the toilet, I would pass out and sleep in my own vomit all night long. I stopped going to classes and spent most of my time looking for drugs or another drink to dull the pain of being alive. Day after day, my journey into darkness grew deeper and deeper.

It was very late one night and I had been drinking a lot. I looked up at heaven and began cursing God with the loudest, most vile words I could possibly think of. I had experienced so much pain and rejection in my life that I believed God hated me—and I hated

Him right back. I cursed Him for as long as I could until I fell to the ground, sobbing in drunken despair.

What I did not realize that night was that while I was cursing God, He was hearing the cry of a lost, broken young man who desperately needed to be redeemed. While I was cursing Him, He was loving me. Little did I know He had a plan for me, and He was working it out.

I eventually dropped out of college and essentially became homeless. Thankfully, I never had to sleep in a park or under a bridge, as I usually found a friend who let me crash on their floor. Other times, I would break into my old dorm and find an empty room where I could sleep and shower.

One hot day in mid-July, I was walking down the street in my flip flops when I suddenly stopped. I stood there for the longest time, looking in every direction. The Oklahoma sun beat down on my head and my empty stomach growled with hunger. It suddenly dawned on me: I had nowhere to go. I was walking nowhere with no destination. I stood there, staring down the street. It was the most empty, hopeless feeling I'd ever experienced.

Thoughts of suicide filled my mind, and I began to think of how to kill myself. I was nineteen years old, and I had no reason to be alive. Death had to be less painful than this.

The words my stepmother had spoken over me all those years had come true.

I wasn't worth a hill of beans.

Chapter 3

The Violent Take It by Force

And from the days of John the Baptist until now the kingdom of heaven suffers violence, and the violent take it by force.
Matthew 11:12, NKJV

A few days after that moment on the street, I was at my friend's one-room apartment, where I had been sleeping on the floor. Huge Mexican cockroaches would crawl all over me at night, but at least I had a roof over my head.

My friend had left for the day, and, for one of the very few times I can remember, there were no drugs or alcohol to be had. I was sober and bored, so I began to rummage around the room and found a book called *The Cross and the Switchblade*. It was a true story about a man named David Wilkerson, who had gone to the streets of New York City to work with gang members and drug addicts.

I lay on the floor and began to read. I became captivated by this amazing story. The more I read, the more I became lost in its pages as I learned about a young man named Nicky Cruz. He seemed to be even worse than me! I could identify with him so much that I felt I was not reading about him anymore, but about myself!

This book was talking about a Jesus I had never heard of before. This Jesus was alive! He was powerful! He could see me and wanted to be a part of my life. He could heal and deliver. He could remove all my anger and hatred and give me a reason to be alive. He could give me worth and purpose. This Jesus had the power to love someone like me! As I read, my soul was crying out, *If I could have a Jesus like this, I'd be a Christian!*

That night I thought of my sister, Sharon. I knew she was married to a preacher somewhere in Kansas. I had not seen or spoken to her in several years. But that night, I felt I needed to call her.

"Sharon," I said, "I'm really messed up. I've been doing a lot of drugs and I'm probably an alcoholic. I have been playing with witchcraft, and I am pretty close to being homeless. I'm so depressed and just want to die. I don't know what to do or where to go. I'm feeling really lost right now."

My sister was very quiet on the other end of the line. She was trying to process what I had just confessed to her. How could her little brother end up in such a bad way? What happened to the cute, redheaded kid she used to tell Bible stories to?

"Well, Daniel, God loves you . . . and I love you." That's all she could muster at the time as she was overwhelmed with so many feelings of grief and sadness for me. I hung up the phone and went to sleep. I was not born again that night, but the hook had been set.

It was just a matter of time.

That phone call motivated Sharon to start praying for me. Every day, three times a day, for eight months, she prayed for me, asking God to intervene and save my life.

During those eight months, I got a job at a pizza parlor. I thought at least I wouldn't go hungry working at a restaurant. I was able to get my car repaired and even secured a little ramshackle apartment. After a while, I called Sharon again.

"I'm just sick of being here. This place is a dead end for me. I'm so tired. If I stay here, I will die."

"Daniel, is there anywhere you can go?" she asked.

"No," I said, "I have no idea where to go. I think I'll just get in my car and start driving and see where I end up."

"Well, Daniel, just come and stay with us for a couple of weeks and maybe you can figure things out."

I wasn't thrilled with the idea of staying at a preacher's house, but for some reason something jumped inside of me. I knew I had an open door out of where I was. I had no idea where it would lead, but I knew I had to take it.

I loaded everything I owned into the back of that Ford Pinto wagon and headed out on a five-hundred-mile journey to northern Kansas.

Sharon and her husband, Tim, pastored a congregation of about sixty farmers out in the middle of nowhere. It was called Pleasant Green, and it was twelve miles from the nearest town, which had a population of about three hundred people. If I wanted to get away from my past, this sure would be a good place to do it.

I arrived late at night. They had been sitting up waiting for me. I'm sure when they first saw me, they thought I looked like something the cat had dragged in. I was down to about a hundred and twenty pounds, skinny as a rail. I had long, shaggy red hair with some semblance of a mustache, and I had a pack of cigarettes in my shirt pocket. I had the spirit of death all over me, and they could feel the darkness in me as I entered their home.

They didn't say much but showed me to a room that I would share with their oldest son, Corey, who was eleven years old. In fact, day after day, they did not say much. They were polite and kind, and, while I felt welcome, there was a huge gap between us that was impossible for them to bridge. I was so far gone that Tim and Sharon had no idea how to reach me. So, my sister did all she knew to do. She went to God.

Or maybe it was God who went to her.

I felt guilty about getting high in a preacher's house, so I left my drugs out in the car. There was no alcohol, and the nearest store was twelve miles away. My car had a flat tire, so I wasn't going anywhere. I tried to go out back to smoke a cigarette, but it was February in northern Kansas and the windchill was below zero. That cigarette just wasn't worth the frostbite that accompanied it.

Sharon was so wise. She never once tried to preach to me or talk to me about Jesus. She never once told me how bad I was or judged me. She never told me I needed to get right with God. She knew there were no words that could ever reach me. She knew I didn't need words. I needed God. But there was no mistaking the deep sadness in her eyes every time she looked at me.

It was February, Friday the 13th, 1981. I had been on a two-day road trip with Tim to Oklahoma and had just returned. I walked into the house late in the evening. Sharon was sitting in a chair doing her macrame, and I sat on the couch opposite her.

She didn't say anything; she just put her macrame down in her lap and looked at me with an intensity in her eyes that I had not seen before. My body began to get very warm and shake a little. A few tears welled up in my eyes.

"Sharon," I said, "I don't know what's going on, but I just feel like crying."

This was strange for me. It had been a long time since I had shed any tears without being drunk, and I had no idea why I was doing it now.

"Daniel, that's the Holy Ghost working on you!" she said. Her voice was strong and intense. She was dead serious. Suddenly, tears came into her eyes, and I felt bad I was making her cry. I stood up to give her a little hug, but when I touched her it was like touching a live electric wire.

My body began to shake uncontrollably and now the tears turned into deep sobs that welled up out of the deepest recesses of my soul. Years of pain and trauma came pouring out of me. I sobbed so hard, Sharon had to hold me up or I would have fallen over. As she held me, I could literally feel a hand—a huge, strong hand—reaching down through my head and down into my chest. I could feel that hand ripping the darkness out of my body.

Suddenly, in the blink of an eye, I felt the years of hatred and anger leave. Depression, hopelessness, and the desire to die were gone. All the pain and darkness instantly left. I could feel light radiating through me, transforming me, making me new.

Now the sobs turned into joy. Laughter began to flow out of me. Sharon looked over at Tim, who had come in to see what was going on, and said, "He's getting saved!" I had no idea what that meant, but I knew I was getting something really good!

Then the most wonderful feelings of love filled me to overflowing. For the first time since my mom had died, I could actually feel someone love me, and that love was completely overwhelming. I was loved! I had value! My life suddenly mattered! In an instant, I knew: *I am a child of God!*

Tim and Sharon got down on their knees by the couch to pray and I joined them. I didn't know much about prayer. All I could do was laugh and cry and say, "*Wow!*"

For years, I had cursed prolifically. It was almost impossible for me to speak a sentence without it being full of curse words. Now, suddenly, all the curse words were gone, and I was completely at a loss to speak. With my vocabulary substantially depleted, all I could think was, *Wow*. I was so excited I said it backwards: "Wow!" On my knees by the couch, I looked up at heaven and said, "Okay, God. You are for real. I know You are powerful. You see me, I know You love me, and I am coming after You with all I've got!"

I ran out to the car and got my drugs and flushed them down the toilet. I took my cigarettes and ripped them up and threw them away. I knew I did not need those things anymore. I was free; I was clean. I had been a dead man walking but now I was alive! I was so full of energy I couldn't sit. For three hours, I walked back and forth in that little living room, clapping my hands, crying, laughing, and saying, "Wow!"

What I came to discover was that while Tim and I were on that road trip, the Holy Spirit had come on my sister with a spirit of deep intercession. She began to weep as she prayed for me, and the longer she prayed, the deeper the weeping became. She could not sleep all that night as she paced the floor, crying out for God to save me.

All through Friday, the burden for my soul intensified to the point that she cried out in agony. She said the travail she felt for me was more painful than giving birth to her own children. She had been pacing in a circle in her living room for hours until she fell on her knees and lay curled up in a fetal position on the floor. With loud groans that came from the innermost parts of her soul, she wrestled hell for me. She knew she was in a life-or-death struggle, and there was no choice but to win.

It wasn't just Sharon who was praying for me. It was the Holy Spirit living in her who was praying and fighting for me. God wanted me, but He had to find someone who cared enough to become truly violent in intercession to rescue me from hell.

When I was at my darkest and lowest moment, wishing I was dead, God raised up someone who would believe Him for the impossible. Someone who was not intimidated by what they saw with their eyes. Someone who knew God and His ability to do miracles. Someone who would wrestle hell and rip me out of the hands of Satan himself. Someone who would crawl up into heaven on my behalf, stand before God, and say, "I will not let You go until You answer me!"

So, by the time I walked into that living room and sat on the couch, Sharon knew the battle had already been won. She knew that I was going to meet God that night. She just knew it!

Sharon's violent prayers brought me out of darkness and delivered me into the kingdom of light. The same fearless warrior spirit she had when facing Daddy's drunken tirades was now being used to bring me into the kingdom of God.

I never said a sinner's prayer asking Jesus to come into my heart. Prior to this, if Sharon had asked me if I was ready to receive

Christ, I would have said no. This was never going to be a mental decision for me. My mind could never understand what my heart was crying out for. God simply bypassed my mind and went straight to my spirit.

That night, Jesus walked through a garbage dump and saw me crawling in my own filth. He reached down, picked me up, and made me His own.

John 1:12–13 (NKJV) says, "But as many as received Him, to them He gave the right to become children of God, to those who believe in His name: who were born, not of blood, nor of the will of the flesh, nor of the will of man, but of God." I had been born again by the will of God!

The next morning, I woke up early, went into the kitchen, and sat down at the table with my sister. I looked at her and just started crying again. Tears of joy, tears of knowing I was loved, tears of knowing I was free. The tears just kept coming, and as they came, my soul continued to heal.

Later that day, Tim asked me, "So, Daniel, what do you think you will do now?"

I was standing in the living room, looking out the window. When I heard his question, I spun around and said, "I'm supposed to be a preacher. How do I get to be a preacher?"

I knew instantly that I was called by God. After what He had just done for me, how could I not give Him my entire life? I had to serve Him. There was no other choice.

That night, Saturday, February 14, St. Valentine's Day, Tim took me into town to attend a Youth for Christ rally. I walked into a high school auditorium filled with about two hundred young people. Tim introduced me to Randy, the leader of YFC, and told him I had just been saved the night before.

Randy looked at me and asked, "Would you like to give your testimony tonight?"

"Sure," I said.

"Okay, just be ready to come up when I call you."

After he walked away, I looked up at Tim and asked, "What's a testimony?"

He laughed and said, "Just tell them a little about who you are and how you got saved."

I can do that, I thought. After all, I had gone to school on a drama scholarship. I was comfortable speaking in public.

That night, less than twenty-four hours after being born again, I stood in front of two hundred people and spoke about Jesus for the first time.

I have never stopped.

Chapter 4

Early Lessons

My sheep hear My voice, and I know them, and they follow Me.
JOHN 10:27, NKJV

Six months after being born again, I moved to Kansas City to attend Christ Unlimited Bible Institute, sponsored by Kansas City Youth for Christ. It was a small class of about eighty students, and we went to class four hours a day, five days a week, for one year. It was straight Bible courses that gave me a very strong foundation in the Word of God. That Bible education became the compass for the rest of my life.

KCYFC conducted more than one thousand Bible clubs throughout the Kansas City area, and many of them would invite CUBI students to speak. One night, after speaking at one of those clubs, I began to chat with the host while I waited for my ride to pick me up.

Her name was Donna, and she attended CUBI with me. She was in her mid-forties and had a charismatic background, although I had no idea what "charismatic" meant at the time.

EARLY LESSONS

As we chatted, Donna paused and looked at me intently. "Have you been praying for the baptism in the Holy Spirit?"

I thought that was a strange question, as I had just been asking God for this gift the past two weeks. "Yes," I said.

"Well, you have it!"

I was a little taken aback. "What are you talking about?" I asked.

"You have had two words running around in your head for the past two days that are not English," she said confidently.

Now, I just about came up out of my chair, because that was exactly true. *How does she know that?* I thought. Two days earlier I had prayed with a friend, and, in my passion, I said, "God, just give me more words to praise You with!" I wasn't thinking of tongues, it was just an impassioned desire to love God more. But, after praying that, two words kept running around in my head that were not English. I kept thinking, *Is this it?* How did this woman know about that? In my head I prayed for God to protect me from this crazy psychic lady!

Suddenly, she began to write something down and then read it to me. "This is a word from the Lord for you," she said.

A word from who? You mean this lady can talk to God and He talks back? Who is this woman?

"My beloved son," Donna read, "I am well pleased with your growth. I have many frontline battles in store for you. Stand strong. My blood is covering you. I love you. God, your Father."

Donna's gift had totally piqued my curiosity and I wanted to learn how to hear from God. She hosted a charismatic meeting at her house each week, so a few friends and I began to attend. It was a wonderful balance of getting grounded in the truth of the Word of God during the day and learning about the gifts of the Spirit in the evening.

I became a follower of Jesus because I experienced a demonstration of the Spirit's power. I knew firsthand His power to set me free from demons and trauma that had kept me bound for years. I knew

He was alive, interactive, and powerful. I was hungry to know Him in His Word, and I was hungry to learn the ways of the Holy Spirit.

Donna became a spiritual mom to me over the course of that year and taught me about prophecy, deliverance, hearing the voice of God, being sensitive to the Holy Spirit, and much more. God was equipping me for my future.

Go Directly to Jail

God had set me up for the best training available, but He also had His very own, unique methods of teaching me to grow deeper in Him.

On my first weekend as a Bible student in Kansas City, I decided to attend church on a Sunday night. As I drove, a car crossed into my lane and sideswiped me. I was not at fault, and it wasn't very serious, but the collision did crunch up the side of my car. The police were called, and when asked for my driver's license, I realized I had left it in my apartment.

"Sir, you will need to get into your car and follow me to the station," the officer said. "You are under arrest for driving without a license."

As I sat in the holding cell that evening, wearing my new three-piece suit, I reflected on my situation.

Hmmm, this makes no sense at all, I thought. *I used to sell drugs and never went to jail. In fact, I used to lie, steal, cheat, and do all manner of evil, and I never went to jail. But here I am on my way to church, and I end up in jail, and the accident wasn't even my fault!*

"God, what are you doing to me? I don't understand!" I prayed.

What I did not realize at the time was that God had created the perfect situation to reveal Himself to me as the God who provides and the God I could fully trust. Daily, I had been crying out to God to increase my faith. This was His way of answering that prayer; He placed me in a position that required more faith.

After several hours, a friend came and bailed me out. My Bible college career was getting off to a stellar start.

The next day, I took my car to the shop for the repairs. My insurance covered most of the cost, but I found I had a two-hundred-dollar deductible I would need to pay before they would release the car. This was an enormous sum as I barely had two cents. My car was the only transportation my two roommates and I had to get to school every day, so we were feeling quite desperate to get that money. The three of us sat on the floor of our apartment to pray and ask God for a miracle.

As we rose from the floor one of my roommates said, "Hey, Dan, an envelope came for you in the mail today. I laid it on your desk."

I opened the envelope, and there was a check for exactly two hundred dollars!

While we sat on the floor crying out for a miracle, God had already answered. Before I even knew I had a need, God had moved on a person's heart to send the exact amount necessary.

He was teaching me I could fully trust Him.

Hearing the Voice of God

Another important lesson I was learning was how to hear His voice. Jesus said, "My sheep know My voice," so I was determined to become spiritually sensitive to hear Him speak to me.

One day, on my way to school, I got a flat tire. I happened to be near a police station and I got out to change it. I jacked up the car, removed the lug nuts, and tried to remove the flat tire, but it was locked against the rotor, as if it were welded. No matter how hard I tried, I could not get the tire to come loose so I could remove it. I hit it, kicked it, and pounded it with a lug wrench, all to no avail. The Bible college required us to wear a suit to class every day, so by that point, my suit was covered in dirt, grease, and sweat.

Finally, I paused and prayed. "Jesus, can You please tell me what to do? Please help me."

I waited quietly and then heard Him say, "Put the lug nuts on, but don't make them real tight." Now, I did not hear Him audibly, but that's the thought that came into my mind. But now I was confused. How could I get the tire off if the lug nuts were on? But I obeyed and put them on.

"Okay, what's next?" I asked.

"Let the car down off the jack."

Still confused, I obeyed the small voice in my head.

"Now, get in the car."

Again I obeyed.

"Start the car."

I started the car.

"Now drive."

Finally, I couldn't take it anymore. None of this made sense! How could any of this help me get the tire off? I was just making up stuff in my own head. "This is a waste of time!" I exclaimed. I pounded my fist into the steering wheel in frustration and turned off the car.

I decided to go into the nearby police station and ask for help. Maybe they had a sledgehammer or something I could use to knock the tire loose. I went up to an officer, explained my problem, and asked for help.

He said, "I don't have a hammer, but I know what you can do. Put the lug nuts on loose, let it off the jack, and then drive it and bump it against the curb. That should work to knock it loose, and it won't fall off because you have the lug nuts holding it on."

I just stared at the officer for a moment. He had just told me to do exactly what I had been hearing in my head from the Lord! I walked out of the station, got into the car, and bumped the tire against the curb. Sure enough, it came loose and I was able to change it. I felt very humbled and sheepishly prayed: "I'm so sorry for not trusting You, Lord. Please forgive me."

While I did not necessarily miss hearing God, I did flunk the test in trusting and obeying Him fully. My lack of understanding overrode His voice. God does not ask us to understand; He asks us to trust (see Proverbs 3:5–6).

During that year of Bible college, God was revealing to me He is a good Father, and as a good Father, He is always at work to teach us spiritual disciplines that will conform us to the image of His Son (see Romans 8:29). Our heavenly Father is a master at creating the perfect situations that will reveal His character—and develop ours.

That year was an intensive time of learning God's Word, experiencing the realms of the supernatural, growing in character, and receiving the tools to grow in Christ. But most of all, I learned my God is faithful and worthy of my absolute trust. Without learning these early lessons, I would never have been ready for what He had prepared next.

FLASHBACK

My Indian friend, Samson, who had been driving the car with the rest of our team, stood next to my gurney, looking at my broken leg. By this time, it was swelling into a very large purple balloon. Tears were streaming down his face as his lips moved, praying quietly.

"Hey, Samson," I said.

"Yes, Pastor?" he replied.

"Why are you crying? Are you hurt?"

"No, Pastor. You are the one who is hurt. Your leg is broken very badly!"

"Yeah, but it's my leg, not yours. What are you crying about? I'm not crying, so what's your problem?" I was laughing as I teased him, but I was concerned for my team. It was a traumatic experience for them, and they were not only concerned, but very much afraid and feeling helpless. I tried to use humor to help set their minds and spirits at ease.

"Samson, God has us in His hands. Everything is going to be fine. Right now, we are in the perfect will of God. Just relax and trust Him. I'm just glad it was me on the bike and not you. Your wife would have been so mad at me; she would have broken my leg anyway!" I continued to crack jokes with him through the fog of the painkillers, and I actually got a little laugh out of him a time or two.

From time to time, I could hear Ishan groaning in pain. I found out his leg was broken in three places, but he had no head or spine injuries, and with proper surgery he was going to be fine. He was only twenty-two years old, and slamming into that truck terrified him beyond measure. Now, he was in enormous pain and very scared. I wished I could get to him and encourage him, but he was far on the other side of the room. I prayed for God to comfort him and give him peace.

The doctor approached us with the X-rays they had taken. Holding them up to the light, I could see a major break in the middle of my right femur. The ends of the bone were sharp and jagged, like it had been shattered.

"Will I need to have surgery?" I asked.

"Yes, most definitely," the doctor replied. "But we cannot do that here. We must get you to a city where they have a proper facility. For now, we need to have a brace for your leg to keep it immobile while you travel. We do not have a brace here to do that."

Samson jumped to the rescue. "Doctor, I will go into the town nearby and see if I can find something that we can use as a brace." I was glad Samson had an assignment that would keep his mind busy for a while. It made him feel a little less helpless by doing something for me that I very much needed.

After taking measurements of my leg, Samson left and began his search for the brace. After some time, he found a metal shop where they had a welder. He approached the owner, asking if he could make a brace for my leg.

"It's the end of the day. I'm closing the shop and going home. I cannot help you," said the man.

"No, no, please, sir. I desperately need your help. My friend has a badly broken leg. Please, you must help him. We must get him down the mountain for surgery and he cannot travel unless he has the brace. Please! You must help us!" Samson was fighting for me as much as he could. He knew I desperately needed that brace, and he was not going to leave without it.

The man must have heard the desperation in my friend's voice. He paused for a long moment and finally said, *"Bahut acha*—very well—I will make it."

EARLY LESSONS

He proceeded to take a thick sheet of aluminum. He shaped it, cut it, and welded it, following the measurements Samson had provided.

Samson rushed back to the hospital, praying the brace would fit me correctly. The doctors lifted my leg and slid the brace on. It covered my entire leg from my hip to my ankle and fit wonderfully. Samson took a deep breath and smiled broadly. He had accomplished his mission and had helped his friend. He was now feeling a little less helpless and a little more at peace.

Now I was set to travel. But it was at least an eight-hour drive down the mountain to a proper hospital. How in the world were we going to get there?

I tried to lift my head up enough to see my friends in the corner, who were in a serious discussion. My friend Ashish, who had organized the prayer journey, came to me.

"Dan, it is a very difficult journey down the mountain to the hospital. The roads are very rough. We are going to get an ambulance for each of you, but it will be a very hard journey."

"Just do whatever you have to, and we will deal with it," I replied.

My dear friend Jacob, who was also on our team, would not leave my side. Just before they loaded me into the ambulance, they gave me another pint of blood. The blood had been refrigerated, so as it entered my system, it made me cold and I began to shiver intensely. Now, Jacob sat with me in the ambulance, holding the bag of cold blood under his shirt, tight against his chest, to warm it for me. I cannot overstate how much I appreciated this man at that moment, staying at my side, holding my blood. I looked at the ceiling and thanked God for my dear friend.

The ambulance began the journey down the mountain, bouncing so much that my broken leg fell off the gurney. The driver stopped and came back to reposition my leg, tying it down to keep it in place. With every jolt, I groaned from the pain. Mile after mile, the rough mountain road kept me awake with the pain shooting through my leg. Samson was with Ishan in another ambulance, experiencing the same rough journey.

PART II
CHICAGO MINISTRY

Chapter 5

At the Gates of Hell

*On this rock I will build My church, and the gates
of Hades shall not prevail against it.*
MATTHEW 16:18, NKJV

Upon graduating from the Bible program at CUBI, I was invited to go to Chicago to work with the youth in a local church. My brother-in-law, Tim, knew Pastor Dave from their Bible college days and had referred me to him. Pastor Dave was a wonderful man of God who had a unique vision of planting churches among the most broken and distressed neighborhoods of the city. It was through his visionary leadership that our denomination became much more involved in planting churches in the inner cities of America.

I was now twenty-one years old and excited to actually begin my life of ministry, although being in the huge city of Chicago was intimidating for this small-town country boy.

During this time, I met Jan, and nine months later, she became my wife.

Jan was born and raised in Chicago and worked as a travel agent. She had traveled all over the world and stayed in some of the finest resorts in some of the most exotic locations. She was accustomed to fine food and fine entertainment. For me, fine dining meant a Whopper at Burger King.

We met at the church where I was working as a youth pastor, and somehow we caught each other's eye. We began to spend a lot of time together and became close friends.

I worked as a bag boy at a grocery store during the week and would get paid every Friday. I then would take Jan out to dinner or a movie over the weekend. I would spend my entire paycheck on her, and then, because I had no money for gas or a bus, I would walk three miles to and from work all week long.

And I couldn't wait until the next weekend to do it all over again.

Somehow this amazing, beautiful, intelligent girl fell in love with me, an uneducated former drug addict. The one thing we had in common was we both loved Jesus intensely and we wanted to pursue Him with all our hearts.

We were married October 1, 1983, in a lakeside gazebo in Green Mountain Falls, Colorado, in the shadow of Pikes Peak. To this day, I can't believe how much God loved me to give me Jan.

For the next five years, we worked with Pastor Dave in the inner city of Chicago. We fed the homeless, conducted crusades, and ministered to the poor in any way we possibly could. Through Dave, I learned the value of hard work, being a servant, taking Jesus to the streets, and extending compassion to the poor, although that was not difficult for me. I knew exactly what it meant to be poor. I could see myself in every one of those families we were reaching out to.

Ministry in Cabrini Green

It was summer 1987 when Dave called me into his office and introduced me to a Salvation Army chaplain who was doing Bible clubs for children in a housing project called Cabrini Green. Cabrini Green housed nearly fifteen thousand African Americans and was the most violent and notorious housing project in America. It had a reputation so bad that no white person would ever go there. Even the police were afraid to go into Cabrini and would only do so in large groups. Gang violence dominated this neighborhood, which was located near downtown Chicago. Shootings were an everyday occurrence. If there were anywhere in America that could be described as the gates of hell, Cabrini Green was it.

"Dan, I would like for you to take a team and go help this man do Bible clubs in Cabrini."

Say what? I thought. *Cabrini Green? You have to be kidding me.* I knew I was a difficult person to work with, but sending me to Cabrini and risking me being shot was a little over the top. I sat looking at Dave for a few moments, trying to discern if he was serious. He was.

I thought this was a crazy idea, but I had no choice but to submit, so the following Sunday, I loaded up the church van with twelve volunteers and headed to Cabrini Green.

When we arrived, we met the Salvation Army chaplain on a corner and I asked him, "Where do you have this Bible club?"

"Hmmm," he said, "Where is a good place to start one?"

"*Start* one? I thought you already had one established and we were supposed to come help you with it."

"No, this is our first day being here. We have nothing going on yet," he replied.

Oh boy, we are starting from scratch, I thought.

The chaplain pointed to a park bench behind one of the buildings and said, "That looks like a good place to do the Bible club." He handed me a few bottles of juice and some cookies. "You just go on up in those buildings and round up the kids and have a good time. Watch out for the gangs, now!" he called out as he walked to his car and drove away. Now, here I was, standing on a corner in Cabrini Green, with twelve people looking at me wondering, *Now what?*

"Okay, guys, let's do it. Let's focus on these two buildings. Go to each one of the twelve floors, knock on the doors, and invite the kids to come down to the park bench." After my training at CUBI, it was second nature for me to conduct a Bible club. So, we rounded up the kids, told them Bible stories, played games, gave them refreshments, and prayed with them. Since it was summertime, all the windows to the apartments were opened, so the adults could hear everything we were saying down below.

And just like that, a Bible club was established in Cabrini Green.

Candy Bars and Football

We were faithful to do the Bible club every Sunday afternoon throughout the summer, after which I thought we were done. It was supposed to just be a summer program, and once the school year started, we ended it.

The problem was that school did not begin that fall. There was a teachers' strike that lasted several weeks, and the kids were on the streets with nothing to do.

One day, as I was sitting in my office (which was a broom closet under the stairs in the basement of the church), I sensed God telling me to go to Cabrini Green.

"Go to Cabrini?" I replied to the Lord. "Why? The summer Bible clubs ended. What am I supposed to do in Cabrini Green?"

"Go to Cabrini and take some candy bars with you," He prompted me. I had tried to do a youth group fundraiser selling candy bars, and they were not selling. I had cases of them sitting in my office. I had no idea what God was doing; all I knew was I was supposed to go to Cabrini and take candy bars.

That decision to obey His prompting changed the course of my life.

I loaded up my backpack, jumped into the church van, and headed to the projects. The peace of God settled on me as I drove.

His Presence was tangible. I had no idea what I was going to do, but I knew I was driving into His perfect will.

I drove up to the buildings and saw a bunch of kids outside, playing football. I handed out some candy bars and they allowed me to join their game. They called it "kill the white man with the ball." They would get the ball to me every chance they could so they could have the joy of plowing me into the hard ground. In between the times of picking myself up and wiping off the blood, I began to get to know some of their names.

Each day, I returned and did the same thing. I was slowly winning their trust, and they began to look forward to hanging out with me. Eventually, I invited some of them to go get sodas and we would all load up in the big, white church van and go all over the city. We would laugh, memorize verses, and sing songs. It got to the point that I would drive up to the buildings, honk the horn, and instantly the van would be overflowing with kids.

I realized that for those couple of hours in the van, they did not have to worry about being shot or live in fear of the gangs. That van became their daily refuge and escape. It was the only safe place they had. Everything else was a war zone.

"Dying for Me Is the Easy Part"

I continued to do the Bible club every week at the park bench. When it became too cold, we were given a meeting room in one of the buildings. When we outgrew that, God gave us an old, abandoned church building directly across the street from the projects. There were two bullet holes in the front door of the church, a daily reminder of the neighborhood I was working in.

One day, I was on the second floor of one of the project buildings when I heard gunshots ring out. I was on the balcony, looking out across the playground, when a young man with a gun looked up and saw me. He raised the gun and pointed it at me. I simply stepped back behind a wall for a moment, and when I peeked my head out again, the young man had run away. It really was no big deal, but it did get me thinking, *I could actually get hurt doing this.*

I sat down and talked to God about it. "God, do I love You enough to die for You?"

"Son," He replied, "You don't even love Me enough to *live* for Me yet. Dying for Me is easy. Living for Me is the hard part."

Be Strong and of Good Courage

At this time, the major gang in the area had broken up into different factions, which were at war with each other. They would fight over who would control the drug trade in each building. The shootings were constant, and one never knew when something was getting ready to go down, whether day or night. The people, especially the mothers, lived in constant fear of their children being killed.

God gave me great grace and favor to walk in the midst of all this with no fear. I could go anywhere I chose, day or night, and was never shot, beaten, or stabbed. I was never touched. Rather than the gangs confronting me, I was the one confronting them.

When I committed to God to go to Cabrini, He gave me a verse: "Have I not commanded you? Be strong and of good courage; do not be afraid or dismayed, for the Lord your God will be with you wherever you go" (Joshua 1:9, NKJV). I knew I was sent by God and everywhere I placed my foot belonged to Him.

I worked in Cabrini Green for three years, confronting gang members, working with the youth, and establishing a church. God gave great grace, and many youth and gang members came to Christ and were filled with the Holy Spirit.

Because I was a white man working in such a notorious place that was all African American, I began to develop a reputation in my denomination for being fearless and a little crazy. I began receiving invitations to speak about what God was doing in that infamous housing project.

In the summer of 1990, I decided to expand the ministry and went to the South Side of Chicago to plant a church in another housing project called the Robert Taylor Homes.

Chapter 6

I Believe in You

Ask, and it will be given to you; seek, and you will find; knock, and it will be opened to you.
Matthew 7:7, NKJV

It was a hot midsummer day when I pulled my big, blue van into the playground area of the Robert Taylor Homes on Chicago's South Side.

The playground was strewn with broken glass and damaged equipment. It had been years since there had been any proper maintenance here. For the most part, it was known as no man's land, since it was rarely used as a playground. It was mostly a place the gangs ran through while shooting at each other and fighting for control of the buildings.

In this area, there were three sixteen-story buildings that stood in a horseshoe formation. As I pulled my van up, I had one building in front of me, one to my left, and one to my right.

I pulled large, blue tarps out of the van and laid them on the ground. I pulled out my small sound system and ran an extension cord to one of the buildings for power. Then I turned on the microphone.

"Bible club starts in ten minutes!" I called. "Come on down! We are going to play some games, and I have a bunch of candy! Come on down and learn about Jesus! Bible club starts in ten minutes!" I continued to shout this until the blue tarps were covered with children whose eager faces looked up at me with anticipation. There was very little for the children to do in the projects, and my presence there was a pleasant diversion for them.

We would play music, play games, and tell a Bible story, all while the gang members stood along the buildings, watching from a distance. The smaller children would sit on the tarps, but some of the older ones felt that was not cool and stood in the back or along the edges to watch and listen. These kids who wanted to remain on the edges were anywhere between twelve and fourteen years old. They were young enough to not have been fully recruited by the gangs yet. These kids were the ones I focused on.

As I ended the Bible club, I would call out to some of these older kids.

"Hey, guys, I could really use some help doing this Bible club. I need you guys to step up and be my leaders and help me with the shorties." (This is what they called the younger kids.) I made sure I looked them in the eye and made them feel important and valuable. "I need you guys to help me set things up, lay out the tarps, hand out the candy, sing the songs, everything. When you do that, all these shorties are going to look up to you and give you respect because you are the leaders."

It didn't take long before I had a core group of twelve-to fourteen-year-old boys and girls whom I was able to disciple and train to be leaders.

During the week, I went by the buildings and rounded up this group of kids, drove around town, and bought them sodas. Through them I was able to meet their moms and siblings and get to know more people. Because of the Bible club having high visibility right in the middle of the playground, all the residents in those buildings knew who I was.

What was amazing was the respect I received from the gang leaders. Whenever I was there doing the outdoor Bible clubs, the gangs would call a pause on their war: "No shooting when the preacher is out there with the shorties!" God gave us His protection every time.

Miracle Provision

I began to look around the area to find a building where we could start a church. Just three blocks away from the projects was an old, abandoned Catholic church. It had a gymnasium, a rectory for the priests, a convent for the nuns, and a large church building on the corner. And it was for sale!

All I really wanted was the gym. That was like having a gold mine in the inner city. The kids loved basketball and would flock to the gym. Attached to the gym was an old bingo hall we could convert into a chapel. This was all I really needed to establish a strong work in this neighborhood. But the seller did not want to divide the property. I could take all of it or none of it.

I stood there looking at those four large buildings on three acres of land on the corner of one of the busiest expressways in America. It was prime real estate, but the buildings were over one hundred years old and in terrible shape. The place was a total mess. It would take millions of dollars and thousands of man hours to renovate them correctly. But I had a big God. Nothing was impossible for Him, right?

So, I prayed, "Well, God, if you want to give me the entire thing, I'll take it."

In September 1999, the phone rang.

"This is Pastor Bob."

Pastor Bob? Why was he calling me? This man pastored the largest, wealthiest church in Illinois. Every year they gave more money to missions than any other church in the nation. Talking to Pastor Bob was like talking to God. That is how highly regarded he was.

"Dan, I heard you were starting a church on the South Side. Is that true?"

"Yes, sir," I responded.

"Have you found a building yet?"

"Well, I have, but I'm not sure I'm going to be able to get it." I proceeded to tell him about the Catholic church property that was available.

"Well, I know you are going to the pastors' conference in Cincinnati next month, and I will be there. Let's meet with the district superintendent during that time and we can discuss it."

I was very excited! I needed twenty-five thousand dollars for a down payment on the property. I was hoping they would consider helping me with that.

At the conference, I met with Bob and our district leader. I shared about the vision I had to start a church on the South Side of Chicago and told them about the property. I also told them I needed the twenty-five thousand dollars for the down payment. They politely listened and we finished our lunch.

That evening, after the service, Pastor Bob approached me. "I've decided we would like to help you get that property," he said.

"Wow, that's great! If you could help us out with the down payment, that would get us started," I replied.

"Well, that would be good, but what we would *really* like to do is just buy the whole thing and give it to you."

I just stood there staring at him. I didn't know what to say. This was so far beyond anything I could have ever hoped or imagined.

Bob laughed and put his big arm around me and said, "I believe in you, Dan."

Those words went deep into my soul. To have this man's support meant the world to me.

Chapter 7

Slavery

The son said, "Father, listen! How many years have I worked like a slave for you, performing every duty you've asked as a faithful son? And I've never once disobeyed you. But you've never thrown a party for me because of my faithfulness."
Luke 15:29, TPT

We closed on the property on Halloween, October 31, 1990. I think that should have been a sign to me because the following years became a nightmare.

The purchase of this property garnered a lot of attention in our denomination all over the state of Illinois, and at our national offices. Suddenly, my name became synonymous with inner-city ministry. What we were doing on the South Side of Chicago was now a major focus for our denomination.

I knew I was in way over my head, so I formed a board of advisors to counsel me and bring guidance to the overall project. The board consisted of very influential leaders from the national, state, and local levels.

During the first board meeting, I was asked how I planned to raise the millions of dollars it would take to renovate the property.

"Well," I said, "I plan to pray, believe God, and live by faith."

The men around the table stared at me for a long moment. "Are you saying you have no plans to raise the money? You aren't going to travel, do fundraisers, apply for grants, or send out support letters?" they asked.

"Yes, that is correct," I responded.

Another long moment of them staring at me in silence.

Then the district superintendent let out a long, loud laugh that the others joined in with. "Dan, obviously you do not understand the situation. You will need millions of dollars. You will need thousands of volunteers to help do the labor. There is no way that is going to happen with you doing nothing! You must develop a strategy to raise this money! If you can't do that, we will bring someone else in who can."

Bring someone else in? I thought. *They would really do that? They would just toss me to the side?* Suddenly I realized things had changed. This wasn't just between God and me anymore. This project now belonged to the denomination, and so did I. If I wanted to be a part of this, I would need to toe the line and do what they expected of me.

Live by Faith

Prior to this, I had had two different men contact me at different times to talk to me about living by faith and trusting God for all my needs.

They both told me if I depended on men instead of God, I would be obligated to them, and that dependence on man would bring bondage while depending on God would bring freedom.

I deeply respected each of these men and I knew I needed to listen to them. They were adamant that they were sent by God to give me this message, and I took it to heart. I wanted to be a man who trusted God. I knew the only reason I was here in the first place was because the hand of God was on my life.

Yet, as I looked at the men around the table during the board meeting, I realized I was proposing something that was outside the purview of their religious system. Living by faith and being totally dependent on God was not how religious systems operated.

Living by faith would put God in control. Religious systems prefer that man be in control. After all, the spirit of religion and the spirit of control work hand in hand.

Those men at the table did not mean to operate under a spirit of religion. They were good men who loved God to the best of their ability, and this way of thinking was all they knew. It was just the way things were done.

As the men laughed, I lowered my head, feeling ridiculed and ashamed. These were men I respected; some, I was even in awe of. I was just an ex-drug addict who didn't know anything about how to run a project of this magnitude. Maybe I was being foolish and naïve to think I could just believe God would supply my needs. I did not have the strength and courage to take a stand against these men.

Looking back, I know it was not their fault; it was mine. I simply did not trust God enough, and I was going to pay a high price for that.

"Okay," I said. "I will do it the way you want me to, and I will begin raising money the best I can."

I did not realize it at the time, but I had just exchanged the supernatural power of God for my own strength. I had just sentenced myself to years of hard labor rather than opting to trust God and live by faith. I had exchanged the hand of God on my life for the hand of man.

I found out that if you live by faith, you get what God can produce. If you live by your own abilities, you only get what you can produce.

Doing things on your own also displays a spirit of pride. Pride, self-reliance, religion—all go hand in hand. The book of James says, "God resists the proud but gives grace to the humble" (James 4:6, NKJV). God was going to have to deal with my pride before He could give me His supernatural grace. Proverbs says, "Pride goes before destruction, a haughty spirit before a fall" (Proverbs 16:18, NIV). I had no idea how full of pride I was or how much it would take to humble me.

Paul said, "Your new life began when the Holy Spirit gave you a new birth. Why then would you so foolishly turn from living in the Spirit by trying to finish by your own works?" (Galatians 3:3, TPT).

That board meeting was my turning point, the moment I gave up my life of "living in the Spirit" for a life of working in my own strength to accomplish the work of God.

Yes, as Paul would say: How foolish could I possibly be?

For the next six years, I did all I could to raise money. I traveled all over the nation doing missions services for an offering. I sent out support letters asking for funds. I constantly asked churches to send work teams to help renovate the property.

I spent every spare minute trying to work on the property: leading the volunteer work teams, procuring supplies, painting, hanging drywall, sanding walls, repairing the old boilers, sanding and repairing the old gym floor, putting in new windows . . . the list was endless. When I was not working on the property, I was out in the projects trying to stop the gang war and lead people to Jesus.

Often, I would walk back and forth in the no man's land between the buildings and pray. Whenever I would do this, the shooting would stop. They would never shoot when the preacher was out there praying. I would then go into a building on one side and the gang members would come up to me, begging me to pray for them because they were afraid they would die that day. Then I would go across to the other side and pray for the others the same way. I don't know for sure, but I hope those prayers helped save some lives.

The Older Brother

Once I committed to fundraising, the traveling increased dramatically. I constantly needed to be on the road bringing in money. Because I was gone so much, the ministry suffered. I had a wonderful team of workers, but they were not called to do what I could do, and I wasn't there to do it.

I became a workaholic, working eighty to a hundred hours a week, but no matter how hard I tried, it was never enough. There was never enough money, never enough workers, never enough supplies to repair the property, never enough time to be with my family, never enough time to do street ministry. I slowly began to slip into depression as I began to blame God for what I was doing wrong.

Somehow, I had changed so much that, instead of seeking God because of His wonderful love, I was only seeking God to get things from Him.

I did not realize I had begun to try to use God to build my ministry instead of God using me to build His kingdom. I was no longer His son; I had slipped into becoming His slave.

Slaves work very hard but never have anything to show for it. No matter how hard a slave works, he only has enough to barely survive. No matter how hard a slave tries, he can never be part of the family. A slave can never know the love of a father or the rights and privileges of a son. A slave can never truly belong. They are always on the outside, looking in.

I prayed for two hours every morning, but if you are praying out of the wrong relationship and with the wrong motives, the heavens can be as hard as brass. I began to believe one more "not enough" about myself: I believed God did not bless me because I wasn't good enough.

I grew angry with God and jealous of others. If a fellow pastor was blessed in some great way, I was not happy for him. All I could think was, *Why him? Why not me? Why can't I get blessed? I have been working as hard as I can, and I get nothing!* It never occurred to me that I had no love for my brother. In fact, I was actually quoting the older brother in the prodigal son story!

> The son said, "Father, listen! How many years have I worked like a slave for you, performing every duty you've asked as a faithful son? And I've never once disobeyed you. But you've never thrown a party for me because of my faithfulness." (Luke 15:29, TPT)

The older brother's own words exposed his wrong attitude: "I have been working as a slave for you." This is the spirit of religion: trying to earn God's favor by working hard enough or being good enough.

The older son wanted to be loved for his hard work and faithfulness. The father wanted to love him simply because he was his son.

Religion produces slaves. God produces children.

I was learning the hard way that a major key to answered prayer is to pray out of the correct relationship with the Father.

Paul explains this very well in his letter to the Galatians:

> So that we would know that we are his true children, God released His Spirit of Sonship into our hearts, moving us to cry out intimately, "My Father! My true Father!" Now we are no longer living like slaves, but we enjoy being God's very own sons and daughters. And because we are His, we can access everything our Father has, for we are heirs because of what God has done! (Galatians 4:6–7, TPT)

The Pharisee

This same spirit of religion also operated among the Pharisees. They obeyed the Law perfectly and thought they were so good that God must approve of them, but their works and obedience to the Law only filled them with pride.

In Luke 18:10–14, Jesus tells us the story of the Pharisee and the tax collector. The Pharisee says, "God, I thank You that I am not like other men—extortioners, unjust, adulterers, or even as this tax collector. I fast twice a week; I give tithes of all that I possess" (Luke 18:11–12, NKJV). The Pharisee is essentially telling God, "Look, I am giving you my very best. Now tell me how good I am! Surely you must bless me based on my good works!"

On the other hand, the tax collector simply prays, "God, be merciful to me a sinner!" (Luke 18:13, NKJV).

The Pharisee was exalting himself in his pride. The tax collector humbled himself, fully aware of his need for God's mercy. Jesus said it was the tax collector who walked away justified. The Pharisee walked away rejected and condemned, and he didn't even know it.

Paul had discovered the truth of this revelation of the Pharisee when he made this statement:

> But what things were gain to me, these I have counted loss for Christ. Yet indeed I also count all things loss for the excellence of the knowledge of Christ Jesus my Lord, for whom I have suffered the loss of all things, and count them as rubbish, that I may gain Christ and be found in Him, not having my own righteousness, which is from the law, but that which is through faith in Christ, the righteousness which is from God by faith. (Philippians 3:7–9, NKJV)

When I read the stories about the older brother and the Pharisee, I identified and agreed with them. In my mind, I knew it was wrong to side with them, yet my heart was still blind to the fact that I was operating under the same spirit.

I had a long way to go before I was delivered of that hideous spirit of religion.

Depression

My wife and three small children suffered as well, as I sacrificed time with them to focus on the ministry.

"What's wrong, buddy? What's happening?" I was talking to my four-year-old son, Josh, on the telephone. I had been gone for four weeks doing missions services.

At first, he didn't want to talk to me, but finally he answered, "I am angry with you."

"Why are you angry with me, Josh?"

"Because you never come home anymore."

His words cut me to the heart. I was failing my own son. I was sacrificing time with my son on the altar of building a ministry. He was feeling unloved by his own father, and to be honest, I was feeling unloved by my heavenly Father. I sat on the edge of the bed in the hotel and wept.

We would have Sunday services every week, and every Sunday, the church would be virtually empty. I would stand there, and as the tears of depression and failure rolled down my face, I would say, "I'm sorry, God. I will try harder this week. I will pray more, I will do more visits, I will do more outreach. I promise I will try harder."

But when you have the wrong mindset and the wrong motivation, trying harder at what you are doing wrong is not the answer.

Wanting to Die

While this was happening, I was still overseeing the work in Cabrini Green. One day, I stopped by the old church to check on how the ministry was going. A young black couple had taken the lead and were doing a good job working with the kids.

As I got out of my car, I noticed that, directly across the street, several young men were darting around the corners of the project buildings. A few shots rang out as they ran from building to building, shooting at each other. I saw that one of the young men was Charles, someone I had spent countless hours counseling and praying with. He had actually left the gang at one point. But now, here he was, back in the gang and in the middle of a gunfight.

I walked across the street and called his name. I could see the look of surprise and shame on his face when he saw me. He came over to talk to me, his eyes darting all over the place to see where the other gang members were. He was on high alert as we were standing directly in front of the building where the gunfight was taking place.

As I talked to him, trying to get him to go home before he got killed, a gang member stepped around the corner of the building and pointed a gun at us. Charles stood behind me and began to yell at him, "Go ahead and shoot! You can't kill me! You will never be able to kill me!" That sounded really brave, but I was thinking it would've been better if he weren't standing behind me while he was saying it.

The other guy yelled back, "Get out from behind that white man and I will kill you!"

Charles took off running as fast as he could, getting into the building and ducking for cover.

I walked back to my car and sat there for a few moments. Then I slammed my fist into the steering wheel. I cussed and said to God, "You are going to make me *live* through this, aren't you?"

I'd secretly been hoping I would get shot that day. It would look like I died as a hero working in the inner city, gunned down while trying to bring Jesus to the projects. No one would have to know how much of a total failure I really was.

From time to time, friends would stop by to try to encourage me. Over and over, I would hear the same thing from them: "God says, 'Seek my face and not my hand.'" I was so blind; I had no idea what that meant. I just kept thinking, *I don't care which body part I get; I just need God!*

Failure

We never had enough money, and the ministry was always in debt. One cold November day, I was supposed to host a pastors' luncheon in our chapel. I could not afford to pay the bills, so the gas had been cut off. I was so embarrassed that all my guests had to keep their coats on and stay bundled up while eating lunch. It was just another thing that added to my shame of being a failure.

The dark blanket of depression became heavier day by day. I would sit in my office, lay my head on my desk, and cry from hopelessness.

All of this put a heavy strain on my marriage as well. I had married the most wonderful, supportive woman who was willing to follow me into the dangerous housing projects and support my crazy dreams. Jan loved God deeply and did her best to keep the family together while I was gone so much. But the strain of me being such a mess was wearing on her.

On the outside, I was a very popular public figure. I could preach well, tell stories, and make people laugh when I was out ministering. People would tell me how courageous I was and that I was a great man, but they had no idea of the truth: I was a broken man. A failure. A man who believed he had been rejected by God. A man who was not good enough.

Chapter 8

The Lord of the Journey

*Blessed is the man whose strength is in You,
whose heart is set on pilgrimage.*
Psalm 84:5, NKJV

In August 1995, Jan and I made the commitment to move our family to the ministry location. We moved into the third floor of the former rectory and turned it into a three-bedroom apartment. Somehow my wife had agreed to raise our children in the inner city of Chicago. Our youngest, Josiah, had just turned three. Jennifer was six and Joshua was eight.

Josh and Jenni began to attend a charter school directly across the street from the projects. Their white skin and blond hair stood out in a sea of black faces, as they were the only white kids in the entire school.

Jan began to homeschool a few kids from the neighborhood. Their actions at school had become so bad that the teachers would place a desk in the hallway and make them sit there all day, learning absolutely nothing. Jan began to work with these kids, and they blossomed as she would speak life into them and encourage them. For the first time, these kids felt important and valued. You could watch hope rise because they had finally found someone who believed in them.

What Jan did with those kids was truly miraculous, all the while raising our three children and being the bookkeeper and administrator for the ministry.

While Jan was taking to her new role wonderfully, I was still a depressed and broken man. One night in December 1995, a couple who were dear friends came to visit us. They could see I was discouraged and in emotional pain. My friend began to give me a prophetic word from God. I was so burned out and hopeless that I stopped him.

"Please, just stop. I don't want to hear it. I am tired of prophetic words. I don't need another word; I need action!"

My friends went silent. They had no idea how to help their hurting friend.

The Toronto Blessing

In January of 1996, I began to hear chatter about a move of God that was taking place in Toronto, Canada. I had heard the story of a woman named Heidi Baker, who was a missionary in Mozambique. After years of fruitless ministry, she had become burned out and depressed. She went to the services that were being held in Toronto, and God met her in a tremendous way. She was set free from the hopeless depression and filled to overflowing with the love of God. Hearing her story gave me a spark of hope. Was it possible that, if I went to this place, God could do the same for me? I loaded up my wife and our staff and made the trek from Chicago to Toronto.

The services were being held in a large warehouse. Word had gotten out that the waters were stirring, so thousands of desperate, broken people came flocking to this place, hoping they could receive a touch from God.

I was one of those people.

For three days we went to services, heard the Word of God preached, worshiped, and prayed. Everywhere I looked, people were manifesting the Presence of God. While the manifestations were everywhere, I remained as dry as toast. I felt like I was walking around in a shower but not getting wet.

On the third and last night, a woman preached and then asked for anyone who was involved in ministry to come forward. Hundreds of us responded and lined up on the red tape they had placed on the floor.

The woman began to pray for us from the platform and as soon as she did, every single person standing on the tape went down, slain in the Spirit. Hundreds of people fell backward simultaneously. No one had touched them. It looked like machine gun fire had just taken them out; every one of them was on the floor—except me.

I looked to my left, looked to my right, looked up to heaven, and laughed. *How could you miss?* I thought. But the thing about not going down was that now I stood out and was about to get more prayer. The woman stepped off the platform and walked toward me. She must have thought I was a challenge. I just didn't feel anything and wasn't going to fall down pretending that I did. I closed my eyes as she prayed.

That night there was a violinist and a guitarist leading worship. I could hear the music playing through the speakers as the woman prayed for me. I happened to open my eyes for a moment and was shocked to see the guitarist on my left and the violinist on my right. They had come off the platform and were standing right next to me, sending the music straight into me.

A powerful surge of the love of God overwhelmed me and I fell to my knees, weeping. It was as if God really did see me and somehow, He still loved me. My soul felt a glimmer of hope.

That night in Toronto, God encountered me and gave me grace to begin my journey of seeking His face.

Upon my return to Chicago, I could feel my spirit changing ever so slightly. Now, I wasn't trying to get things from Him, seeking His hand. Instead, I was seeking His Presence, seeking His heart. I would spend hours in the dark chapel at night, pacing the floor, praying, and listening to worship music, asking God to change me and make Himself known to me.

The Pilgrimage

I had set my heart on a pilgrimage. A pilgrimage is not a short trip, but a long journey that can take weeks or even months to complete.

The problem with this pilgrimage was I had no idea where I was going, or how to get there. Thankfully, Jesus is the Lord of the journey, and He is faithful to complete the good work He has started (see Philippians 1:6).

A pilgrimage takes time, and it has the power to change you forever.

We read in Scripture: "Even when their paths wind through the dark valley of tears, *they dig deep to find a pleasant pool where others only find pain*" (Psalm 84:6, TPT, emphasis added).

I had begun my journey and I was digging deep. God was with me on this journey, and He alone would lead me to find that pleasant pool of intimacy with Himself.

I found a workbook called *Experiencing God* by Henry Blackabee, which God used tremendously to change how I perceived Him. Before, I was the one coming up with the vision and all the ideas, asking Him to bless them. But this teaching showed me God is always at work, that He loves me, and that He invites me to join Him in what *He* is doing. So, instead of trying to get God to do my agenda, my job was to look to see where He was working and join Him there.

It was a simple concept that I had not seen before. In the former, I was in charge, telling God what to do. In the latter He was in charge, inviting me to come join Him. I began to see the latter was certainly better than the former.

The lights were beginning to come on.

Grace

I found a verse that hit home to me: "Come to me, all you who labor and are heavy laden, and I will give you rest. Take my yoke upon you and learn from Me, for I am gentle and lowly of heart, and you will find rest for your souls. For my yoke is easy and my burden is light" (Matthew 11:28–30, NKJV). Tears came to my eyes as I read it again and again.

God spoke to my heart, "If you are working harder than I am, something is wrong. I will do the heavy lifting. I simply invite you to come alongside me and participate in what I am doing."

It would still take some time for me to understand what that truly meant, but God had begun the conversation.

Day after day, I would pray, worship, and seek God, and although I was doing that, I was still under a strong spirit of depression and despair. I had still not gotten a breakthrough with God.

The concept of grace frustrated me. I wanted to be seen as someone special to God based on what I accomplished. I wanted Him to love me because I stood out as something special, which I based on who I was and what I did for him. I wanted God to see me as someone significant, not because of what He had done for me, but because of what I had done for Him. (This is the spirit of religion.)

I felt that grace just made me like everyone else and stripped me of my individuality. I eventually found it was quite the opposite.

Grace was stripping me of my pride, and my old identity was fighting it.

The book of Hebrews says, "There remains therefore a rest for the people of God. For he who has entered His rest has himself also ceased from his own works as God did from His" (Hebrews 4:9–10, NKJV).

"Ceased from his own works." What did that mean? Was I just supposed to sit and stare at the wall and do nothing? My frustration level continued to grow. I felt like a brute beast with no understanding.

But the beautiful thing about frustration is it leads you to seek the truth until you truly find it. Frustration can be God's vehicle to change.

In May of that year, I thought maybe I should fast, so I went on a three-day fast. It didn't seem to help a bit. So, I did a seven-day fast. Once again, no breakthrough at all. Then I went to a pastors' meeting, and there, I met a man who had just finished a forty-day fast. He was so full of joy, and his countenance shined like the sun. *This guy is insane*, I thought.

As I drove back to my office, I began to talk to the Lord. "Forty days! I can't fast for forty days! I'll die!"

Softly, gently, I heard the Lord say, "That's the point."

The irony was that all this time that I wanted to die, God had wanted me to die as well—just not in the way I had thought.

I walked into my office and glanced down. Someone had placed a book on my desk. It was called *How to Do a Forty-Day Fast* by Bill Bright.

You have to be kidding me! Who in the world put this here? I wondered. I wanted to toss it in the garbage can, but even I had enough sense left to know this was God talking to me.

Chapter 9

The Death

*Most assuredly, I say to you, unless a grain of wheat
falls into the ground and dies, it remains alone;
but if it dies, it produces much grain.*
John 12:24, NKJV

I began the forty-day fast in May of that year. I figured, *If I'm going to die, I might as well die God's way.*

I didn't go into the fast with an attitude of hope; it was an expectation that I was simply going to die, and that death would be better than the life I had been living. What was strange was that during the entire fast, the depression was lifted from me.

God gave great grace as each day I drank a glass of vegetable juice and a glass of apple juice. I had plenty of energy to stay active and fulfill my duties at the ministry, although I did stop traveling during that time—at least up until the last few days of the fast, when I traveled to Minneapolis, Minnesota, for a conference on inner-city ministry hosted by a local Bible college.

THE DEATH

Three Questions

Billy Graham happened to be in town doing a crusade at the same time, so after the last evening of the conference, I decided to walk over to the stadium and attend the crusade. (I figured I needed to get saved all over again anyway.) A woman named Carolyn, who was the vice president of the Bible college, decided to walk with me. Along the way, we began to have a conversation about what God was doing in my life. We stopped and sat on a park bench—we never did make it to the crusade.

"Dan, you do realize God wants to kill you, right?" Carolyn asked.

"Yeah, I have that part figured out. Is there anything I can do to speed up the process?" I responded.

"No, He is in charge of all that. You just have to continue to surrender to it. Dan, God wants to ask you some questions. Are you ready?"

"Sure, fire away," I replied. I had no idea what was coming.

"All right," said Carolyn. "Here they are. 'Daniel,' says God, 'if I move you out from your place of ministry and bring someone else in, and give them massive revival, and they get all the credit for it, is that okay with you?'"

"Say what?" I exclaimed. "Seriously? He would do that to me? After working as hard as I could for six years, I wouldn't be able to see any of the fruit of my labor at all? That's not fair!"

"'Oh, I'm sorry,' God says, 'I thought you were doing this for Me, but I guess you were just doing it for your own fulfillment and for your own pride.'"

Ouch! It was like a knife pierced my heart. My motives of selfish ambition had just been exposed. Carolyn was speaking, but it was certainly the Lord giving her the words to say.

Figuratively, she reached over and pulled the knife out. God wasn't done with it yet.

"'Daniel, if I never use you publicly ever again, if you never preach for Me again, and no one ever knows your name, but you have Me, is that okay with you?'"

"Oh man, I like preaching. I like people giving me compliments. I like the attention I get when the spotlight is on me," I answered.

God was exposing my false identity. My identity was not in Christ; it was in what I did and how people looked at me. My reputation had become my identity.

Once again, she reached over and pulled out the knife. God was still not done with it.

"'Daniel, your reward for seeking Me is Me. Is that enough for you?'"

With this simple little question, He exposed the selfish, self-centered desires of my heart. I didn't want God; I just wanted to use God to get what I wanted, and He was not going for it.

Those three questions cut me more deeply than I can explain. Those three questions helped me change my relationship with God. Those three questions would eventually change my life forever.

That evening, Carolyn took me back to her office and had me kneel down. She opened a bottle of fragrant anointing oil and poured the entire contents over my head.

"I believe God wants me to anoint you for your burial," she said as the oil flowed over my head and down my face.

At the end of the forty days, I was expecting a major breakthrough in my life. The problem was, I wasn't quite dead yet. Within a week of finishing the fast, the depression had returned with a vengeance.

My Resignation

After the fast, the hopelessness and despair came flooding back deeper than before. I was totally lost. I knew I could not continue in ministry like this. If I could not get a breakthrough with God, I would have to quit. Maybe I wasn't called by God to be in ministry after all. It was time to leave and go get a regular job, so I wrote my letter of resignation.

"It's time for me to quit," I said to Jan. "I have done everything I know to do to find God, and I can't find Him. I'm done. I have nothing left. It's time to go." Tears were streaming down my face as I sat in front of my wife, ashamed of being a total failure. I had shown her my letter of resignation.

"Well," she said, "I will follow you wherever you want to go, but I just have to tell you, you are wrong! I know God is not done with you! I know who you are. Just give it a little more time. Please, just a little more time."

I sat, shaking my head slowly. I couldn't believe this amazing woman still believed in me after all she had witnessed. I had no faith left, so I chose to hang on to hers for a little while longer. I put the letter in a drawer of my desk.

Ironically, God did want me to resign. While I had written that letter to my board, God was receiving it as if it had been written to Him, and He gladly accepted it as my act of surrender. My works had ceased, now He would be able to do His works.

During the next seven months, I fasted, worshiped, and prayed. I would fast for ten days, then twenty-one days, then thirty days, and then forty days with one day on and one day off, and then I would fast some more. I didn't know what else to do. As I fasted, my hunger for God grew until it became insatiable.

I began to think that if God did not come down to me, I was going to crawl up into heaven and get Him myself! I just knew I had to find Him in a way that I had never known Him before.

Jesus Comes to My Door

One night I was lying in bed, staring at the ceiling as I had done on countless nights. I glanced over at the doorway to my bedroom, and I saw Him. I don't know how to explain it; I didn't see Him physically, but I knew He was there. I could see Him in my spirit.

Jesus was standing in the doorway; He lifted His hand and beckoned me to come.

I rose from bed and followed Him to the kitchen and sat at the table. I took a pad of paper and a pen, and I began to write. He directed me to make a list of everything I had done over the years, as leader of the ministry, that was not of His will.

I listed decision after decision that I had made that came from my own mind rather than being led by the Holy Spirit. The list grew to about thirty things that needed to be rectified and brought into His will. It only took a few minutes. It was as if Jesus sat at the table with me and was saying, "Fix this, change this, let this go. . . ."

Interestingly, I knew instinctively which decisions I had made that were not of Him. He had given me my to-do list, but it would take months to correct all that I had done wrong. I did not make all those decisions overnight, and it would take time to correct them.

Change of Philosophy

The next morning, I went to work on the list. I had staff who were in the wrong positions. I had staff who did not belong there at all. I had people living in our ministry house who did not belong there.

The entire way I had approached ministering to the poor had been wrong. I had given and given, but no matter how hard I tried to help people, it was never enough. And because I tried so hard to be the solution to people's problems, they never prayed to God, they never exercised faith. They simply came and "prayed" to me, and when I was not enough for them, they became angry and jealous of those I did help.

I never realized I was placing myself in the position of God and teaching them to depend on me rather than Him. In my

THE DEATH

effort to bring them to God, I had become a roadblock to their faith in God.

They would never experience the relationship with God that created supernatural miracles as long as they depended on me instead of Him.

God instructed me to tell the people, "From now on, I have nothing for you. I can't buy your groceries, I can't pay your bills, I don't have a job for you. I have nothing except Jesus. I can't do anything for you except bring you into the Presence of Jesus. If you want that, He will be everything you need." I was beginning to learn the lessons Jesus had been trying to teach me all those years, and now I was applying them to how I did ministry.

Obeying God became another way of pursuing Him; it also became my way of worshiping Him.

I began to have a holy fear that I must do exactly what He told me, no matter the consequences. As I obeyed Him, I was coming into alignment with His heart. I was no longer in charge. He was now the one leading the way, and He was inviting me to come join Him.

It was no longer my strength, my strategy, or my work. I was moving into His supernatural grace, and what had been hard was becoming easy.

It was as if I were removing Saul's armor, which represented doing things in the natural, and being clothed in God's supernatural grace. Grace is the supernatural power of God that enables you to be and to do what you could never be or do on your own.

I was beginning to discover His grace. I could hear Him inviting me to come closer. He had promised, "And you will seek Me and find Me, when you search for me with all your heart" (Jeremiah 29:13, NKJV). I was now truly seeking Him with all my heart. Not to get things from Him—I was desperate just to find Him for who He truly was: my Father who loved me and had good plans for me. I knew if I found Him, I would find all I would ever need.

The God of More than Enough

During this time of dying to self, I decided it was time for the ministry to die as well. I had spent years working as hard as I could to keep it alive. We were always in debt, and it seemed we were always living on life support. As I sat at my desk, I symbolically reached over and pulled a plug from the wall socket.

"Okay, God, you let it live, or you let it die. Just let me know when it's time to leave."

I was not going to travel anymore. I wasn't going to write support letters anymore. I wasn't going to recruit work teams anymore.

I was done. The ministry no longer belonged to me. I had truly resigned. I had finally begun to live by faith.

At the time I pulled the plug, we were fifteen thousand dollars in debt. Six months later, we had one hundred thousand dollars in the bank.

Chapter 10

The Resurrection

And you did not receive the "spirit of religious duty," leading you back into the fear of never being good enough. But you have received the "Spirit of full acceptance," enfolding you into the family of God. And you will never feel orphaned, for as he rises up within us, our spirits join him in saying the words of tender affection, "Beloved Father!"
ROMANS 8:15, TPT

During those months of fasting and pursuing God, I felt myself changing day by day. Things that used to matter suddenly didn't. I no longer checked the mail for money every day, hoping for some morsel to keep us going. I no longer worked eighty hours a week trying to earn God's approval. The depression had faded, and my spirit was feeling lighter. My heart had become tender and sensitive to His Presence. The deeper I pressed in for more of Him, the more I was transformed and renewed.

My Two Sons

One day, I was in the living room when my son Josh, who was nine years old at the time, came in and handed me a piece of paper.

"Here, Dad, I drew this for you."

(Josh is a very talented artist and to this day has a fine career using this gift.)

"Josh," I exclaimed, "this is simply amazing! You have so much talent, and I am so proud of you. Thank you; I love you very much." I gave him a big hug, thinking we were just having a nice father–son moment. What I did not know was that my other son, five-year-old Josiah, had been watching this and had run into his bedroom. After several minutes, he came back into the living room and handed me a piece of paper.

"Here, Daddy, I drew this for you. Will you love me too now?"

His words cut me so deeply. It was as if a knife had stabbed me in the heart. I was so hurt by his words that tears filled my eyes. "No, no, no, Jo! I'm your dad! I love you! You are my son! You never have to draw me a picture to get me to love you. I always love you! The picture is very nice, but that's not why I love you. I love you because I am your dad, and you are my son. I will always love you!"

At that moment, I felt as if Father God was standing in front of me, looking deeply into my heart. In an instant, I felt the intense Presence of God as I became keenly aware that this was exactly what I had been doing to Him. I had been trying to draw Him the best picture I could, hoping that if it was good enough, He would love me. He, on the other hand, simply wanted to be my Father and wanted me to be His son, to know the deep security of being forever loved by Him.

Suddenly, I understood how much my wrong mindset had deeply grieved His heart.

This revelation reverberated in my spirit like an explosion. God had just used my two boys to teach me one of the greatest truths that would transform my life forever. He is my Father and I am His son and that is why He loves me. There is nothing I can do to make Him love me more than He loves me right now.

The journey to the end of yourself can be long and painful, but the Lord of the journey will guide you each step of the way. When you reach the end, He will be there, waiting with open arms, to embrace you in His overwhelming, unconditional love and fulfill every promise He made to you. That is the place where you no longer live, but now the life you live is for the one who loves you and gave Himself for you (see Galatians 2:20).

One morning during our staff prayer, He finally brought me to the destination of my pilgrimage: the end of myself. I began to weep, and I fell to the floor with deep sobs that came from my innermost being. This time it was not out of hopelessness and despair, but because I could feel the love of God penetrate my heart to the deepest recesses possible. I could feel His love permeate my soul. It was like the very first day when He had come and saved me and filled me with His love.

He had brought me all the way back to the starting point. He loved me. He had chosen me, and He had plans for me.

Digging Deeper

The psalmist writes, "Even when their paths wind through the dark valley of tears, they dig deep to find a pleasant pool where others only find pain" (Psalm 84:6, TPT).

I had dug deep for months; where I had found only pain, I now found the pleasant pool of His love and grace. Suddenly I was no longer the older brother in the prodigal son story, slaving away for his father's approval. Somehow, I no longer carried the spirit of religion, serving the God of never enough. I was now His child!

That morning during staff prayer, His Presence came upon me and tangibly rested for the next eight months. Every time I thought of Him, I would cry. Every time I prayed, I would cry. Every time I spoke His Name, I would cry. I was overflowing with His love. My spirit was leaping with a joy and freedom I had never known. I was free! I was loved! I was alive again! I thought back to that moment

I saw Momma on her knees in her bedroom, weeping and crying out to Jesus. Maybe, just maybe, I was understanding just a touch of what Momma had felt.

Momma's prayers were still being answered.

Loving Much

It became embarrassing to be in public. Once, I was asked to attend a board meeting at Moody Bible Institute in downtown Chicago. I sat around the large walnut conference table with ten very distinguished Christian leaders in the city. The person in charge asked me to open in prayer. Big mistake! As soon as I said the name "Jesus," I began to cry. In moments, my head was down and the tears were flowing.

I could not open in prayer; all I could do was praise, worship, and lavish my love on Him as a pool of tears formed on the beautiful table.

When I finally stopped, they all sat in silence and stared at me. I felt like the woman who had gone into the Pharisee's house, anointed Jesus's feet with oil, and washed His feet with her hair. There was no way they could understand how much I loved Him.

"To him who is forgiven much, that person loves much" (Luke 7:36–47, NKJV)—and I had been forgiven for so much!

Suddenly, everything that had been difficult became easy. People began to get saved. The Presence of God filled our services. I had become a worshiper of God, and that became our primary focus: to worship Him and experience His tangible Presence.

I formed a discipleship group for the teens called Warriors. We focused on prayer, worship, and experiencing God at the deepest levels. The kids living in the projects who had experienced so many wounds and so much trauma in their lives began coming in. They would spend hours at the altar, weeping and praying, allowing God to bring healing and deliverance to them.

The God Who Provides

"Dan, I do construction and build homes for a living. I believe God wants me to move down to your ministry and oversee all your work teams and all the renovations. Would that be okay?"

I couldn't believe it. Renovations of the property were a black hole that consumed hundreds of hours of my time and hundreds of thousands of dollars. Now God had brought me a man who knew what he was doing and would oversee all of it. I just laughed.

"Yes, I think that would be just fine," I answered.

About that same time, my nephew Nathan, who is one of the most anointed worship leaders I have ever met, came to our church and began to take us into the Presence of God. The worship in that little inner-city church was some of the best in the world.

Tim and Sharon, who had led me to Jesus and had been planting churches in Chicago, decided to come work with me. Now we had mature, godly leaders to disciple and mentor the people who were coming to Christ. It was such an honor to have them by my side, working together for the kingdom. God was bringing everything He needed to build His church.

One Saturday morning, I was invited to speak at a men's prayer breakfast in a nearby suburb. I was invited not as a missionary, but as a man speaking to other men.

That morning, I spoke about being a failure as a man. I told about how I had tried to have an identity based on who I was, what I did, and what I accomplished. I spoke about how I was a total failure until I found my true identity in Jesus Christ. It was not about what I had done for Him; it was about what He had done for me. As I spoke, the Presence of God settled on the men, and some of them began to weep.

I stood there watching the Holy Spirit minister so beautifully to those men. It was the first time God used my experiences to set others free from the same mindsets that had kept me bound for so many years. I realized the reason God had taken me through my experiences in such great depth was because He was preparing me to set others free from the same bondage I had lived under.

After the meeting that morning, the church administrator approached me.

"Dan, after you spoke, a gentleman came to me and gave me something for you. He did not want you to know who he is." He reached out his hand and gave me a piece of paper. I looked at it. It was a check for seventy thousand dollars!

I had just preached on being a failure, and the man gave me seventy thousand dollars!

Man, I'm sure glad I didn't preach on being a success! I thought.

Chapter 11

The God of Breakthrough

*As waters break out, the Lord has broken out
against my enemies before me.*
2 Samuel 5:20, NIV

The ministry continued to grow and be full of God's grace. His supernatural favor energized me daily and made easy what had previously been difficult. I finally had come to the place where He was doing His work and I had ceased from mine.

Reesie

One day, our chapel was filled with kids for a youth service, and several of them were causing a disturbance, so I asked them to come outside so I could talk to them. There were four boys, and I could see that three of them always deferred to the same boy. I could tell he was the leader, so I spoke directly to him.

I told him God had created him to be a leader, and he needed to stop wasting his time on the streets. I told him I wanted to start training him to be a leader for God. To my surprise, he came back into the service. His name was Maurice, and we called him Reesie.

Reesie joined the Warriors discipleship program, a group of fifteen kids I poured my life into, teaching them everything God had been teaching me. Reesie was filled with the Holy Spirit and became one of our top leaders.

At Christmas, we had a special party for the Warriors. After the party, we turned off the lights in the room and gathered around the Christmas tree. In the soft glow of the Christmas lights, I asked the kids to give thanks to God for something.

Each one of them gave their thanks to God in different ways. When it was Reesie's turn, he looked at me and said, "I want to thank God for PD saving my life." (They called me PD, short for Pastor Dan.)

I looked at Reesie and said, "What are you talking about?" I was totally clueless as to what he was referring to.

"Don't you remember, man? When I was bleeding to death, you found me and took me to the hospital and saved my life."

"What?" I exclaimed. "You are *that* kid? Are you serious?" I couldn't believe it.

The memory came flooding back: Five years earlier, a friend and I had been going from door to door in the projects, visiting people and inviting them to come to church. Suddenly, a door flew open and a woman yelled at me and my friend.

"Come help! This boy is bleeding to death! Come help!" We rushed into the apartment and a boy about eight years old was sitting on a chair with blood streaming out of his leg like a fountain. The wound was just above the knee. The chair was soaked with blood. I quickly had him lie down, then elevated the leg and tied a towel around the wound as tight as I could to serve as a tourniquet.

His mom told me he had fallen off a bunk bed and his leg had been punctured by the thick, sharp glass of a broken ashtray. He was already beginning to faint from the loss of blood, so I knew there was no time to wait for an ambulance. Besides, because of fear of going into the projects, the ambulance may never have come anyway.

I picked the boy up in my arms and ran down the seven flights of stairs with his mom right behind me. I put them in the van, and I drove as fast as I could to Michael Reese Hospital. I picked him up again and ran into the emergency room.

In Chicago, you have to be near death to get attention in an ER, and Reesie must have been really close, because the nurses immediately jumped into action and took the boy into a room, where then fought to control the bleeding. I went into the room with him, and he lay on the bed gripping my hand as tight as he could with tears in his eyes.

As I held his hand, he passed out from shock and loss of blood. The doctors pushed me to the side as they worked on him, and they made me leave the room. Eventually, they told us they had everything under control and the boy would be all right.

Now, it was five years later, and that boy was Reesie, sitting in front of me thanking God that I had saved his life. I hadn't realized this was the same boy until he said something.

Only God could take a seed that was sown five years earlier and cause it to produce fruit at just the right moment.

Stopping a Gang Fight

One hot summer day, I was driving my Jeep Wrangler down State Street, where the housing projects were. My friend, Kenny, a black brother, was with me. Kenny lived in the suburbs and would volunteer every chance he could. His love for God and his humility stood out to me as a constant.

We noticed a commotion and saw more than a hundred people pouring out of the buildings. We could see that a huge gang fight was getting ready to break out, as many of the young men were screaming and cussing at each other. Whatever was about to happen was going to be bad, and people were going to get injured; some could possibly die.

I pulled over and jumped out of the Jeep as quickly as I could and ran over to the scene. They had not really begun to fight yet; they were mostly yelling at each other, trying to muster up the courage to get violent. There were fifty to sixty young men on each side, all waiting for someone to get brave enough to start the rumble.

When I saw a few gang members really getting ready to escalate things into an all-out fight, I walked right up in between them. I did not say a word, but I stood nose to nose with the loudest one, praying in tongues under my breath.

It was the strangest thing. They acted like they did not see me. It was as if I did not exist. They did not acknowledge my presence, but as I stood there praying, they backed off and quieted down. Then some others in the mob grew louder and ready to fight, and I walked over to them and did the same thing. I did this again and again, and each time I did, they did not look at me, but they backed off and quieted down.

There was one young woman out there in the melee, trying to get the gangs to stop before someone was hurt. I heard her yell at one of the young men I was standing in front of.

"Can't you see this man? Can't you see him? Listen to him!" Even she thought it strange that none of them looked at me or acknowledged me, yet each one responded by backing down and becoming quiet as I stood directly in front of them and prayed.

During this chaos, there were hundreds of people out on the balconies and hanging out the windows of the surrounding buildings, watching what was happening down below.

Eventually, police cars began to pull up, and all the gang members scattered and ran back into the buildings. In a moment, what could have been an all-out bloody war ended without anyone getting hurt.

I had been so intensely focused on getting to the hotspots that were escalating that I had totally forgotten about Kenny. I had no idea what had happened to him. I looked over at the Jeep, and he was not there. As I looked around to find him, I suddenly realized he was right behind me. I couldn't believe it. The entire time I was putting out the fires, he was right behind me, praying in the Spirit as well. I was so impressed with his courage to literally have my back in a situation where we both could have been greatly harmed.

This was not like the time I walked into a gang war in Cabrini Green, wanting to get shot because of my depression. This time I felt the authority of God on me and moved in perfect peace, knowing I was completely safe.

It wasn't me and my friend that showed up that day. It was Jesus walking up into the middle of that chaos to bring peace. Through us, Jesus had just come into the projects. When Jesus shows up, everything else must bow.

Some of the people who had witnessed what happened that day began to come to our church. They had expected bloodshed, and they watched Jesus step in, take authority, and put a stop to it. They saw that the Presence of God was more powerful than the gangs, and it made them curious to know Him. The name of Jesus was being glorified in the projects.

Lavon

One night, someone came to our house banging loudly on the back door. I rushed to open it and found a young woman panting heavily with panic in her eyes.

"PD, my brother had an asthma attack and his lungs collapsed. The ambulance came, but they said he is in bad shape and may not make it. They took him to the emergency room. Please go pray for him!"

Her brother was Lavon, a young man in his early twenties who was a gang leader I had been working with for several months. I had a special affection for Lavon as we had spent hours together talking about his future and his need to have Jesus in his life. I jumped into my Jeep and rushed to the hospital.

When I walked into the emergency room, Lavon was surrounded by ten to twelve gang members, most of whom were dressed in long black trench coats and wearing red-and-black Chicago Bulls caps tilted to the side. The doctors and nurses were frightened and completely intimidated by these young men who refused to leave their friend. The nurses seemed to be relieved when I walked up and shook hands with all of them. All of these young men knew me because they had come to my gym to play basketball many times in the past.

Lavon lay in the hospital bed, unconscious and connected to a ventilator to keep him breathing. I looked at the nurse and asked, "How is he doing?"

"He is in critical condition."

I took his hand in mine, leaned over the side of the bed, and put my face next to his. I began to pray in the Spirit and kept praying for several minutes. The gang members stood around me in respectful silence as I prayed for their friend. As I prayed, I saw tears begin to roll down Lavon's cheek, and then suddenly his eyes opened. His hand gripped mine tightly as he looked at me, thanking me with his eyes.

A couple of days later, I answered a knock at the door. I was shocked to see Lavon standing in front of me. He grabbed me and hugged me as tightly as he could for the longest time.

"PD, thank you for saving my life. All I remember is waking up and hearing you speaking that funny language in my ear, and I could feel God. I knew right then that God was healing me and I was going to be okay. You saved my life, man, and I wanted to come say thank you." Lavon had tears in his eyes as he once again hugged me tight.

"Lavon, I'm not the one who saved your life," I said. "Jesus saved you that night. He loves you and He wants to have a relationship with you. He has great plans for you if you will fully give yourself to Him. He saved your life for a purpose, Lavon."

Because those gang members who were in his room that night had witnessed the miracle, they, along with Lavon, began to tell everyone in the neighborhood about what God had done. Lavon and many others continued to come to our gym, but now they would stay for our devotionals and prayer times.

God is always intent on showing His love and power. He always wants to make Himself known, especially to the hardest, most broken people. That night, Jesus walked into a hospital room and changed a young man's life forever.

Blind Eyes Opened

During this time, we had many volunteers from a large church in the suburbs who would come and help our ministry in different ways. One day, we received an emergency phone call from one of these couples we had come to know through the volunteer program.

"Our four-year-old son was playing and suddenly went totally blind for no apparent reason. We are rushing him to the children's hospital downtown. Is it possible for Dan to meet us there and pray for our son?"

I couldn't imagine the fear and concern those parents were feeling at that moment, let alone the fear of a small boy who suddenly was blind. I jumped into my Jeep and went to the hospital. I found their room and saw that the little boy was asleep. I looked at the mom and dad and could see the fear in their eyes. In fact, you could feel fear dominate the atmosphere of the entire room.

I leaned over the little boy, gently placed my hand on his head, and began to pray in the Spirit. I continued to pray for quite some time, and then I gathered his parents and their friends who had come to support them. We held hands as I prayed, asking God to do a miracle for this family. The Presence of God was tangible. Tears ran down the parents' cheeks as the Holy Spirit filled them with hope.

As I left their room, I knew fear was no longer there. It had been replaced with faith that came from the Presence of God. By the time I had reached home, the call had already come with the news. Jan met me as I walked in the door.

"He is completely healed," she said. "When he woke up, he saw his stuffed animal and reached for it. He can see perfectly." The doctors never did find the cause of the blindness. There seemed to be no physical reason for it. But for myself and the people in that room, we knew God had given us faith to pray. And then He answered those prayers.

God initiates our faith to believe Him for what He wants to do. He is the author and finisher of our faith. Within us, we have nothing to accomplish anything of significance. But it is God who shows us what He wants to do, and then He invites us to partner with Him, to believe, and then to become spectators of His glory.

Mexico Crusades

In 1999, I was invited to go to Mexico with David and Kathy Walker. They were going to conduct large evangelism and healing crusades and asked me to be part of the prayer and ministry team.

David had been part of the Voice of Healing Crusades with Jack Cole, William Branham, and A. A. Allen back in the 1950s. As a young man, David had died in a skiing accident and his mother prayed for him and raised him from the dead. David experienced being in heaven during that event and returned with a powerful gift of healing. It would be the greatest honor to travel with him and do crusades in Mexico.

We traveled from city to city, hosting crusades in bullrings and auditoriums. It was a joy to get to know David and Kathy and experience their humility. They simply loved God and loved people. I saw God do many amazing miracles on those journeys. I saw blind eyes opened, people delivered from demons, and many, many physical healings. But one of my greatest joys was being able to minister to the pastors.

In each city, during the day, we would have gatherings for the local pastors to encourage them and pray for them. When I was asked to speak to the pastors, I would share my story of failure and how God had led me to find His grace. I told of my brokenness and my depression and how I had slaved for God for so many years with no results. I shared about how He brought me into the place of being His son and overwhelmed me with His love.

So many of those pastors could relate to my story. So many of them could connect to the feelings of never having enough, never being enough, or never doing enough.

Over and over again, God used my past failures to minister His truth to hurting men who needed a revelation of the love of Father God. Each time I spoke, hurting pastors would be set free from the spirit of slavery and receive supernatural grace.

At the crusades, thousands of people were being healed, but in these small gatherings of pastors, spiritual leaders were being set free to have powerful, fruitful ministries. Each time I watched God set the captives free in those meetings, I rejoiced and thanked Him for all I had gone through.

What I had experienced now gave me authority to minister to others.

Leaving the Inner City

I continued working in the projects for a total of thirteen years, including my time at Cabrini Green. Over time, I began to feel that my assignment from the Lord there was coming to an end. During that time, He was also letting me know that it was time for me to leave the denomination. After nearly twenty years of being part of a religious structure, it felt strange to separate. I felt like I was sailing off into a great big ocean; it felt lonely and a little scary. *Okay, God, what next?* I thought.

I had no idea what the next phase of my training was going to be like.

FLASHBACK

The ambulance lumbered along, bouncing over a rough stretch for such a long time that I cried out, "You have to be kidding me!" I looked over at Jacob, still holding my bag of blood against his chest.

The bumpy mountain road, with all its twists and turns, was not sitting well with him. He had slid the side window open, stuck his head out, and was emptying his stomach along the road. I felt so bad for him as the car sickness caused him to retch even after his stomach was long empty. I reached over and patted him on the knee. We looked at each other with compassion in our eyes, but there was nothing either of us could do to ease the pain of the other.

Suddenly, the van came to a stop.

"We aren't there already, are we?" I asked.

"No, they just stopped for a chai break," Jacob replied.

"A chai break?" All I could do was laugh. We may have been in an emergency situation, but in India, even in the most severe of times, a good chai break is mandatory. After all, it was a long drive, and it was probably a good idea for our drivers to take a break and refresh themselves.

Ishan was in another ambulance making his way down the mountain as well. At this point, I had no idea how he was doing, but I knew Samson had stayed by his side and was in the ambulance with him. As I lay in the ambulance, I prayed for God to comfort and strengthen him.

My phone rang, and I saw it was my wife. Because of the twelve-and-a-half-hour time difference, she had been sleeping at the time of the accident.

THE GOD OF BREAKTHROUGH

Jan woke to her phone blowing up from people trying to reach her with the news. She fought the initial fear that tried to grip her and instantly began to pray.

I answered my phone. "Hey, hon, how are you doing?" I was trying to sound as cheerful as I could through the pain and the effect of the drugs. I felt so bad for her, knowing how helpless she felt knowing her husband was ten thousand miles away, in a foreign country, in bad condition. I proceeded to give her the report about how the accident had happened and that my leg was broken.

"Where are you now?" she asked.

"I'm in the back of an ambulance. We are waiting for our drivers to finish their chai break," I said, laughing. "I'm fine. They are going to take me to a hospital, and I will get surgery." I tried to sound as reassuring and jovial as I could, making jokes and making her laugh a little. The last thing I wanted to do was make her more fearful or worried about me. "My friends here are taking very good care of me and are doing everything they can to get me proper care. I am surrounded by the best people possible, and God has completely filled me with His peace. There wouldn't be anything you could do for me if you were here anyway."

"All right, I'm going to get the word out and start getting people praying for you," she said.

And that she did. Jan is a woman of prayer and great faith. She is also an amazing organizer and administrator. Over and over again, throughout our years together, I have seen her remain perfectly calm in the midst of a storm. Jan is rock solid, emotionally and spiritually. She has always been my backbone and the backbone of our ministry.

Within a few hours, she literally had hundreds of people praying for us. My wife may not have been by my side physically, but at that moment, she was carrying me with her love and prayers. Jan went to battle and did what she did best: mobilize an army of prayer warriors.

PART III
BASEMENT YEARS

Chapter 12

Lessons in Time

But those who wait on the Lord
Shall renew their strength;
They shall mount up with wings like eagles,
They shall run and not be weary,
They shall walk and not faint.
Isaiah 40:31, NKJV

We left the ministry on the South Side of Chicago in September of 2000. I was very much looking forward to the next chapter in my life.

Our family moved to a nearby suburb where the kids could walk to school, ride their bikes, and go to the park. They were thrilled with their newfound freedom and were quick to make new friends and settle into a new life. It was a great joy to watch them blossom outside the confines of the ministry house in the inner city.

Jan, our three children, and I were settled in our new house in the suburbs, and I began working odd jobs, mainly in construction. Our house had a large, finished basement, and I took one end of it and turned it into my office. I would spend hours at my desk reading the Word and studying.

I would spend every spare minute pacing the length of that basement, praying in the Spirit and seeking God. Every day I could not wait to get home from work and pace that basement.

On Saturday and Sunday mornings, my son Josiah would come down to the basement. He would curl up on the couch in a blanket and sit quietly as he watched me pace the floor and pray in the Spirit. It was strange, but those were not only intimate times with God, but also with my son.

That basement became my refuge, my secret place with the Lord, and I deeply cherished it. These would become known as my basement years.

Called Out by Name

During this time, I began to attend a charismatic black church on Chicago's South Side. The first service I attended there was on a Tuesday evening, and there were several hundred people in attendance. I had heard that this church had a reputation for being very prophetic and moved in deliverance as well. I was just trying to find a place where I could learn more about these things outside the confines of my previous denomination.

On my first visit, I walked into the building and sat in the back. Kenny invited me to come sit with him near the front. (This was the same friend who was with me when we stopped the gang fight.) Working for years in all-black neighborhoods, I was accustomed to being the only white person and standing out, but this night I only wanted to experience the service and have no one pay any attention to me. I just wanted to blend in, but God had other plans.

"Is there someone here named Dan?"

Worship was just ending, and a woman had taken the microphone. I looked around, waiting for someone to respond, when Kenny elbowed me and said, "That's you!"

I slowly raised my hand and the woman said, "Come on up here, brother; God has a word for you."

I made my way to the aisle and began walking up to the platform thinking, *God, You sure have a funny way of helping me blend in.*

As I approached the platform the woman lowered the microphone and asked, "Taylor? I think I am hearing your name is Dan Taylor?" Now, I knew we had never met before and there was no way she could know who I was. God had just called me out by name!

She proceeded to prophesy over me, and while I don't remember all of it, it was filled with promises, as well as admonition. God was telling me He was going to take me through a time of deep training to prepare me for what He had in the future.

The last part of the prophecy was: "Cross over, cross over. I will cause you to cross over your Jordan, and you will take cities for Me."

That prophecy sent me into the wilderness for the next eleven years. It was that prophecy that sustained me as God continued to do a deep work in my life.

Sometimes, only time can accomplish what God wants to do in a person's life. Time can be a powerful tool in the hands of God.

Waiting

It was twenty-five years from the time Abraham received the promise that God would give him a son to the time of its fulfillment. Scripture says, "Abraham believed God, and it was accounted to him for righteousness" (Romans 4:3, NKJV). Twenty-five years of waiting. Waiting until it was humanly impossible and only God could fulfill the promise with a miracle.

Waiting can develop an enormous amount of character in a person, especially if he chooses to keep believing in the waiting, no matter how long it takes.

From the time Joseph received dreams about being the savior of his people to the time of fulfillment, it was approximately thirteen years. Scripture says, "It was Joseph, who was sold as a slave. His feet were bruised by strong shackles and his soul was held by iron. God's promise to Joseph purged his character until it was time for his dreams to come true" (Psalm 105:17–19, TPT). In the fullness of time, God brought Joseph from the prison to the palace and fulfilled every promise to use him to save his people.

From the time David was anointed by Samuel to be king to the time he took the throne, it was approximately thirteen years. In fact, just prior to him becoming king, he experienced his lowest moment. His village of Ziklag had been attacked. Everything had been burned down, and the women and children taken captive. His own men were so distraught that they wanted to kill him. In the face of this destruction and loss, Scripture says, "David sat down and encouraged himself in the Lord" (1 Samuel 30:6, NKJV).

But how did he do that? I believe he sat down and remembered the prophecies that had been spoken over him—the promises of God. He remembered when Samuel had anointed him to be king. He remembered that Saul had, on two occasions, declared that he knew David would be king. He remembered Jonathan telling him he would be the next king, and he remembered Abigail, who had come to him in the wilderness and told him he would be king. David sat down and encouraged himself with the promises of God, and he chose to believe them, even in the face of failure and loss. God was molding and shaping his character to prepare him to receive the promise.

As David was sitting at Ziklag, Saul was fighting the Philistines and was killed. Within weeks of David's lowest moment, he became king. Paul tells us:

> Even in times of trouble we have a joyful confidence, knowing that our pressures will develop in us patient endurance. And patient endurance will refine our character, and proven character leads us back to hope. And this hope is not a disappointing fantasy, because we can now experience the endless love of God cascading into our hearts through the Holy Spirit who lives in us! (Romans 5:3–5, TPT)

We are God's workmanship. We are His creation. He is very good at developing us into the exact person He intended us to be from the time He formed us in the womb. He is an expert at using time and circumstance as powerful tools to shape us into ones who produce fruit for the kingdom. He is faithful, He is wise, and He can be fully trusted to accomplish His good pleasure in us.

As I look back today, I cherish my time in the wilderness with deep fondness. I know it did a deep work in me that caused me to mature, and I grew in deeper surrender and intimacy with Jesus. And when it was time, He brought me out in the power of the Holy Spirit.

Chapter 13

Forgiveness

For if you forgive men their trespasses, your heavenly Father will also forgive you. But if you do not forgive men their trespasses, neither will your Father forgive your trespasses.
Matthew 6:14–15, NKJV

During those basement years, God continually taught me about Himself. Glorious revelations of His goodness, grace, and love would overwhelm me. But things He showed me about myself could be especially painful. Hebrews tells us, "For the word of God is living and powerful, and sharper than any two-edged sword, piercing even to the division of soul and spirit, and of joints and marrow, and is a discerner of the thoughts and intents of the heart" (Hebrews 4:12, NKJV).

God is a master at seeing what is in our hearts, separating the good from the bad, and then removing what is not pleasing to Him. He is never finished with the task of conforming us to the image of Jesus Christ, and as always, God is really good at what He does.

It was this time in my life that God wanted to reveal my heart and do some very serious conforming to the image of His Son.

Spirit of Offense

Most often, I have a very thick skin, and it takes a lot to offend me. But there was one situation that occurred when I was deeply hurt by a local pastor. It's not necessary to go into the details, and in fact, looking back, I was as wrong in my behavior as he was in his. Suffice it to say, he did something to me that greatly offended me to the point that I was deeply hurt and filled with anger.

Day after day, night after night, I was consumed with the anger and pain this man had caused me. I would constantly have scenarios running around in my head of what I wanted to say to him, or even worse, scenarios of what I wanted to do to him. I had lost all peace and had no desire to pray. I must have had a thousand conversations with that man in my mind, and none of them sounded a bit like Jesus. At night, I lay in bed and went over these conversations again and again until my mind and body were totally stressed. These intense feelings continued every day for nearly three months.

Finally, as I paced my basement, trying to pray, God broke through the cloud of anger and pain and asked me a simple question:

"So, are you going to be a Christian or not?"

"Wait, what was that You said?" I asked, not really wanting Him to repeat it.

"Are you going to be a Christian or not?"

"Of course I want to be a Christian."

"Then you are going to have to forgive that pastor."

"But I don't want to forgive him," I declared.

"Then I can't forgive you. I meant it when I said, 'If you don't forgive men their trespasses, neither will your Father in heaven forgive you' (Matthew 6:15, NKJV)." The Holy Spirit was digging deep and forcing me to confront the truth about myself.

I inwardly groaned. All of a sudden, this wasn't about what the man had done to me; now it was between me and God. Was I going to be a Christian or not?

"Yes, Lord, I choose to be a Christian," I said quietly. "I forgive him. I release him from anything that I feel he owes me. I forgive him, and he owes me nothing."

Throughout the day, as I prayed, I would repeat this over and over again: "I forgive him. He owes me nothing."

As I continued to repeat this, I actually began to believe it. And as I believed it, I could feel my soul changing. The torment I had been feeling constantly for the past three months began to leave my mind. The feelings of anger and revenge were suddenly gone. Depression and darkness lifted off of me. Peace began to return to my heart and mind.

Forgiveness was setting me free from demonic oppression.

The Holy Spirit led me to Matthew 18:22–35. This is a parable Jesus told about a man who owed his employer a huge sum of money that would be impossible to pay back. The debtor fell on his knees before the master and begged for more time to pay back the overwhelming debt. The master looked upon the debtor and was moved with compassion for him. He did not just give the man more time to pay the debt; he actually erased it, released him from all he owed, and allowed him to go free.

The former debtor should have been humbled by this great mercy that had been shown to him, but instead, he saw a fellow employee who owed him the equivalent of five dollars. He took this man by the throat and demanded his money. This debtor also fell to his knees begging for more time to repay the money owed, but the man who had been forgiven so much refused to forgive and had the man thrown into prison. Now, an employee of the rich man observed this and was disturbed by what he saw. He went to the master who had shown mercy and told him what his fellow worker had done.

The rich man was deeply grieved and angry with the one who had been forgiven so much, and he called him back to stand before him.

"You wicked servant! I forgave all your debt because you begged me. Should you not also have had compassion on your fellow servant, just as I had pity on you?" (Matthew 18:32–33, NKJV).

The next two verses brought revelation to me that I had never seen before.

"And his master was very angry and delivered him to the torturers until he should pay all that was due him" (Matthew 18:34, NKJV).

Now, in the last verse of this story, Jesus goes from telling a parable to revealing the lesson of the story: "So my heavenly Father also will do to you, if each of you, from his heart, does not forgive his brother his trespasses" (Matthew 18:35, NKJV).

Wait—was God really serious? Would He actually deliver me to the tormentors if I refused to forgive my brother? The answer was a definite *yes*—in fact, that was exactly what I had experienced for those three months. My unforgiveness had opened the door to anger, resentment, bitterness, jealousy, revenge, depression, and deep darkness. Those spirits tormented me day and night, and they had the legal right to do so until I released forgiveness and was completely set free.

I believe God allowed this situation into my life for me to learn one of the greatest truths of my Christian life: Unforgiveness brings spirits of torment, but forgiveness sets the captive free.

I also believe God allowed this situation to occur for the purpose of helping me become more like Jesus.

Becoming more like Jesus is a powerful act of spiritual warfare.

Deliverance and Forgiveness

God highlighted this spiritual truth to me again, as at about that same time, I went on a prayer journey to Mexico. While there, we had an opportunity to minister to a woman who taught public school. She had explained she had been under demonic torment in her mind for some time and requested prayer. As my small team and I prayed for her, she felt more and more freedom. It was a peaceful and wonderful time of prayer as God ministered to His beloved daughter.

Suddenly, the woman winced with pain as a demon began manifesting in her. We attempted to cast it out just like we had done with the others, but it refused to go. The woman was physically manifesting and appeared to be in agony. We continued to pray for some time, but to no avail. We began to get tired and frustrated as we seemed to be impotent against this dark spirit.

Finally, I paused and stepped back to ask the Holy Spirit for help. I looked up at one of the team members, and we both received the same revelation at the same time.

"Unforgiveness," we said in unison.

"Ma'am, is there anyone in your life who has hurt you and whom you need to forgive?" I asked.

"Yes," she replied. "My husband has forced me to have sex with other men so he could make pornography videos. He has been sexually and emotionally abusive to me for years."

"Jesus is asking you to forgive him. Are you willing to do that?" I asked gently.

"He is an evil man. He does not deserve forgiveness!" I could see in her eyes the depth of the pain this man had caused.

"No," I said. "He does not deserve forgiveness, but this is not for his benefit. You forgive him for your own sake. Forgiveness will set you free from this demonic spirit of torment."

The woman continued to manifest even as she thought about what Jesus was requiring of her. Finally, she said, "What about the woman he is having the affair with? Should I forgive her too?"

I looked at her with a little smile. "Yes, ma'am, I think that would be a good idea."

The woman proceeded to forgive her husband and his mistress. As she prayed, she began to weep. God was setting her free and healing her wounded soul at the same time. Instantly, the tormentors were gone, and the woman was at peace.

Because of this experience, from that time forward, before doing any type of deliverance I always led the person through forgiveness first. I have found that this removes the legal right for the demon to remain, and they must bow their knee to Jesus and leave immediately.

Nearly one year after these experiences, I was taking a walk and I began thinking of the pastor who had hurt me. Suddenly, all the old feelings of anger and pain popped up inside of me as if it had just happened yesterday.

"What is this, God?" I asked. "I forgave and forgave. I don't want these feelings inside of me anymore. Why are these feelings still here after all this time? I thought I had been set free."

"Yes, son, you forgave him. But you did not ask *Me* to forgive him," Jesus said.

"I didn't want You to forgive him. I wanted You to get him for me. Whatever happened to 'Vengeance is mine, says the Lord'?"

Secretly, on the inside, I was still hoping something bad would happen to that man. I wanted justice to be served. Justice means to make something right. But I found that sometimes, the way God makes things right is by forgiving the guilty person.

"All right, Jesus, I don't want these evil spirits tormenting me anymore. I want to be totally free and full of Your Spirit. I want to be clean." I stopped walking and stood in the middle of the sidewalk.

"Father, I ask You to forgive that man and treat him as if he had never done anything wrong to me. I ask You to love him and bless him and bring great things into his life."

Now, finally, I was free! And I was becoming a little more like Jesus.

Offended by God

Over the years, God has taught me many aspects of forgiveness, but I was surprised when one particular revelation became personal between Him and me.

After my radical salvation experience, I still had to deal with many wounds and traumas from my childhood. In the months following my salvation, I dealt with forgiving the people who had injured me, whether they did it on purpose or unintentionally. I felt that God had ministered to my heart at a very deep level, and I felt His love and freedom as I pursued emotional wholeness.

Then, nearly ten years later (during the time of brokenness and failure I experienced in Chicago's South Side), all of the emotions and pain from my childhood resurfaced. I was shocked that this was happening. I thought I had dealt with these issues and walked through forgiveness. I thought I had been healed of the childhood trauma, yet here I was, with the pain so raw it was as if it had all happened yesterday.

"God, I don't understand. Where were You when I was going through all of that pain? Why did You allow all of that to happen to me for so many years? I can understand how later in life my own sins brought me pain, but what about when I was just a little boy? That pain wasn't my fault. Why, God? Why?"

I was sitting on the edge of my bed with tears running down my face as I prayed and questioned God. Why was I feeling these emotions so intensely after all these years? Where was this coming from? I did not understand what I was experiencing.

Then, in the middle of my pain, I heard God say, "Son, I am asking you to forgive Me."

"Say what?" I asked, totally confused. "Are you telling me You made a mistake, that You were wrong?" Even though that was what my heart felt toward God, my mind still could not comprehend the idea that He had made a mistake.

"No, son, I have not made any mistakes in your life. I am perfect in all My ways," He replied. "But you have pain that you don't understand, you are blaming Me for it, and you are holding it against Me. You have built a wall between you and Me, and you do not fully trust Me. I am asking you to release Me from the pain you are blaming

Me for. In this life you will understand some of what happened to you, and some of it you will never understand until you come home, but I am asking you to trust Me, even in the middle of your pain."

I lowered my head and began to sob deeply. I knew that if I did not fully trust God, our relationship could never grow past this point. This was as far as I would ever go with Him until I dropped my walls of mistrust. As I released God from the blame for my pain, healing began to take place in the deepest recesses of my soul.

Yes, I would love Him. Yes, I would trust Him, even in the pain I did not understand.

I had no idea that moment of surrender would set the course for the rest of my life. That decision to trust Him and never doubt His goodness became my new identity. It is the rock I will forever stand on.

Many of us have experienced pain that was not our fault. Sometimes that pain can be extremely intense, and it makes us question God's love and faithfulness. In these times, we must trust God and not lean on our own understanding (see Proverbs 3:5). God has never asked us to understand, but He has asked us to trust Him and keep our hearts open to Him, even in the middle of pain.

For many, forgiveness can seem to be an impossible request. Some people have suffered so deeply and for so long that forgiveness can seem to trivialize what happened to them.

But God is not asking us to make light of what happened to us, or to treat it as if it never happened. The bad thing *did* happen. It was painful, it was devastating, and it crushed your soul. It robbed you of your identity. The pain and suffering turned you into someone you never intended to be. Forgiveness is not for the one who hurt you. Forgiveness is for you, because it restores your identity.

It is said that time heals all wounds. I have no idea who came up with that, but it certainly wasn't from God. Time does not heal wounds. Only God can do that. And to bring healing to our hearts, He asks us to forgive. Forgiveness heals our wounds. Yes, there may be scars for the rest of our lives, but God glorifies those scars and turns them into badges of authority.

Now, because of my scars—because of what I have gone through and have overcome by His grace—I have greater spiritual authority to minister to others.

Paul says, "From now on let no one trouble me, for I bear in my body the marks of the Lord Jesus" (Galatians 6:17, NKJV). I believe Paul was pointing to his scars as a signet of his authority to speak and to be heard.

We also read, "And they overcame [the Enemy] by the blood of the Lamb and by the word of their testimony" (Revelation 12:11, NKJV). It is our testimony of suffering and overcoming that gives us authority to set the captives free.

I have learned to thank God for every wound, every scar, and every moment of suffering, because now, He is using those experiences to minister to many others.

Chapter 14

Equipping the Saints

For the equipping the saints for the work of the ministry, for the edifying of the body of Christ.
Ephesians 4:12, NKJV

Our family began to attend a local church near our house. It was a great church that had a good mix of black, white, and Hispanic believers. Pastor Tom was highly gifted in music and a very anointed man. We became good friends and he would invite me to preach from time to time, which I enjoyed.

One Sunday, we had a missionary couple from Peru visit the church and share about their ministry. Israel, a young Peruvian man, was married to an American woman named Jen. We all listened intently as they spoke about ministry in the Amazon jungle.

When they finished, Pastor Tom stood and looked out at me as I sat in the audience.

"Dan, I believe God wants you to take a team to Peru and work with this couple. You are not to do anything except pray. This will be a prayer team. You will not do evangelism crusades or help build anything. You are to go there and pray. I want you to put together a team from our church, train them, and set a date to go."

I was a little shocked to hear this. Pastor Tom had no idea that I had been learning about prayer walking and spiritual mapping. It could only have been the anointing of the Holy Spirit that prompted him to say this to me. It was more of a prophetic directive than something that came from his own mind.

Informed Intercession

I had been reading several books about informed intercession and breaking demonic strongholds. The basic principle behind this teaching is akin to doing spiritual demographics. The idea was to study the history of a given territory or region and ascertain what spiritual strongholds were there and how they came to be. One would then use this information to attack these strongholds in the name of Jesus and remove them, thus changing the spiritual climate of the region. Then, it would be as if the veil had been lifted and people would have clarity of mind to receive Jesus as their Savior.

Pastor Tom had no idea that I had been doing all this research, so when he said to take a prayer team to the Amazon, my spirit jumped. God had already been preparing me for this. But take a team from this church into a place that had some of the highest-level witchcraft in the world? *There is no way these people are ready for that*, I thought. *They have no clue what they would be walking into.* I would need to do some very intensive training with this team.

As I began to prepare the team, I wanted to make sure Jen and Israel were open to the type of prayer I wanted to do. If we were not on the same page, then it would not be effective at all. I emailed Jen, explaining I had been reading books by C. Peter Wagner and others about spiritual mapping and doing informed intercession.

"Are you familiar with any of these teachings?" I asked. "And if so, would you be open to us doing this type of prayer in Peru?"

"Yes!" she replied. "I went to Fuller Theological Seminary and had C. Peter Wagner as one of my professors. I took his class on informed intercession and have been asking God to send us a team to do that here!"

The stage was set. God was putting everything together for a very powerful time in Peru.

Targeted Prayer

For the next three months, I met twice a week with the team of ten people who had volunteered to go. We learned about spiritual warfare, demonic strongholds, and spiritual mapping. We learned how to hear and be sensitive to the voice of God, how to discern flesh from Spirit, and how to pray specific, targeted prayers.

I taught them how to listen to the Holy Spirit and allow Him to pray His prayers through us, rather than just praying out of our own minds. I taught them to stay focused on one prayer target, hitting it over and over again, until we knew we had breakthrough. The Holy Spirit would then lift off that topic and move on to another one.

I have been in many prayer meetings where people pray and bounce around from topic to topic. One person prays for revival and the next person prays for their business to prosper and the next prays for their family and so on. All of those are great prayers, and at the end everyone says, "Wow, that was a great time of prayer." But what was actually accomplished? Was there a breakthrough with results to those prayers?

I have found that praying Spirit-led, targeted prayers is a powerful and effective way to achieve breakthrough; this is what I taught the team.

They Shall All Prophesy

Another topic I focused on with the team was teaching and activating them to prophesy. Paul says, "Pursue love, and desire spiritual gifts, but especially that you may prophesy" (1 Corinthians 14:1, NKJV). And again in verse 3 of that same chapter: "He who prophesies speaks edification and exhortation and comfort to men."

Prophecy is a powerful tool to be used in ministering to others, as it reveals the heart of God toward the individual. It reveals to the person that God knows them, sees them, and has a plan for their life. Prophecy is also a powerful gift to be used in the life of an unbeliever. It instantly connects them to a living God who loves them and wants to have a relationship with them. It makes God real and alive and accessible to them.

One day, my daughter Jenni brought her friend Katie home to meet me. Katie referred to herself as a "white witch," who used her powers to help people. She told me all about her crystals that exuded spiritual energy, and how she had two spirit guides that would visit her through portals in her house.

I listened intently as this beautiful young lady shared openly about her magic powers and how she communicated with her spirit guides. After some time, I looked at her and said, "Katie, you are a very spiritual person, and you have a very powerful gift. I believe God gave you that gift from the time you were born." Katie smiled as I gently affirmed her gift. "But Katie, if you connected your gift to the Most High God who gave it to you, you would be amazed at what He could do with you."

Katie looked at me with a quizzical look on her face.

"Katie, would it be okay If I prayed for you?" I gently asked.

"Yes, please," she replied.

As I began to pray for her, God showed me a picture. I saw Katie as a little girl, maybe six or seven years old, wearing a sundress and sitting on the living room floor playing with a doll. She kept looking at the door, waiting for her father to come home, but he never came. Then I saw Jesus walk into her house, pick her up, and hold her.

As I told Katie what I saw, she laid her head on my shoulder and began to weep, and after several moments of praying for her, she gave me a tight hug, thanked me, and left.

Three months went by without hearing anything from Katie again, until she called me one day.

"Mr. Taylor, can me and my mom come over to talk with you?"

"Sure, Katie, I'd be happy to meet with you," I replied.

I had no idea why they wanted to talk to me, but when they arrived, Jan and I took them to the basement and we sat down.

"When I was here and you prayed for me, you told me about the picture you saw of me when I was seven years old, waiting for my dad to come home," Katie began. "You had no way of knowing my dad committed suicide when I was seven years old. And when you said Jesus came and picked me up, I could feel God's Presence. It wasn't like what I feel with my spirit guides; it was a feeling of love and security I had never experienced before." Katie paused and looked at me. "I want to be a Christian," she said with great confidence.

"Katie," I said, "If you are going to give yourself to God with all your heart, you are going to need to break up with your spirit guides, and renounce being a white witch and everything that goes with that. Are you willing to do that?"

"Yes, I am very willing to do that!" she answered emphatically.

That night Katie prayed and gave herself to God. She asked the Holy Spirit to come live inside of her. As she did so, His love overwhelmed her and she wept deeply. I asked her to stand and laid hands on her, asking the Holy Spirit to come baptize her and fill her with His Presence. Almost instantly, Katie began to speak in tongues as the Holy Spirit filled her to overflowing.

I looked at Katie's mom, who had been sitting quietly all this time.

"Have you ever given yourself to God before?" I asked.

She looked at me with her eyes opened wide in amazement at what she was witnessing. "Not like that!" she replied.

"Would you like to?" I asked.

"Yes! Most definitely!"

Katie's mom prayed and gave herself to God and as I laid hands on her, she also was filled with the Holy Spirit and began speaking in tongues.

All of that happened because of the spirit of prophecy being used to see a picture that opened Katie's heart to the God who saw and loved her.

If I was going to take a church team to a place of high-level spiritual warfare, I wanted to arm them with everything I could for them to be effective. Learning to use the gift of prophecy would be a tremendous help.

Activated

"All right, guys," I told my team, "On Tuesday night I have invited a team from another church to come and teach on prophecy, and they will activate you to do it." (This was the same charismatic black church on the South Side where the prophet had called me out by name and given a prophetic word.)

"Activate? What do you mean activate? You're going to activate me to do what?" asked TC, one of the team members. "I'm not sure I want to be activated. What are you going to do to me?" TC was an ironworker, and among the trades, ironworkers were known to be a little mentally whacked. TC was the poster child for that reputation.

"Well, the Bible says we can all prophesy, so that means you have the ability but you just need to become active in using the gift that is already in you," I replied. "The people who are coming will help you do that."

"Well, I'll show up, but I'm not sure about getting activated to do anything!" said TC.

That next Tuesday night the prophetic team came and TC was sitting in the back row, his arms folded on his chest with an eye on the door just in case he needed to escape. The prophetic team

EQUIPPING THE SAINTS

did a great job giving a biblical teaching on prophecy and how God administers this gift to minister more effectively for Him. TC listened intently, and eventually, his folded arms came down and he began to lean forward, wanting to catch every word of the teaching.

The prophetic team separated our group and began to do exercises, encouraging them to hear from God and speak something encouraging to another person. It was a joy to watch my team begin to say things that came straight from God and not their own minds. They were blown away by not only what they were hearing for themselves, but what they were saying by the Spirit to others. Some of them were laughing loudly, and others were crying, as they never dreamed that God could use them in this manner. I looked over at TC. He was now on his knees, head in his hands, weeping softly.

He looked up, and turned his head toward me. With tears running down his face, he said, "I got activated!"

FLASHBACK

Chai break over, the ambulance resumed its journey. It continued to bounce along the narrow, winding mountain road. The hours passed as my leg banged against the steel gurney, causing me to cry out.

Finally, we came into the city of our destination and the ambulance pulled up to the main entrance of the hospital. I had been to this hospital nearly ten years earlier—not as a patient, but to visit and pray with people.

The ambulance pulled to a stop. It was now four-thirty in the morning, and Jacob had been awake, bouncing and throwing up all night. I could see he was totally exhausted. The back doors to the ambulance opened. I expected to see the hospital staff but instead I saw my friends, Pastor Daniel and his wife, Poonam, and about fifteen of his church members waiting to receive me and care for me.

I had ministered in this city many times over the years and had many wonderful friends here. Now they had come out in the middle of the night to care for the one who used to care for them. The tables had turned. The missionary that had come to give of himself and to minister to others was now the one who needed their ministry.

I was taken aback. I had not expected to see anyone I knew at that time of night, but here they were. They had heard the news of the accident and had immediately gone to the hospital to wait for my arrival. They had reached several hours earlier and prayed together for Ishan and me. Tears filled my eyes as I looked into their faces, seeing their deep love and concern for me.

In times past, I had prayed and prophesied over each one of them, ministering to them as effectively as I could. Some of them received physical healing and some had been set free from demons. Others had become followers of Jesus through my time with them. I had sat in each of their homes talking about Jesus and drinking chai. Now, it was their turn to minister to me and they did it with the most generous love I could have imagined.

That night, those beautiful believers became the angels I desperately needed. They came to be by my side, and they were not going to leave me.

Many hands reached into the van to pull the gurney out, and immediately they went to work caring for me. They gently lifted me to another gurney and took me for a fresh set of X-rays. As they wheeled me through the hospital, I could glimpse how dirty and primitive it was.

Ashish, who had followed us by car, was there and explained, "We planned to take you to a private hospital, but we learned they did not have a proper surgeon, so we had no choice but to bring you to the government hospital."

By this point my leg had swollen to double its normal size and looked like a black-and-blue balloon. They finished the X-rays, lifted me back on the gurney, and wheeled me into the emergency room, where there were lines of patients lying in beds waiting to be attended to. They lifted me onto a hospital bed and the nurse gave me an IV with painkiller, which I gladly welcomed.

I looked over at the bed next to me and saw Ishan. I tried to smile and give him a thumbs up, but the mixture of pain and fear in his eyes told me he was having a really rough time.

As soon as I settled into the bed, I was surrounded by the local believers who had come to pray for me. At the moment, I was greatly encouraged by this wonderful show of love and support. I did not realize then that this injury was going to cause major problems for me.

"This, we are not concerned about; we can fix the broken bones."

The doctors were showing Ishan's X-rays to Ashish and Jacob. They had hung them on the lightboard for them to see clearly.

"The breaks we can repair, but this is what we are concerned with. This could kill him," the doctor said, pointing to a blood clot that had moved from his broken leg into his lungs. The black spot on his lung was very visible. "There is nothing we can do but wait and see if it moves or if it dissipates. It is too dangerous to do surgery on his leg now; we must wait until the issue of this blood clot is resolved."

Ashish called Jan with the prayer request that Ishan was in a life-or-death situation, and within minutes she had hundreds of people praying for him. It was such a huge blessing having Jan organize and execute the prayer support. She was the lifeline of our little missions team. We all could feel the prayers of the intercessors carrying us each moment of the day.

PART IV
SOUTH AMERICA MINISTRY

Chapter 15

Building Spiritual Foundations

You are rising like the perfectly fitted stones of the temple; and your lives have been built up together upon the foundation laid by the apostles and prophets, and best of all, you are connected to the Head Cornerstone of the building, the Anointed One, Jesus Christ himself!
EPHESIANS 2:20, TPT

We arrived in Iquitos, Peru, deep in the Amazon jungle, and got settled into our hotel. The next morning we met at Israel and Jen's house for breakfast. A short, stocky Peruvian man in his midsixties joined us. It turned out this man was Israel's father, Jose. He had been planting churches in the jungle for more than thirty years.

As a young man, Jose had read about Jim Elliot and four other American missionaries who had been killed by the Auca Indians in Ecuador in 1956. It was this story of their martyrdom that provoked him to go into the Amazon to share Christ with those who had never heard of Him before. There were hundreds of unreached tribes in the jungle, and Jose felt compelled to go where no Christian had ever gone.

Jose was a fearless pioneer and a veteran of years of ministry in places that were extremely dangerous and difficult to get to. He had dealt with anacondas, tigers, flooded rivers, violent natives, and intense witchcraft from the brujos. The brujo was considered a shaman, or a witch doctor. These individuals controlled every level of society through enchantments, spells, and curses that would be cast on the victim. Even government officials and priests would pay brujos a lot of money to bless them or curse their enemies.

The stories of people being killed by brujos' curses were countless. They were very powerful and greatly feared by everyone. Well, everyone except Jose. He had encountered them many times and was always able to defeat them with a demonstration of the Spirit's power.

Connecting in the Spirit

I sat at the breakfast table across from this veteran missionary and instantly connected with him. I looked into his eyes and thought, *I really like this guy.*

"Israel and Jen tell me you have come here to pray," he said. "We have many teams come here from America because of Jen's connections there, but we have never had a team come here to just pray. God told me to prepare for your coming. He directed me to fast for three days, and He told me to set everything aside to be with you the next ten days and pray with you. I know He sent you here, and I need to give you my fullest attention."

Jen was sitting next to me, translating in a soft voice. She looked at me and added, "This is true. We have many teams who come here, but Jose has never cleared his schedule to be with any of them. It's always Israel and me who work with them. This is very significant that Jose is giving you his focused attention."

I sat quietly, taking in the importance of this moment. It was another clear sign that we had been sent here by God and He had a very specific assignment for us. It piqued my curiosity and raised my faith. Surely God was going to do something very special during our visit here.

After breakfast, Jose took us to their church property. It was just a slab of concrete with a canopy built over it to protect from the torrential rains that could come at a moment's notice. After all, we were in the Peruvian rainforest.

We had a wonderful time of worship in that place, feeling the Presence of God so strongly that Jose and I both went down to our knees as we prayed for one another.

Finally, I stood as Jose remained on his knees. Preston's wife, Paty, who was born in Mexico, stood beside me and translated as I laid my hands on Jose's head and prophesied over him: "God says that this day He is establishing you as an apostle of Jesus Christ. He is giving you a new mantle of authority to advance His kingdom, and He is giving you new strategies to build. He will cause you to be a master builder as he shows you when, where, and how to build. From this day, you will carry this mantle of authority, and nothing will be able to stand against you all the days of your life."

I could feel the Holy Spirit surging through me as the words came out of my mouth. The anointing was heavy. It was such an honor to pray for this man and even more of an honor that God would connect us at such a deep, supernatural level.

Apostle Jose

That evening my team and I attended Jose's Sunday service. I sat in the front row with Preston, who was fluent in Spanish. Pastor Jose stood to speak and as he spoke, Preston kept saying, "Wow!"

I looked at him and asked, "What's going on? What is he saying?"

When Preston translated Jose's words, it was my turn to say, "Wow!"

"For years I have had people say that I am an apostle," Jose said. "But I have never received that and had rejected that title. Today, this man prophesied over me that God was placing me in the office of apostle, and I received a mantle of authority for this office. God has shown me that this is not a title, but a gift of His grace in my life, and I now fully receive that gift. From today on, I am now an apostle of Jesus Christ. And now," he continued, "because I have accepted this new mantle, I am going to make some changes here at the church."

For the next half hour, Jose laid out the blueprints of an entirely new strategy for the church. He removed people from certain positions they had held and moved them into positions where they could be more fruitful and productive. He established an entire new focus for the church to win souls and make disciples. Then came the change no one had seen coming.

"Since I am now an apostle, I will be gone more, planting churches in the jungle. Therefore, I am placing my wife, Carmen, in place as your senior pastor."

I looked over at Carmen, and she did not look happy. She had a very concerned look on her face as she was trying to grasp what had just happened to her husband. What was she supposed to do with all these new changes?

I sat in shock as Preston continued to translate for me. *Oh man*, I thought, *I sure hope I was right!* I was amazed at how deeply Jose had received the Word from the Lord and had immediately responded to it. I was thinking, *Don't you want to pray about this for a while before you make all these changes?* But Jose had heard from God, and he knew exactly what to do. Jose was a man of action. There was no need to sit around praying about what God had told him.

I was astounded at what had transpired. At this time I was working as a handyman and janitor at my local church. Through a prophetic word from my pastor, God singled me out and sent me on an assignment to South America. And while there, He used me to set a man of God in place as an apostle and transform his entire ministry.

Through this, I realized spiritual authority does not come from having a platform, a title, or a position. Sometimes you just need to put your head down, take out the garbage, and mow the yard. God makes you who you are, not a title.

There was another lesson I learned. Immediate obedience moves the kingdom of God forward with authority. Once Jose received his new commissioning, he was prepared to move forward without hesitation, and because of that, the ministry was quickly positioned for exponential growth.

The Assistant Pastor

After the service, we were back at Jen and Israel's house, and Carmen was there. She sat in a corner alone, thinking about what had just happened. I stepped over to her and gently touched her arm. When she looked at me, I saw a face covered in worry.

"I don't know how to be the senior pastor," she said. "I have never been a pastor before. I have always been the assistant pastor. What am I going to do?"

"Well, Sister Carmen, you still are the assistant pastor. Jesus is the senior pastor now, and all you have to do is listen to him and do what He tells you. Nothing has changed at all. You are still the assistant pastor!"

She looked down, thinking intently about what I had just said. After a few moments she raised her head with a big smile.

"Yes," she said, "I can still be the assistant pastor!"

Looking for a Brujo

For the next ten days Jose traveled with us to spiritual power points all over that region. We focused on areas of poverty, business districts, portals in and out of the city, the Amazon River, places of prostitution, and much more.

We traveled in an eleven-passenger van, but usually there were at least fifteen of us counting the driver and a few others Jose would invite. There was no air conditioning, and in the ninety-five-degree heat and ninety-percent humidity, we would sit, crammed in next to each other, sliding against each other's sweaty bodies.

One day, we asked Jose to take us to the place where the brujos lived and worked. Many of them would cater to tourists from all over the world doing ayahuasca ceremonies. In this ceremony, they would give their guests a hallucinogenic drink where they would have visions of demons. Apostle Jose seemed eager to take us out to this location to pray, so we all loaded up in the van and started out.

The driver took us to the outskirts of town along a remote road through the jungle. After driving for a while, the driver pulled the van over and stopped. Apostle Jose jumped out and we all watched as he disappeared into the trees. Preston looked at me.

"Where did he go?" he asked.

"I have no idea," I replied.

Preston, speaking Spanish, asked the driver where Apostle Jose had gone. I could not understand what the driver said, but I was watching Preston's face as the man answered his question. Preston's eyes got a little large, his lips pursed together, and he looked down at the floor of the van. I could tell the driver had said something that had deeply concerned him.

"What's up? What did he say?" I asked.

"The driver said, 'Apostle Jose went to go look for a brujo.'"

Suddenly, the chatter in the van went to dead silence.

"He went where?" asked TC, hoping he had heard wrong.

"He is looking for a brujo," Preston reiterated. I looked around the van and every eye was on me. I was supposed to be the fearless leader, and they were looking at me to see if things were going to be okay. I looked at Preston and began to laugh. All I could imagine was Jose coming out of the jungle dragging a brujo by the leg, shouting, "I got one!"

BUILDING SPIRITUAL FOUNDATIONS

"What's he going to do with him if he finds one?" asked TC.

"Well, I'm not exactly sure," I said, still laughing. After several minutes Jose came walking out of the jungle, and to everyone's relief, he was not dragging a brujo behind him.

"The brujo is not home," Jose said, "but we can go to his house and pray." So, we all unloaded from the van and went a few hundred yards into the jungle to a small hut where the brujo lived.

Jose was not shy. He just marched right into the hut and had all of us come in behind him. I guess if you are going to pray against witchcraft in the jungle, you might as well do it standing in the home of a brujo!

Apostle Jose was bold and fearless, but it was not rooted in pride or a sense of self-reliance. His boldness was rooted in his identity in Christ. He was a man who knew his God, and he knew who he was as a child of God.

If our true identity in Christ is not rock solid, then we have insecurities that rob us of our true authority that comes from God. Jose had no such insecurities. It was that steadfast identity that gave him spiritual authority everywhere he went.

Chapter 16

Interview with a Brujo

[Christ] stripped all the spiritual tyrants in the universe of their sham authority at the Cross and marched them naked through the streets.
Colossians 2:15, MSG

Later on that trip, Jose and his other son, Pablo, took us down the river to a town called Tamshiyacu. This was the town where the number-one brujo in the Peruvian Amazon resided. The brujos actually have an organization where they become certified and are ranked according to their power and influence.

Jose sent Pablo out to find the home of this brujo so we could visit him, but we found that he was out of town. He was actually in America conducting seminars on ayahuasca ceremonies. But his nephew, who was rated the number-two brujo, was at home and welcomed us to come for a visit.

His hut was on the outskirts of the small town. The brujo was a small man of slender build and long black hair. He stepped out of his hut and invited our large group to come in. We all were quietly praying in the Spirit under our breath as he showed us all of the amulets, pipes, charms, and drums he would use for the drug-induced ceremonies.

He passed each one of them around, and we quietly prayed over each one before we passed it on. He then showed us a large bottle of yellow liquid, which was the ayahuasca he had made himself.

We sat in a circle and listened to him explain his craft, and we asked many questions. Through this interview we were able to learn much about what the brujo did, what motivated him, and how he operated in the spirit world. He was very honest and forthright about what he did and how he did it. It was an amazing learning experience.

At one point he began to sing in demonic tongues. Jose sat on his right and I on his left and we prayed intently in the Spirit, canceling anything he may have been releasing into our group. He then gave us a CD of him singing in demonic tongues accompanied by the Peruvian flute.

"I sell these in New Age stores all over the United States," he said. He allowed us to pray for him and we gave him some money for his time, then we made our way to the boat to head back to Iquitos.

On that boat ride back, I meditated on what had just happened. I had been spending a lot of time in my basement, praying and seeking God. Now, He had picked me up, taken me to South America, and dropped me in the home of a high-ranking brujo to learn about spiritual warfare.

"God," I prayed, "please help me understand what I just experienced, and teach me to apply it correctly wherever You may take me."

The Brujo at the Tourist Market

The next day, in Iquitos, Jen took me to a local tourist market to buy some trinkets to bring home to my kids. As we went from stall to stall looking at the knickknacks laid out on the tables, we noticed a stall that had many works of art that were painted by a brujo while doing ayahuasca. The paintings were all very dark and full of demons. *Why would anyone want to experience such things and then want to paint them?* I wondered.

Jen, who spoke Spanish fluently, began a conversation with the young man behind the tables. It turned out he was the brujo who had painted the pictures. Jen introduced him to me—his name was Alejandro—and she translated as I began to share Christ with him.

"You are a very spiritual man," I said. "God has given you a gift of being able to see into the spiritual realms, but you are connected to the wrong power source. There are only two power sources. One is from the Most High God, and the other is a counterfeit source from Satan. You must choose which power source you want to be connected to. Jesus Christ, the Son of God, died for you on a cross so that you could be delivered from the power of darkness and be filled with His love."

He listened intently as the Presence of God enveloped us. I felt great confidence, and I was able to speak with authority because of what I had just learned the day before from the high-ranking brujo. That experience helped me understand the brujo had a certain amount of power, but it was counterfeit and would immediately bow before the true power of Jesus Christ.

God had seen the heart of this young man and had set things up perfectly for me to meet him at just the right time. If I had met him prior to the interview with the brujo, I would not have had the confidence to speak the way I did.

Let's jump ahead one year later for a moment: I returned to Iquitos for another prayer journey and went back to the same market to buy souvenirs. As I made my way through the narrow lanes between the stalls, a young man ran up to me and grabbed my arm.

"Do you remember me?" he asked.

"Yes! Alejandro! Of course I remember you," I responded, a little startled at the sudden reappearance of the young brujo and the fervency of his greeting.

"I asked God to let me meet you again," he said. "After you left last year, I had three dreams about you. When you were here talking to me, I was terrified of you."

"Terrified of me? Why?" I asked.

"When I saw you in the Spirit, you were a huge giant! I had never seen anything like that before. When I saw you like that, it scared me. I know what you told me is true and I want to be connected to God."

"Well," I said, "If you want to be connected to God, you will have to break up with Satan, renounce being a brujo, and ask Jesus to forgive you. Are you willing to do that?"

"Yes!" he said emphatically. For the next several minutes, Jen and I had the most wonderful time leading him to Jesus and praying with him.

Later, I questioned God about how the man had seen me as a giant.

"What was that, Lord? Why did he see me like that? I certainly don't feel that way at all."

I felt God say to me, "Even a child who is filled with my Spirit is a giant compared to the god he served."

Breaking the Fear of Witchcraft

On my next trip to Peru, I was at Apostle Jose's church in Iquitos, teaching about spiritual warfare and our authority in Christ over all the power of the Enemy. As the conference was during the daytime, it was mostly attended by women. About eighty of them were there.

As was customary, Paty translated for me. She had become invaluable to me in our South American ministry, with her strong and sensitive spirit helping to bring in the Presence of God. It always felt like we were in perfect unity as the Holy Spirit would move through us, breaking strongholds and setting the captives free, and this conference was no exception.

The subject of spiritual warfare was of huge interest as everything in the jungle was controlled by the brujos. Every person at the conference had stories of the power of witchcraft that had affected their families in devastating ways.

On the third day, a woman approached me holding a large cloth bag. Her eyes were wide with fear and her hands trembled as she opened the bag. She slowly reached in and brought out a full-length skin of an anaconda with the head still attached. The snakeskin was nearly twelve feet long, and the head was larger than my fist. It was the biggest snake I had ever seen.

"A brujo became friends with my husband and gave him this snakeskin. The brujo placed it under our bed and ever since he did that, we have had sickness and conflict in our marriage. I can feel the evil in my house, and it has been controlling my husband. He has begun drinking and is violent and abusive to me. Before, he was a good man, but now he has changed. I have not been able to sleep as I have been tormented by nightmares. Can you please help me?" Tears began to fill her eyes as she looked at me in desperation.

I was overwhelmed with compassion for this dear woman who was under so much torment, but I was also feeling angry that the devil was doing this to her. I took the snakeskin to Jose and said, "We need to destroy this." I was thinking we would do it privately with the woman, but Jose had other ideas.

He took the long snakeskin and spread it out on the concrete floor of the church. Immediately, every person in the church jumped from their seats and ran to stand against the walls of the building, getting as far away from it as they could. The fear in the room was tangible.

As I saw their fear, I became even more angry. Every one of those people had suffered from witchcraft, and it was time for it to come to an end. I walked over to the snakeskin and began to stomp on it, praying loudly in tongues as I did so. I stomped and stomped as the women watched in fear.

Suddenly, I felt an arm reach around mine. Surprised, I looked over and one of the women had come from standing by the wall and had taken my arm. She looked at me and then began to stomp on the snakeskin with me. She shouted in Spanish as she stomped as hard as she could, releasing all of her pent-up fear and anger.

In a moment's time, eighty women came rushing over to the snakeskin and began stomping on it, shouting in Spanish. That spirit of witchcraft was taking a beating it had not seen since it had been cast out of heaven.

The women were shouting, "We aren't putting up with this anymore! We will never be afraid of you again, devil! You are under our feet! Jesus has defeated you! His blood has given us the victory!"

As the women stomped and shouted, someone handed me a knife. I grabbed the head of the snake and cut its head off in one stroke and raised the head in the air. The women shouted in victory and began to dance all over the room. I took the snakeskin and proceeded to cut it up in small pieces. Then Apostle Jose took a can of gasoline, poured it on the cut pieces, and set them on fire. As the smoke rose, the women danced and shouted. The fear of witchcraft had been demolished.

Not long after this event, the husband of the woman who brought the snakeskin came to the church and gave his life to Jesus Christ. The power of Satan in that home had been defeated.

The Prophecy

The next evening, Jose took us to a large church in the city that was hosting two prophets from Brazil. I was told these two men were very well known in South America and had a reputation of being extremely accurate in their prophecies. Jose took me to sit in the front row and I sat attentively as they called people out and prophesied over them.

As the service was coming to an end, Jose went to one of them and asked him if he would prophesy over me. He came and sat next to me and looked me directly in the eye. He had been flowing in the anointing of God all evening, and that anointing was still on him. I could feel the Presence of God as he looked at me. He looked at me so intently, it was as if he was looking directly into my soul.

"War!" he said emphatically. Then there was a long pause as he continued to look at me. I patiently waited, thinking there would be more to this powerful word from God. The man kept looking into my eyes. He continued to pause, and I could see that he was asking for more from the Lord, but not getting anything.

Finally, he just shrugged his shoulders and said, "That's all I see: war." And he proceeded to walk away.

Over the years, I guess that word has been confirmed many times. As David once said, "Praise be to the Lord my Rock, who trains my hands for war and my fingers for battle." (Psalms 144:1, NKJV) This is how He formed me. As long as I keep my eyes on Him, I will not fear. I will go anywhere He directs and do anything He instructs me to do. I don't look to avoid risks or question what may go wrong; I just give Him my *yes* because I fully trust the character of the One who called me.

Over the next year, the church in Iquitos doubled in size and the youth group grew from twenty-five to over one hundred.

I continued to go back to Peru once a year for the next four years, taking prayer teams and watching God bring spiritual change to the region. Today, that church has several thousand people in attendance. The believers in the city have come together in unity, having prayer marches and all-night prayer vigils in the football stadium, with tens of thousands raising their voices to God.

I realize that our prayer journeys there were only a small piece of a much larger picture. The change in the spiritual climate did not happen just because of us, but because of the courageous men and women who lived there for years, contending for souls to be saved.

But there is no doubt that by fulfilling our small assignments, it had a great impact and helped release the kingdom of God in that region.

Chapter 17

Ancient Inca Strongholds

And I will give you the keys of the kingdom of heaven, and whatever you bind on earth will be bound in heaven, and whatever you loose on earth will be loosed in heaven.
MATTHEW 16:19, NKJV

For the next several years, I continued working and spending every spare minute I could praying in my basement. Once a year or so, God would release me to lead a prayer team back to Peru or Mexico.

On one of those journeys, Apostle Jose and his son Pablo invited us to go to Cusco and Machu Picchu, high in the Andes Mountains. He had previously visited this place and realized it was a spiritual stronghold of Satan that affected the entire nation of Peru. He was determined to return and pray that God would uproot these ancient demonic strongholds.

Cusco was once the ancient capital of the Inca Empire. To this day, archeologists have no idea how many of its structures were built. Even today, with modern technology, these structures could not be duplicated. Sacsayhuaman and the Temple of the Sun near Cusco are considered spiritual high places from ancient times, and the brujos still go there to do rituals and ceremonies. The walls of Sacsayhuaman are made with hand-cut stones that weigh up to eighty tons each and fit together so precisely that a razor blade cannot fit between them.

They call on their ancient gods, such as the puma (representing the natural world), the condor (representing the spiritual world), and the snake (representing the underworld). But they say that the three gods are actually one, called Viracocha, creating a counterfeit of the Trinity that Christians worship.

Near Cusco, high in the mountains, is the ancient city of Machu Picchu. It was considered the city for royalty and had the highest levels of witchcraft, including astral projection. Both Cusco and Machu Picchu were known to have portals. It was said that an Incan priest could stand in one portal, then appear hundreds of miles away through another. Machu Picchu was not found by Westerners until 1911, when an adventurer named Hiram Bingham uncovered the ancient city.

There are many temples and altars for sacrifice in this place. One of them is known as the Hitching Post of the Sun, where, during the winter solstice, they would sacrifice children to the sun god. They believed the sun god died each year, was dead for three days, and then would rise on the morning of the solstice, once again creating a counterfeit of the death and resurrection of Jesus Christ.

Prayer Walking Machu Picchu

Upon our arrival in Machu Picchu, we were approached by a young woman who worked there as a tour guide. She asked if she could show us the ancient city and explain significant locations therein. We gladly hired her, but after a short time, we realized she was only quoting from a tourist guidebook and had no real knowledge of the many spiritual sites in the city.

We realized that if we were going to learn about the spiritual significance of this ancient site, we were going to need to find a brujo.

Jose disappeared while the rest of us waited. After a short time, he returned with a man who was a brujo and had practiced his craft in this place for many years. He knew the spiritual story behind every portal, every altar, and virtually every stone. To our surprise, he was very happy to share all his knowledge with us. In fact, he seemed pleased that this group actually wanted to know the deep spiritual truths of this place.

For the next several hours we explored the city with our new guide as he explained each location, what the ancients did there, and why it was spiritually significant. The entire time, we prayed in the Spirit under our breath.

Weeping with Jesus

Our guide then took us higher up the mountain to a place called the Seat of the Condor. Here we could overlook the entire region and pray, releasing the Presence of God. The Seat of the Condor was the location the Incan high priest would sit, commune with the demonic realms, and do astral projection. It was said he could move through the spirit world to any place on the earth. In fact, the Inca had ancient aerial-view maps of the world that cannot be explained, except by the possibility of astral projection.

I sat in the seat that had been carved into the peak of the mountain rock by the ancients of long ago and prayed over Peru. And as I prayed, I wept deeply. God was moving through me in a very profound way. It was as if Jesus Himself were sitting next to me, weeping over Peru the same way He wept over Jerusalem. The intimacy of sharing Jesus's heart for the Peruvian people at that moment was overwhelming.

The Condor

We came down the mountain back to the main village as the sun was setting. The brujo left us and we made one last stop before leaving for the night. We stopped at the Hitching Post of the Sun to pray one last time, knowing this had been the place of terrible ritual killings of babies in ancient times. As we looked around, we could see a carving in the stone of a puma. Nearby, we found the carving of the snake near the foot of some steps. We knew these carvings represented their gods, but where was the condor?

Suddenly, Preston pointed and said, "There it is!"

It wasn't a carving, it was the light of the setting sun itself. It hit a certain spot on the altar, and the shadow formed the perfect silhouette of a condor on the wall behind it. The shadow would only be visible for a few moments on certain days of the year as the sun would hit the altar at the right angle. It was not a coincidence that God had led us there at that exact moment to see it.

Over and over again, we felt as if the Holy Spirit was saying, "Look at this. Look at that. Come this way, I want to show you something." He was exposing secrets that helped us pray.

Praying at the River

The following day, Jose wanted us to pray at a river that flowed below the mountain of Machu Picchu. We left our guesthouse and began to walk along the river that ran right through the town of Aguas Caliente. We had been told by the brujo that the ancient Inca had worshiped river gods and considered the river itself to be holy.

As we walked along the river I thought, *We should be able to stop anywhere along the river to pray*, but Jose kept walking farther and farther into the jungle, following the river. I kept waiting for him to stop and pray, but he just kept walking. Finally, I became a little irritated. Why didn't he just stop at any area to pray? Any spot would do, right?

At one point, Jose stopped and looked at me.

"What do you think of this place to pray?" he asked.

"Yes, this place looks fine to me," I said, a little impatiently.

"Let's pray!" He looked at the water for a few moments and then said, "No, this is not the place." He continued to walk. I just rolled my eyes and followed him, thinking this was ridiculous.

After walking about a mile and a half, Jose stopped along the riverbank. He touched my arm to get my attention and pointed.

"Do you see that?"

I couldn't believe it. At that precise location on the river, there was an ancient altar and large stone carvings of the snake, the puma, and the condor.

God had led Jose to the exact spot where the ancient Inca worshiped their gods on the river. I just lowered my head, feeling very embarrassed about my impatience and insensitivity. If it had been up to me, I would have missed the most effective location to pray, wasted our time, and missed the assignment God had for us.

God was teaching me that if I was going to be sent on assignments to do spiritual warfare, I had to be sensitive to Him and be led by His Spirit every moment. On a prayer journey, our job was to listen to what He told us, go where He told us, and pray what He told us. We could not possibly know what He knew, so we had to be fully submitted to Him for Him to accomplish what He desired. Anything else was not only a waste of time, but also dangerous.

The next day, we returned to Cusco, and in the evening, we went to pray in Sacsayhuaman and the ruins of the Temple of the Sun. We found another brujo who guided us through the ruins, taking us to places normal tourists were not allowed to go. He explained in detail how the stones were cut and placed together. He also pointed out particular stones that had spiritual significance based on their shape and placement in the walls of the temple. We stopped and prayed at each of these locations.

As the sun was setting, he said, "I have one more place to show you. It is off the tourist maps and no one is allowed to go there except the shamans. It is a very powerful and spiritual place. I have sensed you people have very strong spirits. It will be my honor to show you this place."

Jose and I looked at each other and said, "Lead on." We were both very curious about what this man wanted to show us.

As it grew darker, the moon began to rise, which gave us a little light to walk by. We walked for about a mile until we came to a large hill. The brujo led us to the top of the hill and showed us a throne that had been carved out of the rock. Here the Incan king would sit as the priests would make offerings to their moon god. It was their version of Baal worship, dating all the way back to Old Testament times. Here, we had a powerful time of prayer.

It was as if God was directing the brujo exactly where to take us and exactly what to tell us so we could pray.

Temple of the Moon

Then, our guide led us down the hill. We used our flashlights to walk carefully through the dark and not stumble over the rocks. He led us to the entrance to a cave.

"This is the Temple of the Moon," he said.

"I don't understand, why would a cave be called the Temple of the Moon?" I asked.

"Turn off your flashlights," he replied. We obeyed and turned off our lights.

It was then we noticed there was a small opening in the ceiling of the cave, and as the moon passed over the opening, its light came into the cave. Not only was the moonlight shining into the darkness of the cave, but its light was also casting shadows onto the walls.

ANCIENT INCA STRONGHOLDS

Each one of these shadows had shapes of phallic symbols, the snake god, and other religious symbols of the ancient Inca.

In one section of the cave was a large stone altar.

"This is where the priests would have sex with the temple prostitutes," our guide said. "This is also where they would sacrifice the babies born to the prostitutes to the moon god."

We were amazed that we were standing in this place. There was no way we could have known about it and been able to come here on our own. We felt God had brought us into this deeply wicked place to bind and cast down ancient strongholds that had been established through human sacrifice.

It was overwhelming to be in this place where so much innocent blood had been spilled, and yet, we felt the authority of God to pray. He alone had brought us here to apply the blood of Jesus.

The prayer journeys in Peru did much to train me in prayer, spiritual authority, and being led by the Holy Spirit, but God was just getting started in training my hands for war.

Chapter 18

He Sets the Captive Free

God anointed Jesus of Nazareth with the Holy Spirit and with power, who went about doing good and healing all who were oppressed by the devil, for God was with Him.
Acts 10:38, NKJV

Upon returning home from Peru, I once again returned to my construction job and my times of prayer in the basement. While each prayer journey was an exciting adventure, they only lasted a few weeks out of the year, and then I would be back in the basement. I grew to love my prayer times in that basement just as much as those in the Amazon jungle and the mountains of Cusco. Where I was did not matter. Who I was with did matter. Just being with Jesus was enough. I needed nothing else. He had burned out all the selfish ambition, all the false identity, and all the effort to try to be somebody or accomplish big things. All of that had become rubbish to me, and I grew more and more content just being close to Jesus.

In 2008, Jan approached me. She had been working for an energy company in downtown Chicago, and now they were planning to relocate their headquarters to Phoenix, Arizona. The company had appreciated her work so much, they asked her to make the move with them to Phoenix.

"How would you feel about moving to Phoenix?" she asked me.

"Phoenix? I love the Southwest, and I don't feel like I have any specific assignment from the Lord here, so yes, let's go." For me it was an easy decision. After ten years in the basement, I was ready for the sunshine of Phoenix, Arizona.

We made the move in August 2009, quickly found a wonderful church to attend, and began to make new friends.

Sickness

Shortly after arriving in Phoenix, I became very ill and was diagnosed with Valley Fever, a fungus that settles in the lungs and can wreak havoc on the body. This sickness can be permanently debilitating and even fatal. For six months, my lungs were badly compromised with coughing fits that would last up to one hour. I actually broke a rib during one of those fits. Deep fatigue settled on me, to the point of barely being able to stand and walk across the floor.

During this time of sickness, I went through training for Healing Rooms, a method of praying for healing established by John G. Lake in the early 1900s. I also attended several local conferences focused on healing. It seemed that during my time of sickness, the subject of healing was sweeping through the body of Christ in the Phoenix area.

I had seen many miracles of healing in the past, but now I was contending for my own. Over time, and much prayer, my faith grew, and eventually, my health returned.

Shortly after my recovery, I was invited to return to Peru, where my daughter Jenni had moved to teach at a Christian school Apostle Jose had established. She had been working there for two years, and I very much looked forward to seeing her again. An added bonus was that my oldest brother, Bill, decided to join me.

Release Healing

It was good to be back in Iquitos and walk the familiar streets once again. The city had been built on the banks of the Amazon River. The streets were lined with small shops and filled with hundreds of small motorcycles that constantly filled the air with the loud roar of their engines. The Peruvians wore bright, colorful clothing and always seemed to have huge smiles on their faces. They were eager to greet us Americans with the best hospitality they could offer.

On the first evening there, the church hosted a midweek service and asked me to preach, which I gladly accepted. My dear friend Pablo, the youngest son of Jose and Carmen, translated for me. The Presence of God flowed between us beautifully as we ministered together.

It had been five years since my last visit, and the building had changed quite a bit as the congregation had multiplied. Now it was a large room with a concrete floor that could seat more than eight hundred people. White plastic chairs were set up in a semicircle facing the large platform that had been built. Large banners with scriptures in Spanish covered the walls.

As I spoke that night I felt the Holy Spirit say, "I want to release healing tonight."

"You want to do what?" I replied.

"I want to release healing. Tell everyone who is in pain or is sick to stand up."

"Oh man," I responded, "what if I do this and nothing happens? God, You really are putting me on the spot. Can't I just pray for a few people after the service where it's not in front of everyone?"

"Release healing," He said strongly. He wasn't suggesting or asking—He was commanding. I had no choice but to obey.

"If anyone is here with severe back pain, please stand up," I said. Pablo glanced over at me, wondering what I was doing, and then gave the translation.

About fifteen people responded and stood looking at me with expectation. *Oh man*, I thought. *I sure hope God does something.* I was more concerned about being embarrassed than I was concerned about people being healed.

I began to pray and commanded healing into their backs and commanded all pain to be gone. "All right, now move around, bend over, stretch out, and see if the pain is gone," I said, holding my breath and hoping someone felt some relief.

To my shock, every one of them began moving and laughing. Some were even jumping. Every single one of them testified to being healed—all pain gone. I had not touched any of them. I had simply declared healing, and God had moved.

Suddenly, my faith level skyrocketed. "Wow! What happened? Where did this come from? I have never done anything like this before," I said to God. Pablo looked over at me with his eyes open wide and laughing. He too had been holding his breath, hoping I wouldn't look like an idiot.

"Do you remember all that teaching you have been receiving about healing? Do you remember your own sickness you carried? This is the fruit of what you were contending for," said the Lord.

I began to realize that out of my severe weakness, He was manifesting His strength. He is the God who heals! Laughing, and now full of bold faith, I asked everyone else who was sick or in pain to stand, and I once again prayed and released healing. Every person in that room who needed a touch from God was healed that night.

God was preparing me for much more to come. Throughout the coming years, I would watch God heal and deliver thousands of people.

Inner Healing

One of the primary reasons for this trip to Iquitos was to do seminars on inner healing. Jen had told me that many of the Peruvians there had suffered much in their lives from physical and sexual abuse within their families. Alcohol and drugs, which were rampant in the jungle, contributed to this, as well as a culture that commonly accepted this behavior.

Jen asked me to minister to the women, the men, and the teenagers. We felt it would be best to minister to each group separately so they could deal with their trauma in a more private way.

Before I began the time of ministry, I took my brother Bill to the side.

"Bill, I am going to be sharing some very deep and personal stories from our childhood as I minister. A lot of the stories are going to be about Dad and what we went through as kids. I am especially going to tell stories about you, because you went through so much more than the rest of us. You may not want to be here to listen to all that. It might bring back a lot of bad memories, so if you want to not be here for this, I understand."

"No, Daniel, I came to support you, so you just do what God tells you to do and I will be okay," he replied.

I put my hand on his shoulder and looked him in the eye. "You do know God brought you here for an encounter with Him, right?"

Bill looked at me intently and slightly nodded his head.

I knew God was going to do something for this man I loved and respected so much. When we were kids, Bill had actually enlisted to go to Vietnam just to escape the torment and abuse of our father. He had suffered PTSD all his life—not because of the war, but because of the trauma he suffered as a child. I knew my stories would be very painful for him, but I also knew he needed God's healing for his damaged soul.

The first teaching was with the women. I shared extensively about the physical and emotional abuse of my childhood, talking about what Momma went through and using my testimony as a way to help them connect with their own trauma and allow God to bring healing.

I spoke about feeling rejected, unloved, and unwanted. I focused on the pain and abuse my mother experienced, and as I did, many of the women nodded their heads, wiping away tears, affirming they had experienced the same things from their husbands.

I told about watching my brothers, sisters, and mother be physically and verbally abused. I also spoke about the journey of forgiveness that set my heart free from bitterness and hatred. Bill sat in the back of the room, listening.

As I spoke, the women wept as the Holy Spirit moved in their hearts. Years of pain and trauma were wiped away as they forgave those who had caused them so much heartache. God was using my testimony to set others free. Once again, I thanked God for all I had experienced as He used it to minister to others.

The next day, we went to a retreat center Apostle Jose had built. It was also used as a Bible school for those from the indigenous tribes who were being trained to be Christian leaders. Here, they brought the teenagers for me to minister to. It was a three-mile hike through the jungle to the retreat center, and upon arrival, we gathered in a large gazebo with wood planks for seats.

Again, I shared my stories and the Holy Spirit moved. When I finished speaking, I invited the young people to respond by coming forward for prayer. Every person who was there came to the altar and God met them in a powerful way.

As I prayed over them, many began to weep and others fell to the floor, wailing and screaming as the spirits of trauma, abuse, hatred, and anger left their bodies. They were not just getting healed; they were being delivered from demonic spirits. God had come to set them free. Once again, my brother sat in the back of the gazebo, listening and watching God do miracles of restoring broken souls.

The next morning, the youth left to go back to the city and we had several hours free while we waited for the men to come out to the retreat center.

Momma's Prayers Still Being Answered

Everyone had left except for my daughter Jenni, Bill, and me. Feeling tired, I found a hammock and rested a bit. As I lay back, gently swinging with the breeze, Bill was pacing back and forth along the edge of the jungle. His head was down, and I could see something was heavy on his mind. From time to time, I would open an eye and watch him pace back and forth. Finally, he walked over to me and fell on his knees, sobbing.

"Daniel, I need you to pray for me! Please pray for me!"

All the while I had been ministering to the Peruvian people, God had been ministering to my brother. There in the middle of the Amazon jungle, the Holy Spirit healed and delivered this amazing man. Years of trauma and abuse were instantly gone. His wounded soul—that had been bleeding for years—was now made whole.

After a long time on his knees, weeping and crying out to God, Bill stood and wrapped his arms around me. We stood there holding each other, feeling the Presence of God sweep through us both. He was a new man. My brother was free.

He had built walls around his emotions that were impregnable, and he had hidden behind them for years. Not knowing how to deal with the pain that would never go away, his solution was to ignore and override. But now those walls were gone, and there was no longer a reason to hide. The captive had been set free from the prison that trauma had built. It was one of the greatest miracles I had ever seen.

That evening the men came, and I ministered again on the same subject, and again God came and brought healing and deliverance. The next morning, they decided to baptize the men in the nearby river. I stood in the water, helping to baptize the men. I looked up to see the next man in line to be baptized. To my surprise, it was my big brother. Jenni had been watching him and seen the great change in his spirit and had asked him if he wanted to be baptized. Bill immediately responded, "Yes, I do!"

All my life he was my hero. I loved him more than words could tell. And now I had the honor of baptizing my brother in a river in the Amazon rainforest. It is a moment in time I will forever cherish.

I know God sent me to that place to minister to the Peruvian people, but more than that, God had a plan to minister to my brother. God had seen his years of pain and suffering, and it broke His heart. Momma had seen so much of the suffering Bill had gone through and had prayed for him intensely.

Momma's prayers were still being answered all these years later.

FLASHBACK

As I lay on the hospital bed, there were many believers in the city who were getting the news that I was there and had suffered a bad accident. There was a constant crowd of people around my bed trying to comfort me and pray for me. It was deeply humbling for me to be in such a weak and vulnerable position in front of so many people I had ministered to over the years.

The head of the emergency room was getting irritated with so many people crowding around my bed. He was a devout Hindu, and seeing so many Christians around the foreigner set off alarms to him. He knew, because of all the Christians surrounding me, I was there as a missionary. To be a foreign missionary in India is highly illegal. I could be arrested and thrown out of the country at a moment's notice. All these years, God had protected me, and not once had I been confronted by the authorities, but now, this man could change all of that.

He rushed over and said, "You must leave! Now! You must leave! I cannot have all of you here interrupting our work!" After he had forced everyone out the door, he approached my bed. "Your condition is very serious and will require our head surgeon to do the surgery."

"All right," I responded. "How soon can we get the surgery done?"

"The head surgeon is out of town. It may be five or six days before he will return. He can do your surgery then."

FEARLESS FAITH

"Five or six days? I'm just supposed to lie here for five or six days?" There was still some concern that a blood clot could move from the fractures into my lungs, heart, or brain. Lying there for that many days would only increase the risk. Even through intense pain and the effects of the painkillers, I could see this man looked at me as his enemy and he was not going to do anything to help me.

"No," I said, "that is not acceptable."

What I did not know at the time was that my friend from Kashmir, Amir, had heard of my accident. When he learned which hospital I had been taken to, he said, "No! That is not the correct hospital for Dan. He will not be well taken care of there. We must get him to a better facility." Amir is a man of great influence and is highly regarded all over that region of India. So, he leveraged that influence and called a friend who worked in the government in the city where I was. He asked his friend to come to the hospital and be an advocate for me.

My team was emotionally and physically exhausted. It had now been more than twenty-four hours since the accident, and none of them had slept or eaten the entire time. At the time I needed it most, God provided a friend five hundred miles away in Kashmir to fight for me.

Amir's friend came to the hospital to speak to the head doctor of the emergency room.

"We are making arrangements to take Dan to a hospital in Chandigarh," he told the doctor. "I would like for you to release him."

The doctor looked at the government official for a moment and asked, "Who is this foreigner? People from all over the city have come to see him. Even in the middle of the night he has many people visiting him. And now he has a government official coming here on his behalf. Who is this man?"

"He is an important man, and we need to get him to the proper hospital to have surgery as soon as possible," he replied.

"No," the doctor answered. "I know he is a foreign missionary, and I demand to have his passport. I will turn him in to the authorities to be arrested and sent out of our country. His presence here will not be tolerated!"

While the doctor was talking to the government official, Amir was busy at work. He had already researched surgeons and hospitals in a large city four hours down the mountain. He was able to find the number-one trauma surgeon in the region, who had agreed to provide surgery for me as soon as I could reach the hospital.

Amir called and told him the news. The official immediately told the doctor, "A hospital and surgeon has been acquired. We will not stay here. We are going now!"

Reluctantly, muttering and complaining, the doctor signed my release.

My friends ordered another ambulance and loaded me in the back. We were off on another four-hour journey of winding, narrow, and bumpy mountain roads. Jacob took his place in the van. He was not going to leave me until he knew I was in good hands and being cared for correctly.

Because of his blood clot, the doctors refused to allow Ishan to travel. It would have been much too dangerous for him to try to make the journey. Hundreds of others and I continued to pray for Ishan's healing.

It was late afternoon. It had been more than forty-eight hours since the accident. I bounced up and down in the ambulance looking out the back window. I could see the mountains in the distance and knew it was another beautiful day in the Himalayas.

As I looked out the window, I remembered the moments before the accident. I had been on the back of the motorcycle with my arms spread wide rejoicing and praising God.

"So, do you still want to praise Me?" I heard Jesus ask.

It was not an audible voice but, in my spirit, I could hear His tone. It was part teasing and part serious, and I could tell He was smiling. I burst out in laughter at the question. I'm sure the driver thought I was delirious and was wondering what in the world the foreigner was laughing about.

I lay on the gurney and spread my arms wide. "Yes, Lord! I still praise You and thank You for allowing me to be here doing what we do!"

PART V
MINISTRY IN TIBET

Chapter 19

Go!

> *All authority has been given to Me in heaven and on earth.
> Go therefore and make disciples of all the nations.*
> MATTHEW 28:18–19, NKJV

Jan and I continued to attend our local church in Phoenix, and every Sunday evening, before the service, they would have a small gathering to pray for missions. During one of those prayer gatherings, I met a man named Steve and his wife, Wei Wei. Steve was from Taiwan, and Wei Wei was from China. Their marriage was a picture of international reconciliation.

As we talked, they told us that earlier that year, they had gone on a mission trip to Tibet with a man named Mark Geppert. They were very excited about the time they had in Tibet and spoke very highly of Mark.

"You have to meet Mark Geppert!" they told me. "He has been prayer walking the nations for nearly thirty years and God has used him in wonderful ways. We are going back to Tibet this year. You should come with us!"

I had no idea where Tibet even was, and I really had no desire to go there, but it was easy to see that Steve and Wei Wei were very much looking forward to returning.

"I don't think I will go with you, but if you would like, I can be part of your prayer team here and pray for you while you are gone."

"That would be great!" they responded. "Mark is coming in next week to recruit people for the trip and give information about it. Why don't you come to the meeting and then you will know more about how to pray for us?"

"Sure, that sounds great," I replied.

I had no idea that this simple, innocent decision would radically change my life.

The time for the meeting with Mark arrived, and I dutifully showed up ready to hear about Tibet. Mark was a heavyset man in his early sixties with piercing gray eyes and a cheerful, outgoing personality. You could tell Mark never met a stranger, as he was friendly with everyone. He also carried an air of authority about him. There was no doubting this man was a veteran and knew how to take charge of any situation.

Proclaiming the Name of Jesus

We met in a small classroom with concrete block walls painted yellow, the typical metal folding chairs lined up in rows. I sat nonchalantly in the back. After all, I was just there to listen.

Mark began telling how he had started a ministry in Tibet ten years earlier. Tibet had been a country that had been closed to the gospel and was nearly 100 percent Buddhist. In 1959, the Chinese had invaded this peaceful country and had occupied it ever since. The Tibetans were a conquered and oppressed people. They harbored animosity toward the Chinese military and had hoped for American involvement to regain their independence, but that help never came.

Mark told us about how he had gone there to pray, and as he did so, God opened the door for him to take medical teams and perform surgeries on children who had heart defects. During the past ten years of this ministry, over five hundred surgeries had been performed, saving the lives of all those children.

Along with the medical procedures, Mark would take prayer teams to sit with the families and pray for the children before, during, and after the surgery. In this manner, hundreds of families had come to know Christ and started many house churches all over the country.

I listened as Mark told his wonderful stories and I thought, *That's a great ministry. I'm so glad that he is doing that.* So far, to me, this was just another missionary telling his stories.

But then he said something that shot straight into my spirit.

"On this journey, we are bringing no doctors, and we will not be doing any heart surgeries. This will be a prayer team, and we will go into regions of the Tibetan Plateau and proclaim the name of Jesus where it has never been proclaimed before."

Those words struck me deeply. *What? Do you mean there are still places on Earth where Christians have never been?* I thought. I was aware of unreached tribes in the Amazon, but I had no idea there were other places around the world that were still completely unreached. I had no idea there were still millions of people who never once heard about the God who loved them and had died for them.

"Proclaim the name of Jesus where it has never been proclaimed before." Those words rang in my spirit, and the Presence of God suddenly came over me. Tears began to fill my eyes. God was doing something in me that was totally unexpected. The thought of being a pioneer, of being the first Christian a people group had ever met, captivated me.

Now, my eyes were fixed on Mark as he continued to speak. Every word he spoke had a profound effect on me. I couldn't help it. I couldn't stop the tears from flowing. Mark noticed this, and his eyes locked onto mine. From that moment on, it was as if there was no one else in the room except Mark, me, my wife, and the Holy Spirit.

I could hear Jesus speaking to me: "Daniel, I want to go to Tibet. Will you take Me there?" It was an invitation I could not refuse.

"Yes, Lord, I will go," I replied.

Jan reached over and took my hand in hers. She could see that I was being deeply affected by what I was hearing. She is my very best friend, and she knows me so well. She looked at me for a long moment and then whispered in my ear, "You're going to Tibet, aren't you?"

All I could do was nod my head as the tears continued to flow.

Chapter 20

The Roof of the World

Oh, give thanks to the Lord!
Call upon His name;
Make known His deeds among the peoples!
Psalms 105:1, NKJV

The Tibet team consisted of fifteen people from different parts of the US and one from Canada. Steve's wife, Wei Wei, was not able to come, so he and I became roommates throughout the trip. Steve is a brilliant man and has a great sense of humor. During the short time I knew him, we became dear friends. It was a joy to be with him and share this adventure together.

After a couple of days getting acclimated in China, we flew into Lhasa, Tibet. Lhasa sits at an altitude of 11,995 feet and is one of the highest cities in the world. In Tibet, foreigners are required to have a certified guide, and Mark had made arrangements to work with his dear friend, Tashi.

Tashi had been with Mark on many of his trips over the past ten years. She was a woman of about forty years of age and had long, straight, black hair and large, round, brown eyes. She had strong facial features as if her face had been carved out of stone, but when she smiled the entire room would light up. After meeting Tashi at the airport, we all felt we were in good hands.

Tibet is one of the most beautiful places in the world. High in the Himalayan mountains, it has some of the most spectacular, breathtaking views imaginable and is nicknamed the Roof of the World, as the average elevation is over thirteen thousand feet.

While in Lhasa we visited Jokhang Temple, a very historic pilgrimage site. Thousands of people walk around the outside of the temple clockwise, holding their prayer wheels and chanting all throughout the day.

The temple had three parts: the outer court where people would walk and chant, the inner court where nearly one hundred Buddhist priests would burn incense and chant throughout the day, and then a smaller room that contained a gold statue of the Buddha. Remarkably, it seemed to have the same concept as the temple built by Solomon with the outer court, the Holy Place, and the Holy of Holies.

Mark led our team into the inner court, and we were almost overcome with the thick smoke of the incense that filled the room like a heavy cloud. It felt like we had just gone back in time five hundred years. We were experiencing something very few Americans had ever seen before.

Suddenly, the inner chamber, where the golden Buddha sat, opened, and we were invited to go in. It was a rare occurrence that his room was open, and by God's design, we were there at the right moment to pray and release His Presence.

Altitude Sickness

After several days in Lhasa, our team boarded a bus and headed to the Tibetan Plateau. We crossed a mountain pass at seventeen thousand feet, and then we came to a spacious plain with a large lake in the distance. At this altitude there were no trees or bushes of any kind. It was a flat wasteland covered with short tundra vegetation that the yaks and goats would eat. Scattered around the edges of the lake were about twenty yurts covered in animal skins that the Tibetan nomads used for shelter. These yurts were easily taken down and moved as the nomads followed their herds across the tundra.

We reached our camping spot just before sunset and set up our small two-man pup tents. The bright-blue tents blended in beautifully with the dark blue of the sky and the deep blue of the lake nearby.

We were now at sixteen thousand feet and struggling with the lack of oxygen. Nearly half of the team was experiencing lightheadedness and nausea, especially my friend Steve, who, the day before, had also eaten something that caused vomiting and diarrhea. At this altitude, his symptoms were becoming more severe.

Even though Steve was feeling ill, he joined us that evening as we sat on the Tibetan Plateau. The sun set behind the mountains, casting red, yellow, and pink across the lake. Our team began to sing worship songs and glorify God. The night air carried our voices to the tents of the nomads, who were very curious about these foreigners who had come to visit them.

I sat, listening to the singing and watching the sunset. We were in one of the most remote places on the face of the earth, and I was full of praise and gratitude to God for allowing me to be in this magical place.

As it grew dark, we made our way to our small tents to try to get some sleep. I crawled into my heavy-duty sleeping bag, which was buried under two horse blankets. I wore multiple layers of clothes and a heavy jacket, but I still shook and shivered until it seemed my bones rattled. The nights were bitterly cold at this altitude.

It was virtually impossible to sleep. As I dozed off, my breathing became shallower, which meant less oxygen in my lungs. Every few moments I would awake gasping for a breath—doze, gasp, doze, gasp. It was a long night.

As the hours of the night slowly passed and morning neared, I could hear thirty-mile-an-hour winds whipping through the camp. I could hear the chomping of a yak herd as it fed on the thick Tibetan tundra, and I could hear the labored breathing of my tentmate as he dealt with the combination of food poisoning and severe altitude sickness.

"Steve, are you okay?" I asked, but got no response. "Steve! Are you okay?" I asked again. No response. A third time I called out; he groaned as he rolled over and laid his head right on top of mine. Steve and I were good friends, but not that good! Especially since he still smelled of what came up from his stomach a few hours earlier.

I rolled out of my bag and blankets and began to shake him, calling his name to get him fully conscious—but to no avail. *This is not good!* I thought. Having my roommate die on my first prayer journey with Mark was not the experience I was looking for!

I jumped up to get help when I saw Mark walking by on his way to the mess tent to get some morning coffee. The sun was just beginning to rise, casting yellow hues across our pup tents. I went over to Mark, trying to sound as calm as I could.

"Steve is breathing, but he is not conscious," I said.

Mark's eyes penetrated mine. "Hmmm, what to do?" This was a statement I would grow accustomed to over the years.

He immediately turned and went to find our guide. Tashi was levelheaded and knew exactly what to do. Calmly, she pulled out an oxygen tank, walked to our tent, and placed a mask on Steve's face.

Slowly, his eyes opened as he began to regain consciousness, and we all sighed with relief.

At the same time, Steve's cousin Cassandra, who had joined us from Canada, was experiencing the same symptoms. Although hers weren't as intense, she also was going to need medical care.

Tashi found the bus driver and gave instructions to take Steve and Cassandra down the mountain. There was a small town about two hours away that had a small hospital where they would be cared for.

Park the Ark

As the bus rolled away, I took a moment to look at my surroundings in the early-morning sunlight. The snow-capped mountains in the background, the herds of yak and sheep tended to by a few Tibetan nomads, the beautiful blue lake glistening with the rising sun, the colorful yurts scattered across the dark green tundra . . . it was one of the most beautiful pictures I had ever seen. I wanted to capture it and hold it in my soul forever.

I glanced over at Mark, who had come to stand beside me and was taking in the same picture I was. *How did this guy get me to come out here to the ends of the earth?* I thought.

"What now?" I asked. "How do we make Jesus known to these people?"

Mark looked back at me and said, "Hmmm, what to do?"

I was prepared to go into spiritual warfare to bind the strong man of the region, casting down the spirits of false religion, attacking any dark spirit I could think of, opening the way for people to hear and understand the gospel freely. This type of spiritual warfare was what I was trained in. I had read all the books. I had been to the Amazon jungle and the mountains of Cusco. I was now in Tibet and ready to go to work. *Let's do this!* I was thinking.

Instead, I heard Mark pray a simple prayer: "Jesus, You brought us here. What do You want to do?" Glancing at me, he said, "Okay, let's now wait and see what happens."

"What? That's it? No spiritual warfare? You pray that little prayer and wait?"

"Our bodies are the temple of the Holy Spirit, and Jesus lives inside of us," Mark replied. "Just as the ark of the covenant carried the glory of God, our bodies now do the same. We are the ark of

God. When Satan looks at us, he sees Jesus, and he must respond by bowing to His authority. If we fully understand Jesus lives in us, we can do what Jesus does."

I thought I was a seasoned veteran in spiritual warfare, but this was different. "So, no strategy? No agenda? No attacking demonic strongholds? No binding the strong man? No plans? We just pray and wait to see what God will do?"

Mark laughed a little. "Our plan is to see where Jesus is working and join Him. Do you think you can come up with a better plan than He can? God wants to reach these people more than we do. He is the one who died for them. He brought us here, and He will show us what to do."

Hmmm, what to do? I thought.

In a Tibetan Yurt

Later that afternoon, a woman came down to the lake to fill water bottles. She looked at our camp filled with foreigners with great curiosity. At sixteen thousand feet and hours from the nearest town, they didn't get many visitors up here. She must have wondered who we were and why we had come. A couple of ladies on our team greeted her with smiles which she returned; her bright smile made her dark, weathered face brighten and glow in the afternoon sun. Our translator spoke to her briefly and then turned to me.

"Come, come! She has invited us to visit her home."

With curiosity, I followed, knowing I was about to step into a new world and a culture that was utterly unknown to me. As we entered her yurt, it took a few moments for our eyes to adjust and see through the smoke of burning yak dung that filled the room. At that high altitude, since there are no trees, locals used dried yak dung for their cooking fires.

As I squinted through the smoke, I could see another woman sitting on the ground tending the fire. She was older with a weathered face that looked like tough leather, seasoned in the sun and the many harsh winters of the Tibetan Plateau.

Our translators spoke with her, asking if she had any pain and if she would like to receive prayer. They had not mentioned anything about Jesus. They just said we had come to pray for people in pain. The woman quickly began to point to different parts of her body that were hurting.

She stood in front of me, her eyes full of expectancy. I gently laid my hands on her head and released the Presence of God into her body.

After I prayed, she chatted with our translators for a few moments, and we made our way out of the yurt. As we left, the woman came to me and pulled at my arm, then touched her head with both hands, motioning for me to pray again. As I did so, I realized she was experiencing something that was supernatural.

Again, we said our goodbyes, and we began to walk away. Again, the woman followed me, pulled at my arm, and touched her head, motioning me to pray for her. For the first time in her life, this woman was experiencing the Presence of God, and she wanted more! Finally, we left and went back to camp.

A Sunrise Visit

The following day, after another sleepless, bone-chattering night, the sun began to come up over the mountains, casting the soft morning light across our camp. As I crawled out of my cocoon of sleeping bag and blankets, I looked up and saw a group of nomad women coming over the hill into our camp. I watched as they spoke briefly with our translator. Quickly, the translator motioned for me, and I walked over, curious about what was going on.

"They want you to pray for them."

The woman I prayed for the previous day had gone from tent to tent, telling her neighbors that there was a foreigner who had prayed for her and that she had experienced God. It was like the woman at the well who met Jesus and had to tell everyone about what He had done.

With great expectation, several of us on the team began to lay hands and pray for these precious women. Our translators were able to speak to them about Jesus, the one true God who loved them, died for them, forgave them, and wanted to give them eternal life.

After prayer, two of the women approached me. In Tibetan culture, it is their custom to honor someone by placing a white scarf around their neck. One at a time, the two women stepped forward and placed a scarf around my neck, bestowing upon me their highest honor.

I could not help but think how God had entrusted us with such a great responsibility of being the first Christians they had ever met. What they now thought about Jesus would be based on what they thought about us.

We had prayed our simple prayer, asking God what He wanted to do. We then waited, and He revealed His plan. He did what we could never have manufactured on our own. People experienced the power and Presence of God and heard the message of Jesus Christ for the first time.

Our act of spiritual warfare was to apply the finished work of Jesus on the cross and watch God do what He did best: show His magnificent love and power to heal and transform lives.

This was the first time I experienced bringing Jesus to an unreached people group. The gospel of Christ had just penetrated the stronghold of Buddhism that had been there for twenty-six hundred years. The kingdom of God had come. And it was accomplished without confronting a single demon.

As I watched the women walk away, I heard Jesus say, "Thank you for bringing Me here, Daniel. I have waited two thousand years to come here and make Myself known to these whom I died for."

The intimacy of that moment with Jesus was like nothing I had ever experienced before.

Overwhelmed with emotion, I went behind one of the tents, sat down, and wept. From that moment, I became addicted to bringing Jesus to places He had never been before.

Chapter 21

Attack Lambs

*Behold, I send you out as sheep in the midst of wolves.
Therefore be wise as serpents and harmless as doves.*
Matthew 10:16, NKJV

The next day the team boarded the bus and headed down the mountain. We picked up Steve and Cassandra, who were doing much better at the lower altitude. As the bus made the twists and turns on the mountain road I sat next to Mark. I was curious about his thoughts on spiritual warfare.

"So, after you get home from one of your prayer journeys," I asked, "do you ever get a spiritual attack? Do you get backlash and retaliation after your victories?" In the teaching I had received, this was a major issue to guard against. If you attacked the Enemy, you could fully expect him to attack you back.

"Do *you* believe in spiritual backlash and retaliation?" he asked.

"Well, yes, after major victories, I feel like I get my butt kicked all over the place. There have been many times it seemed all hell broke loose against me after doing spiritual warfare."

ATTACK LAMBS

Mark looked at me intently for a moment, with compassion in his eyes. "Well, you get what you believe for, don't you?"

Those words snapped my head around. It was like an explosion of truth just went off in my spirit. Mark looked at me and knew what he said had registered.

"If you believe the Enemy is powerful," he continued, "that belief gives him power. Your thoughts and words give power to the Enemy. He is the Father of Lies. The only way Satan can have power over you is through lies and fear. I believe the devil was totally defeated through the cross and has no power unless I give it to him through what I believe.

"The Bible tells us the mighty power of God 'raised [Jesus] from the dead and seated Him at His right hand in the heavenly places, far above every principality and power and might and dominion, and every name that is named, not only in this age but also in that which is to come' (Ephesians 1:20–21, NKJV).' If Jesus has taken all authority away from the Enemy, why would you give it back to him by believing a lie?"

I sat quietly and thought deeply about what I was hearing. What I believed could give power to the Enemy, and that realization shocked me! I had no idea I had been opening myself up to backlash and demonic attacks because I believed the devil had the power to do so. For years, I had been taught that the devil had power and his attacks against believers were to be expected. I was told, "If you are a threat to the Enemy, you can expect to be attacked by him." I would wear his attacks like a badge of honor. But now, I was beginning to see the foolishness of that thought.

During those years working in the projects of Chicago, I had constantly given power to the devil through my thoughts and words. We had an unspoken theme for our ministry: "Whatever can go wrong will go wrong." Problem after problem arose, and after a while, it was just what we expected; and it was exactly what we got, because that is what we believed for. I had no idea I was giving power to the Enemy through what I believed.

Many times, someone would refer to a certain demon by name, and my response would be, "That is a powerful demon." And because I believed it to be so, that gave power to that demon to intimidate and attack me. My beliefs were causing me to lower my shield of authority and give place to the Enemy. When I said, "That is a powerful demon," it was as if the demon would reply, "Thank you very much, I receive the glory you just gave me."

Ouch! How could I have been so foolish?

I studied what I had learned from Mark in Scripture. The Enemy has been totally defeated through the life, death, and resurrection of Jesus Christ. We are seated at the right hand of the Father with Christ, far above all other powers and authorities (see Ephesians 2:4–7), and we trust God to make our enemies our footstool. The psalmist says, "Yahweh said to my Lord, the Messiah: 'Sit with me as an enthroned ruler while I subdue your every enemy. They will bow low before you as I make them a footstool for your feet" (Psalm 110:1, TPT). That was accomplished through the cross of Christ. We have been seated at the right hand of the Father, and Jesus has subdued our every enemy.

"We are attack lambs," Mark told me. "We have been sent as sheep among the wolves, yet Jesus has already defeated those wolves, and we are able to walk in absolute authority."

This teaching completely changed my identity in Christ and how I approached the Enemy. He was not a powerful entity; he was a defeated foe.

The Message paraphrase of the Bible says Jesus "stripped all the spiritual tyrants in the universe of their sham authority at the Cross and marched them naked through the streets" (Colossians 2:15, MSG).

If this is true—and it is—why would we give any power back to the Enemy by what we think or speak?

Paul and Silas

In Acts 16, we have the story of Paul, Silas, and Timothy in Philippi. Paul had led Lydia to the Lord, and now they were going to the river with her and some other women every day to pray. A slave woman with a demon (the Bible calls it a spirit of Python, or a spirit of divination) began to mock the men of God. Day after day this took place until Paul, greatly annoyed, cast the spirit out of her.

It is interesting that it took Paul a number of days to reach this point of casting the demon out. Surely, he recognized it right off as a demon, but it seems he wanted to avoid a confrontation and allowed it to continue day after day. He just wanted to pray and lead people to Jesus. But finally, out of frustration, he confronted the demon and cast it out.

Now that the slave woman had been set free, she could no longer make money for her master, who now stirred up trouble for Paul and Silas. They were stripped, beaten, placed in chains, and thrown in prison.

There is no record of them doing spiritual warfare, attacking the stronghold of divination in the region. They did not attack demons; they did not bind the strong man. They centered their focus on God, and at midnight, as they prayed and worshiped, everyone in the prison heard them.

As they sat in the darkness, covered in blood, their wounds throbbing in pain, they focused on God. Not knowing if they were going to live or die, they focused on God.

God was so pleased with their faith and devotion to Him, He caused an earthquake, shook the prison open, and shook the chains right off of their hands and feet.

It was worship that brought their deliverance, not confronting demons.

Intimacy Is Spiritual Warfare

Dick Eastman, director of Every Home For Christ, once said, "Your greatest act of spiritual warfare is to be intimate with Jesus Christ." I believe this is what Paul and Silas did that night in the prison. In the midst of their pain, they had intimate worship with Jesus.

When we are in pain, confusion, and darkness but we choose to trust Him and praise Him anyway, that is the sacrifice of praise.

Fixing our eyes on Jesus brings us into His Presence, and there, we experience His glory. There are no devils in that place, and if there were, they would have to bow before Him immediately.

Since that day of hearing this teaching from Mark, my life has been greatly affected. Yes, in the past, I had seen many wonderful things using the methods of spiritual warfare I had learned—identifying and confronting the Enemy, attacking strongholds, binding him, and casting him down—but it was also very difficult. Instead of focusing on Jesus, I was looking for demons. While we had many victories, it was exhausting and I was always dealing with spiritual attacks from the Enemy. It took a toll on me spiritually, physically, and emotionally.

Now, I was beginning to understand that by rebuking the demonic principalities and powers and trying to cast them down, I was trying to do what Jesus had already accomplished through the cross. He had already stripped them naked of their sham authority and marched them through the streets in total victory (again, see Colossians 2:14–15).

In this method of focusing on Jesus and giving no power to the Enemy, I have seen greater results and had much less opposition. Prayer journeys became a delight as we were now just spectators of what God was doing. We rejoiced with Him as He led us from victory to victory. Everywhere Jesus goes, demons must bow. I don't have to tell them to bow before the King of kings and the Lord of lords. They simply have to (see Philippians 2:10).

Chapter 22

Throne of Shiva

*The Spirit of the Lord is upon Me,
Because He has anointed Me
To preach the gospel to the poor;
He has sent Me to heal the brokenhearted,
To proclaim liberty to the captives
And recovery of sight to the blind,
To set at liberty those who are oppressed.*
Luke 4:18, NKJV

The following year, in late summer of 2012, Mark invited me to return with him and a team to Tibet. This time, God had laid it on Mark's heart to go into a new region that was completely untouched with the gospel. This was going to be a long, grueling journey across most of the nation of Tibet, going to a place called Mt. Kailash, near the northern border of India.

Mt. Kailash is known as the throne of Shiva, who is regarded as one of the main gods of the Hindu religion and is considered a high holy place. Every year, Hindus and Buddhists go there by the thousands for pilgrimage. This place has stood as a spiritual stronghold of the Hindu people for more than three thousand years.

Mark wanted to take us to this place to release the kingdom of God and gain a foothold for the gospel to be preached for the first time. Our team of fifteen people began our journey, once again starting from Lhasa. This time, due to the length of the journey and the number of days we had to complete it, we did not take several days to acclimate to the altitude. We left Lhasa the very next morning after arriving. We divided up into five different Jeeps and headed out for our adventure.

We traveled the narrow mountain roads, swaying back and forth in the vehicle as it curved around the tight turns of the road. The valleys had rivers running through them, and along the banks you could see thousands of acres of bright-yellow mustard plants that were ripe for harvest. The dark-green birch and aspen trees behind the fields of yellow made for a beautiful landscape.

Tibet is truly one of the most beautiful places on Earth. The tall, snow-capped mountain ranges tower toward the sky, many of them covered with glaciers thousands of years old. Deep-blue mountain lakes that are miles and miles long sit among the mountains.

We traveled for hours that first day, getting higher and higher into the mountains until we went over one of the highest passes in the world at eighteen thousand feet. The higher we traveled, the more altitude sickness gripped most of the team. Fortunately, for some unknown reason, I never experienced this terrible sickness. It seemed that aside from struggling to sleep, I did just fine in the higher altitudes, experiencing none of the negative affects many others did.

At one point, our caravan was forced to pull over, and about half of the team stood on the side of the dirt road and emptied their stomachs, the sound of retching and vomiting filling the night air. We finally reached our camp site, and our guides set up our blue pup tents and we tried to settle in. For most of the group, including Mark and his wife, Ellie, it was a very rough night.

The next morning, Mark came into the mess tent where a few of us were sipping our cups of hot water. He sat across from me and said, "This time I think I may have bitten off more than I can chew."

I smiled a little, as Mark was looking really sick. "Now that is not what the team wants to hear from our fearless leader," I said teasingly.

Mark just rolled his eyes at me and groaned. He knew it was going to be a very long day.

It took us five days to travel across Tibet. Most of that was on dirt roads, and sometimes there were no roads at all. At one point, all five Jeeps were driving across the Tibetan tundra side by side. *National Geographic* could not have published a more beautiful picture of our vehicles cruising across the landscape. Herds of wild donkeys ran near the Jeeps, and far off, we could see many goats that seemed to dance on the mountaintops as they leapt from rock to rock.

As the days passed, we became acclimated to the altitude and started feeling better. Each night we would unpack, set up our tents, and enjoy the countryside. At night, the air was so thin and the stars so bright it was as if we could reach up and pluck them out of the sky. It was the clearest view of the Milky Way I had ever seen.

Let God Arise!

We finally reached our last campsite before Mount Kailash. That morning, we gathered to pray before we went into the small village at the foot of the mountain. As we prayed, I felt compelled to shout, "Let God arise, and His enemies be scattered!" I repeated it three times.

That was the extent of our spiritual warfare: "Let God arise, and His enemies be scattered!" And that is exactly what happened.

We struck camp and Tashi led us into the village.

"I spoke to the local police, and they have given permission for you to stay in one location and pray," she said. "I told them the

Hindus and Buddhists come here to pray, so why not let the Christians say their prayers?"

It was amazing! Here in this Communist-controlled country, Christians had been given permission to pray in the village.

Tashi led us to a vacant lot on a corner in the village. There were a few Tibetans walking to and fro—taking care of their daily tasks—and for the most part, they just glanced at this group of foreigners with mild curiosity.

Mark began to separate the team. "You will stand here and make balloons for the kids," he said, pointing at several people on the team. "You will stand here and play your violins and sing," he told another group. "And you will stand here and pray for the sick," he said, pointing at me and a couple of others.

I stood there watching Mark organize the teams. I was thinking, *What does he think is going to happen?* For now, we were just standing out here alone with hardly anyone in sight.

Healing Prayer

Suddenly, one of our translators grabbed me by the arm.

"Come, come, someone needs healing prayer."

They led me to an elderly man, whom I spent a few moments praying for. When I finished, I turned and saw that they had brought a woman who was blind.

My spirit jumped. Before I had come on this trip, while praying, God showed me that I would pray for a person who was blind. When I saw the woman standing in front of me, I knew she was the one God had shown me. Because of what I had seen in prayer, my faith level soared. If I had not seen this in prayer, I would not have had the faith to pray, but God had prepared me ahead of time for this moment.

I laid hands on her and right there, God opened her eyes. We all stood and laughed as she looked around in amazement, seeing clearly for the first time in years. I found out later that in the high altitudes of Tibet, the sun shines so brightly that over time, it literally burns the eyes. Many people have damaged eyesight or are completely blind.

Immediately, word spread about this group of foreigners praying for people, and a crowd began to form. We laid hands on people as quickly as we could, one after another. They kept coming, and with each healing, the word spread even more. People were running home to get loved ones; others were on their cell phones calling friends. The crowd kept growing.

God healed many eyes that day. Backs, knees, legs . . . everything you could imagine, God healed. For two and a half hours we saw miracle after miracle as God poured out His Spirit at the foot of what is called the throne of Shiva. In a place considered one of the greatest demonic strongholds in the world, God made Himself known.

Suddenly, I looked up and saw Mark standing on the edge of the crowd. He had positioned himself so he could look out for the Chinese police. He knew with a crowd this size, they would be coming, and we would have to make a quick exit before we were arrested.

Mark motioned for me to stop and mouthed the words, "Time to go!" I immediately obeyed. I stopped praying for people and turned and walked away, heading back down the road to our guesthouse. Two Chinese police cars had pulled up and were looking for the instigators of this crowd.

As I walked down the road, some Tibetans followed, tugging at my shirt for me to stop and pray for them. I turned and could see the desperation in their eyes, begging me to relieve them of their pain. I could only imagine what Jesus felt when the multitudes came to Him, desperate for one touch that would change their lives forever. I quickly stopped to pray and then kept walking until I came to the guesthouse. Here, another crowd began to form as I continued to pray for people.

The Presence of God was there to heal, and He was showing Himself strong. It was as if God had been waiting for this moment for a very long time and could not wait any longer to reveal Himself.

These people had been worshiping false gods all their lives, because in their ignorance, it was all they knew. They were a spiritual people, a people who had faith, but their faith had been captivated by lies that led to bondage. Jesus had come to set the captives free.

I Don't Want to Go to Jail

Mark approached me, gently took me by the arm, and pulled me to the side.

"Dan, if you keep doing this, we are going to jail. I've been in a Chinese jail several times, and I really don't want to have that experience again. Would you please go to your room and allow me to disperse this crowd?"

I looked Mark in the eye. He was not demanding; he was not afraid; he was simply saying that if we used a small amount of wisdom, it could prevent potential pain. If I persisted, I could put our entire team in danger. Sometimes, persecution can be avoided by not doing something foolish. Besides, I wasn't sure I wanted to have the experience of going to a Chinese jail either, although I am sure it would have been another great adventure.

I sat in the room with my three roommates. We sat in silence, staring at each other. The Presence and awe of God was thick and heavy in the room. We were all thinking, *Did that just happen?* We had never experienced anything like that in our lives. God had just taken us to the throne of Shiva, and Shiva bowed his knee to the King of kings and the Lord of lords. Not because we told him to, but simply because Jesus showed up and he had no other choice.

After a few hours, Mark came and opened our door and let us come outside. Mark and I sat on the ground against the wall of the guesthouse, looking at the awe-inspiring mountains in the distance.

"On the other side of those mountains, in North India, there are more unreached people groups than in any place in the world," he said. "I am going there next. Would you like to come?"

I laughed. "I would love to."

This experience was nothing short of a book-of-Acts experience. The book of Acts has never stopped being written by men and women of God all over the world.

Generational Mantles

While on our first trip to Tibet, Mark had told our team a story of how he had received spiritual impartation by the laying on of hands. This was like what Timothy had received when Paul had laid his hands on him (see 2 Timothy 1:6–7).

"I received a call from a man named Lester Sumrall, who was a famous teacher on healing and deliverance," Mark began. "He asked me to come visit him because he had heard stories about my ministry over the years. Sumrall told me that when he was a young man, he had been mentored by Smith Wigglesworth in England." (Smith Wigglesworth is famous for having a radical gift of healing and did healing crusades for many years with thousands of miracles. Wigglesworth in turn had been mentored by George Mueller, who was famous for caring for thousands of orphans and building multiple orphanages, all while never making his needs known to man but fully trusting God to provide.)

"Pastor Sumrall told me that Smith Wigglesworth had said George Mueller laid hands on him when he was a young man and imparted a spiritual gift," Mark continued. "Wigglesworth laid hands on Sumrall and said, 'Everything I have received from God and everything I received by the laying on of hands from George Mueller, I impart to you.'

"Pastor Sumrall asked *me* to kneel in front of him, and he laid his hands on me and said, 'Everything I have received from God, and everything I received from Smith Wigglesworth, and everything he received from George Mueller, I impart to you, Mark.'"

Our entire team was silent as we tried to grasp the significance of what had happened to Mark. Even now, years later, we could feel the sacredness of that moment as Mark quietly told his story.

I sat quietly, listening to Mark share this intimate and powerful moment of his life. George Mueller, Smith Wigglesworth, Lester Sumrall. Each generation carried a mantle of spiritual gifting that had been passed down to the next. With each generation the mantles multiplied and now rested on Mark. *That is amazing!* I thought, knowing that I could not fully comprehend the weight of this spiritual transfer.

After our trip to Tibet, our team stopped in Hong Kong overnight before flying back to the States. Late that evening our team went to the roof of our hotel to pray over the city. The nighttime views of Hong Kong were spectacular as we prayed and watched the city lights sparkle across the bay.

I felt a tap on my shoulder and turned to see Mark.

"God told me to do something. Please kneel down."

I wasn't sure what he was doing, but I obeyed and knelt before him.

Mark proceeded to lay his hands on my head and said, "Everything I have received from God, everything I received from Lester Sumrall, everything he received from Smith Wigglesworth, and everything he received from George Mueller, I now impart to you."

There, on a hotel rooftop in Hong Kong, like Elijah did for Elisha, Mark laid his mantle on me.

A few months later, Mark came to Phoenix for a visit, and we had dinner together.

"Mark," I told him, "I feel like God wants me to go to the nations. I feel this stirring in my heart to go, but I don't know how or what to do."

Mark looked at me and immediately said, "Go to India. Go pray. Take teams twice a year and stay about three weeks at a time. Go pray in India."

It sounded so simple. Jan and I looked at each other. She nodded her affirmation. My spirit jumped. In an instant, my mind was clear and I knew what to do. Mark's words had sparked a fire in my spirit and activated me to go to the nations.

"I can do that," I said. I looked at Jan. For several years she had been supporting my journeys, praying for me, organizing my flights and helping to administrate the teams. She was my backbone, and I knew we had to be in agreement if I was going to continue. She nodded, giving me her approval to say yes. It was settled. I would go to India, take teams, and pray.

FLASHBACK

The ambulance finally reached our destination and pulled up in front of the hospital. It now had been two and a half days since the accident, and I was more than ready to get this surgery over with. They wheeled me directly into the operation room where I met the head surgeon for the first time. My X-rays from the previous hospital had been sent to him, so he was ready to go straight into the operation. My friends held my hands and prayed for me for a few moments before they took me into surgery.

Now that I was in the right hospital with the right surgeon, I felt hopeful and ready to get this done. I lay back on the gurney and sighed.

The attendants gave me a shot of painkiller in my lower back that made my entire lower body numb. "You will be awake and aware of what is happening, but you will not be able to feel anything," I was told. I lay still, feeling the effects of the painkiller numbing my legs.

As I lay waiting for the surgery to begin, I noticed some activity in the room. They were having trouble with some of the equipment and were trying to repair it so they could do the surgery. Time went by as they continued to work on the problem. The longer I lay there waiting, the less of an effect the painkiller was having. Finally, all was in order and the doctor made the first incision into my upper leg.

I groaned in pain. Because of the long delay, the painkiller was wearing off and my legs were regaining feeling. I could feel the knife cut through my skin. I felt his hands trying to manipulate the bones to get them lined up properly. First the upper break, and then the lower break. Pain shot through my leg like fire as the bones were being moved.

The doctor was placing a metal rod into my femur. I could feel the hammer hitting the rod again and again, slamming it down through the center of the bone. I tried as hard as I could to maintain some type of control. I groaned loudly. The pain was causing me to rise up and move on the table.

In the effort to hold me still, two attendants wrapped a blanket around my chest and lay across me, holding me down. They had seen that the original painkiller was wearing off, and they gave me an injection of something to try to dull the pain. This only caused me to hallucinate and become completely disoriented.

My mind began to see things that were not in the room, and I felt like I was leaving my body.

"Is this what it is like to die?" I wondered. I truly thought I was dying, as I could not discern if I was in my body or out of it. But since I could still feel pain, I figured I wasn't dead yet.

I could feel the screws being drilled into the upper and lower part of my leg to hold the rod in place. I could feel the staples being slammed into the incisions. Forty-three times, the stapler slammed into my leg. I was completely disoriented from the drugs, and by this time, the original painkiller had completely worn off. The pain had become so intense that I finally lost all control; I just raised my head and screamed.

The doctor finished the surgery and wrapped my leg in bandages. The attendants lifted me and moved me to a hospital bed and took me through the halls to a private room where my friends were waiting for me. The intense trauma of what I had just experienced was still affecting me as I struggled to discern what was real and what was a hallucination. They gave me an IV with drugs that would ease the pain and help me sleep. I lay back and let the drugs settle in. I closed my eyes and for the first time in nearly three days, I felt no pain and slept deeply.

The next morning, I woke up and the doctor was there to check on me. I looked up groggily and asked, "What happened last night?" I was not angry; I just knew something had gone terribly wrong.

"I am very sorry," he said. "A piece of equipment broke, and it took a long time to repair it. I should have stopped and given you more painkillers. I did not realize how fast the drugs had worn off. Normally, those drugs last several hours, but your body reacted differently, and it wore off in half the time. I am very sorry."

The doctor hung his head and was very humble. I could see he felt terrible about what had taken place. He apologized again to me and my friends about what had happened.

"Were you able to accomplish what you needed to with the surgery?" I asked. "Were you able to set the bones correctly?"

"Yes, yes," he replied. "The surgery was successful. The rod has been placed and the bones are set. Everything should heal with no problem."

"How long will it be before I can climb mountains again?" I asked.

He smiled. "You are over sixty years old; do you still want to climb mountains?"

"You better believe I do!" I said emphatically.

"At your age it may take time; probably two years or more, I think."

"But will I heal well enough to go trekking again?" I asked.

"Yes, sir, you will be able to walk fully normal in time."

I lay back and sighed. Even after the intense trauma of the last three days and especially the deep trauma of the surgery, I had perfect peace. God was with me. I was going to be okay.

I called Jan and let her know I was out of surgery.

"How did it go?" she asked.

"Well, if I go back to Kashmir, get captured by ISIS, and am tortured, I am fully prepared for it," I said, laughing.

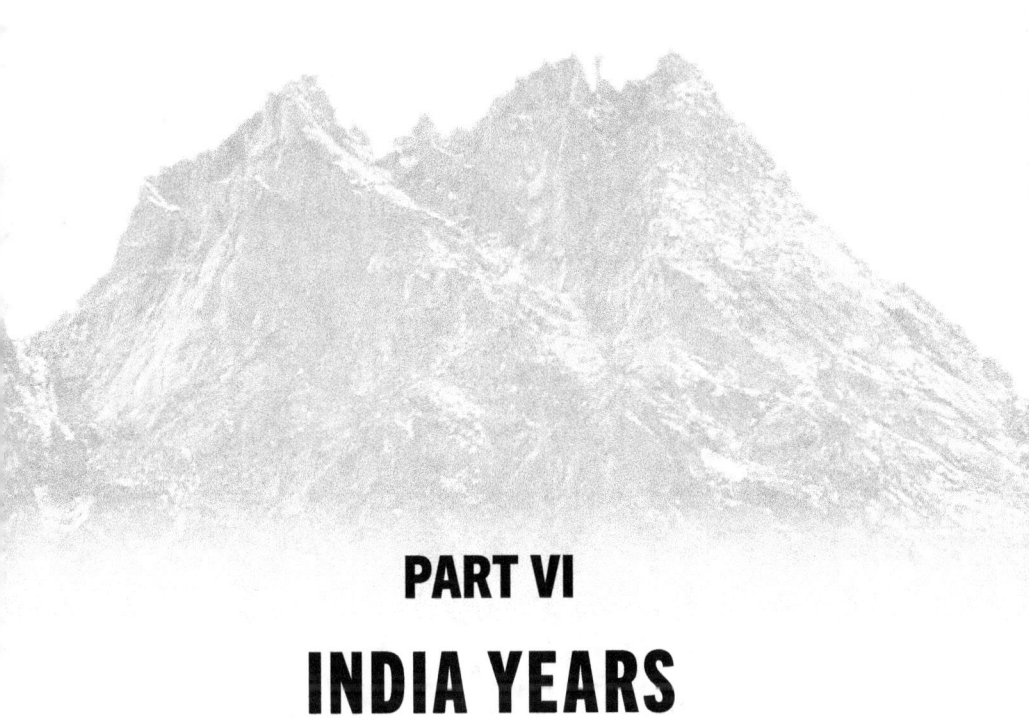

PART VI
INDIA YEARS

Chapter 23

Meeting My Indian Family

I thank my God upon every remembrance of you . . . for your fellowship in the gospel from the first day until now.
Philippians 1:3,5, NKJV

In October 2013, Mark invited me to go to North India with a small team. We made plans that at the end of the trip, the team would leave and he and I would go to the region of Kashmir for a few days.

Mark had scouted out a journey he wanted to do in Himachal Pradesh, a state that has one of the highest numbers of unreached people groups in the world. Mark had also found an Indian tour guide who knew the region very well. He was a young Hindu named Ravi.

Our team of twelve met in Delhi, loaded up in Jeeps, and began our ten-day, eighteen-hundred-mile journey through one of the most beautiful places on earth. As we left Delhi and went through the city of Chandigarh, we began to enter the foothills of the Himalayas and continued to follow the narrow mountain road to Shimla. Shimla was a beautiful mountain city that had at one time been the summer capital of the British Empire. The British had controlled the Indian subcontinent for more than three hundred years, until 1947, when India gained independence.

The Prayer Drive

I sat in the back seat of a Jeep with Mark and Ravi for the entire ten days. I did not know anything about being Hindu, and I was eager to learn about this major religion. Ravi knew nothing about being a Christian, and he also was eager to learn what our group of foreigners believed. Ravi had led many tour groups all over northern India, but this was his first experience with Christians.

I asked Ravi hundreds of questions about the Hindu gods, what Hindus believed, and how they practiced their religion. Ravi was like a walking encyclopedia of knowledge and told many tales of the history of Hinduism. I was surprised to learn that Hinduism is the oldest religion in the world and dates back to fifteen hundred years before Abraham. I was also surprised that they worship more than thirty million different gods. How could they possibly keep up with them all?

Ravi and I bounced up and down in the back of the Jeep and talked for hours each day of the trip. (Mark began to call me Bobble-head Dan.) Ravi would tell me something about Hinduism, and I would tell him something about Christianity. As we spent much time together, we became quick friends.

Several times on the trip, as I would be talking about Jesus, Ravi would look at me with his eyes wide open with curiosity and ask, "What is this energy coming out of you? I feel power coming out of you."

I laughed, because the Presence of God would sweep over us again and again as we spoke. "Ravi, what you are feeling is the Presence of my God. He is letting you know that what I'm saying is true."

Mark sat next to us listening but not entering into the conversation. From time to time, I could see a little smile on his lips as he too felt the Presence of God and knew Ravi was being touched by the Holy Spirit.

For ten days, our group made its way through Himachal Pradesh, our Jeeps winding through the mountains. At one point, our Jeep came around a mountain curve and came face-to-face with a huge truck coming right at us. Ravi jumped and shouted, "My God!" Our driver slammed on the brakes and narrowly missed the truck.

I looked at Ravi and said, "Which god were crying out to, Ravi?"

"Whichever one is most available!" he replied. Mark and I laughed so hard, we had tears.

While I enjoyed the journey, we did not connect with many locals along the way. It was mostly a prayer journey and scouting trip. We stopped at many Hindu temples and spiritual power points and learned much about the spiritual history of this amazing place.

Stuck in Delhi

I found out that the second stage of the trip I had planned with Mark had fallen through, and he was going to return home with the rest of the team. It was going to cost an extraordinary amount of money to change my ticket, so I decided I would just stay in Delhi for a few extra days on my own before returning home on my scheduled flight.

On the morning of the last day with the team, we were asked to visit a well-known Christian ministry in the city. While we were there, I noticed a flyer on a wall advertising a national intercessory prayer gathering. It had just started that day and would go on for the next three days.

That's it! I thought. *I'll go hang out with some Indians and pray for a couple of days.*

I asked our host, "If I give this flyer to a cab driver, will he be able to take me to this place?"

"Yes, absolutely," he replied.

At that moment, Mark received a text on his phone, which read: "Can you stop by a prayer conference and speak before you go to the airport today?" The address was sent with the request. Mark looked at the address, then at the flyer I was holding, then at me. It was the same place!

"Hmmm," said Mark, "What to do?"

The Indian Prayer Conference

Our driver took us across town to the church that was hosting the conference. It was a gathering of nearly two hundred house church leaders representing thirteen thousand house churches in Central and North India. Most of these men and women of God had suffered much persecution and lived in abject poverty, but their faces radiated the Presence of God and their smiles reflected the joy of the Lord.

The worship had just begun when we arrived. Our host led us to some white plastic chairs on the side of the room, where we had a good view of the worship team as well as the congregation. It was a joy to watch them worship with such passion and joy. They clapped and danced and sang at the top of their voices, celebrating their freedom in Christ.

As I watched, I took notice of the young woman who was leading the worship. She didn't just lead worship; she turned the church into a portal where heaven was touching earth. The Presence of God was heavy on her as she shifted back and forth between singing in English and Hindi. The quality and strength of her spirit were easily evident. I wondered who she was.

Invited to Speak

After the worship time, Mark was introduced and preached a powerful message. He then gave me a quick hug goodbye and ran to the car that would take him and the rest of the team to the airport. I turned to say hello to the man who oversaw the meeting. His name was Jacob.

"I have a couple of days here in Delhi with no plans," I told him. "Is it possible I could come back the next two days and pray with your group here?"

"Certainly, you are most welcome. Please come," he graciously responded. "Brother, has the Lord given you a message to share with us?"

I was a little surprised. In America, one does not just show up at a large conference as a stranger and be invited to speak. As I hesitated to answer, his wife came up to us and he introduced her to me. Her name was Deborah.

"Welcome, brother, it is good to have you here. Has the Lord given you something to share with us?" she asked. Her husband and I laughed.

"Well, maybe I am supposed to share something." I said.

The next morning, at the conference, I sat watching as they opened with their first session of prayer. Then Jacob stood to introduce me.

"Come on up here, brother, and share what the Lord has given you." He did not even know my name. I was astounded that he would let a stranger have a platform to speak in this setting. As I stepped to the podium, he whispered in my ear, "Please take about fifteen minutes, brother." I nodded in agreement and stood behind the podium. Jacob walked to his chair and sat down, then jumped up and came back to me. "You take all the time you want, brother." I thought, *This would never happen in America!*

I was hoping the young woman who led worship the day before would be the one to translate for me. But there was another man who had already been translating and was set to do the task. Suddenly, as I began to speak, the young woman stepped up and took the place of the man. As she began to translate, I smiled at her, and my heart said, *Thank You, Jesus.*

As I began to speak, the Presence of God came heavily. I could feel His anointing, but more than that, I felt His Presence flowing through the young woman even stronger. It was like a double-barrel shotgun of the Holy Spirit ministering to those beautiful Indian leaders. I kept looking over my shoulder at the young woman, thinking, *Who are you?*

At one point, I made the comment, "All of us here assume that one day, we will die for Jesus Christ." I waited for the words to be translated, ready to say the next sentence. But when the translation had been given, they began to shout and cheer and clap their hands.

I couldn't believe it. I was stunned. I had just spoken about dying for Jesus, and their response was not rejection of that statement, fear, or intimidation—they cheered! I stood in silence as the Holy Spirit came and swept over all of us. I was standing with a group of people who were not only willing but *eager* to die for their Lord. I was so honored to stand with such amazing men and women of God. I looked at my translator, and her eyes were filled with tears, just as mine were.

Invited to Lay Hands on the Leaders

At the end of the session, Jacob looked at me and said, "Please come up to my flat and have chai with me." I followed him up a flight of stairs when the young woman who translated for me appeared. "This is my daughter, Tara," he said.

"Oh, this is your daughter? It is so good to meet you!" We shook hands and laughed, both of us enjoying the moment. "I kept looking over at you while we were preaching, thinking, *Who is that woman?* It was a great joy ministering with you today. Thank you for your help, and thank you for the Presence of God you carry!"

Neither of us had a clue that day that God would form a deep bond between us. Over the next ten years, Tara and I would continue

MEETING MY INDIAN FAMILY

to minister together hundreds of times all over North India and five other countries.

I sat with Jacob in his home, sipping chai, as he began to share some of his history and ministry. I was amazed that I was sitting with this man of God. He had suffered and persevered with great faith for many years, advancing the kingdom of God in the harshest of circumstances. This was a veteran apostle of Jesus Christ, and he had the scars on his body and his soul to prove it. It was an honor to be in the company of this man of God.

As we sat, Jacob's wife, Deborah, came in with her sister.

"Dear brother, we would like to ask you something," she began. "We have been asking God to send us someone who would lay hands on all our leaders and give them a spirit of impartation for intercession. We believe God has sent you to do that. Would you be willing to stay for tonight's service, preach, and then pray for our leaders?"

This day was just getting crazier by the minute. I looked at Jacob.

"Yes brother, I agree," he said. "Please stay and lay hands on all the leaders and pray for them tonight."

"Yes, it will be an honor," I replied. I lowered my head, thinking, *How in the world did I get here? God, what are you doing?* Two weeks earlier, I did not know a single person in India, and now I was being asked to lay hands on nearly two hundred Indian leaders representing thirteen thousand house churches.

I knew I was experiencing a God moment that no man could ever make happen on purpose. It was only His grace doing what I could never do. As Mark had once said, "Do you think you can come up with a better plan than God?" God definitely had a plan, and He was just getting started.

That evening, Tara and I ministered again and God's Presence came. I laid hands on every person there and prayed for an impartation of intercession. In fact, I think I prayed for every person twice, as after they received prayer, they would run back and get in line to be prayed for again. They were determined to get all they could from God that night.

At the end, Jacob and I went to our knees, holding each other and praying for each other. God had established a spiritual relationship far beyond what we could comprehend at that time.

As I look back on that event, it was as if God was saying, "Dan, meet Jacob, Deborah, and Tara. Jacob, Deborah, and Tara, meet Dan. Get used to seeing a lot of each other. I have work for you to do."

Chapter 24

I Am a Little Bit Angry with You

But God has chosen the foolish things of the world to put to shame the wise, and God has chosen the weak things of the world to put to shame the things which are mighty.
1 Corinthians 1:27, NKJV

I made two more trips to North India with Mark, and then I began to take teams on my own. Every time I went, I stopped in the same city high in the mountains. This city became my home base to work and travel out of while I was in India.

There, at the top of the highest hill, was an Anglican church that was very famous in India. It was here that the viceroy of the British Empire had attended church with other very influential and powerful people during British rule. The church was built in 1857 and has been in continuous use ever since. It stands as the centerpiece of the city and is a major tourist attraction; people from all over the world come to admire its beauty and history.

But to me, it was a beautiful religious structure that had no relevance at all. From what I had heard, the priests of the Anglican Church were very prideful, and many of them were not even born again. The church was for doctors, lawyers, teachers, and other wealthy people of the upper caste system. Most people attended it as a status symbol.

During my first visit to this city, I had walked by the church when the Holy Spirit gently nudged me: "Go knock on the door and say hello to the priest."

"What? Say hello to the priest? Why would I talk to a priest? I have no idea what to say to a priest," I responded, full of doubt and questions.

"Go knock on the door."

Completely confused but also a little curious, I decided to knock on the heavy old wooden door. After a short time, the priest of the church came down the stairs and opened the door. He was short and stocky, with beautiful hazel-colored eyes that stood out against his dark skin.

"Yes? May I help you?" he asked politely.

I had no idea what to say to this man so I simply told him, "My name is Dan. God told me to come to this city to pray, and I thought I would come by to say hello."

He looked at me strangely and after a moment of trying to size me up he said, "I am Mushtaq. Please come in and have a cup of chai."

In India, when you don't know what to do or say, it is always considered a good idea to have chai. In fact, any time you go to visit someone at their house, you are always requested to stay for chai. Anytime someone wants to discuss a matter, important or trivial, chai is required. I believe chai is definitely one of God's better ideas.

We went upstairs to the living area where he introduced me to his wife, Neera, and his son, Arvind. We sat and chatted awkwardly for a few moments and sipped the hot tea. There would be long periods of silence as we tried to think of things to say. After all, I had no agenda, and in fact, I was still trying to figure out why I was there.

After some time, I rose, thanked them for the chai, and said goodbye. As I left the house I sighed in relief and said, "That was awkward and uncomfortable, Lord. What was that all about? I feel no purpose or connection with them at all. We have nothing in common. He is a highly educated Anglican priest, and I am a Pentecostal country boy from America. That sure felt like oil and water trying to mix."

God smiled.

Meeting with Neera

Each time I visited the city, I stopped by and had an awkward visit with Mushtaq and Neera.

Finally, on one of these visits, I was talking to Mushtaq when Neera entered the room. By the sullen look on her face and her stiff body language, I got the impression she was in a bad mood. I politely said hello and she barely acknowledged me. *I wonder what her problem is?* I thought to myself.

As I rose to leave, Neera stopped me and said, "I want to speak to you in private. I want you to come back tomorrow morning and we will talk." She wasn't asking; she was boldly telling me what she wanted and wasn't taking no for an answer.

"Is this okay with your husband?" I asked.

"Yes, yes, of course. Come for breakfast tomorrow and we will talk."

I walked down the hill to my hotel wondering what this was all about. Had I said or done something to offend her? I was still getting accustomed to the culture, so maybe I had done something in my brash American way that did not settle well? All I could imagine was that I was in trouble, and I wasn't sure why.

The next morning, Mushtaq met me at the door. He led me upstairs to their kitchen where Neera served us breakfast. After eating, Mushtaq led us to the living room where he prayed with us for a few moments. "I will now take Arvind to school and give you time to talk. The housemaid is here so you will not be alone."

As Mushtaq and Arvind left the house, Neera sat on the couch across from me and got comfortable. I waited with some trepidation for Neera to speak her mind. I was still trying to figure out why I was on the hot seat.

"I am a little bit angry with you," she started.

Okay, we got that cleared up, I thought. "Angry with me? Neera, I am so sorry, but what did I do to make you angry with me?"

"You come here and help the private pastors, but you don't do anything to help the CNI." (The private pastors she referred to were all of those who did not belong to the Anglican Church but had independent ministries. The Church of North India, or CNI, was the title given to the Anglican congregations.)

"Help you? Help you do what?" In all our times together, it had never crossed my mind that I would ever do anything in an Anglican church. We had absolutely nothing in common. I only came to visit this one because God kept making me do it.

"Our churches are dying! We need revival! We need you to come and preach in our churches and bring the Presence of God!"

"But Neera, you know I am Pentecostal. I pray in tongues and believe in healing and deliverance. I'm not sure the CNI churches would be very pleased. They are very dignified and have many religious rituals. I am loud and passionate. They may not receive me very well."

All I could think of was how I would not fit in with the religious system of this very traditional organization. I'd be like a bull in a china shop. I did my best Moses impersonation and came up with every excuse I could think of to explain I was not the man for the job.

"No problem, no problem," said Neera. "God did not bring you here for us to remain the same. We need God to come and change us, and I know you can help. Mushtaq and I have prayed about you for a long time now. We know you have been sent by God to help us."

I was overwhelmed with the significance of her request. I looked at the floor and shook my head in wonder. *God, I can't believe you brought me here and you are doing this. This is beyond anything I could have ever imagined*, I silently prayed.

As I left their house that day and walked down the hill to my hotel, I was in awe of what God had just done. In simple obedience, I had knocked on the door of the priest, and now the doors to churches where the wealthy and influential attended had opened to me all over North India.

Also, the irony of bringing the Jesus I had come to know into a highly structured religious system was not lost on me. God does have a sense of humor.

Only God could make something like this happen. There was no way I could have ever come up with the idea of working in the CNI churches, and even if I did, I would never have known how to open the door. God simply had me knock on one, and he opened them all.

Coming up with your own ideas and working to fulfill them is a waste of time. Not only is it a waste, but it also keeps you from being available to do what God created you to do. His plan is always better, always more productive, and always takes much less effort.

As Jesus said, "The Son can do nothing of Himself, but what He sees the Father do; for whatever He does, the Son also does in like manner. For the Father loves the Son, and shows Him all things that He Himself does; and He will show Him greater works than these, that you may marvel" (John 5:19–20, NKJV).

God loves you. He will show you what He is doing, and then He will invite you to join Him.

Ministering in the Church of North India

As I continued to visit this city over the next few years, Mushtaq slowly and wisely began to open the door for me to minister in the Anglican Church. One Sunday, he invited me to speak at the English-speaking service. As I stood on the platform, trying to figure out when to sit and when to stand as they went through their liturgy, I told Jesus, "Lord, I am sorry, but I really don't feel very comfortable being in this orthodox religious setting."

"Neither do I," I heard Him whisper back. It made me laugh and set me at ease a bit.

Later, Mushtaq had me preach at the main Hindi-speaking service. As always, Tara was there to translate the message.

The Presence of God came in power that day, and after we finished ministering, Mushtaq asked the congregation, "How many of you would like to have Dan and Tara come back and conduct three days of revival services?" I was surprised, as we had never discussed this beforehand. Everyone in the congregation clapped and cheered, except for two or three sitting on the front row. They did not look like they approved at all.

Later, I asked Mushtaq about what he had done, and about those who did not seem to approve.

"Our church has a few Pharisees," he said with a little smile. "They serve on the board. If I had gone to them to get permission to invite you back for revival services, they would have said no. So, I went directly to the congregation, and because of their overwhelming approval, the Pharisees will have to agree."

I laughed and said, "Mushtaq, you are a very wise man!"

The following year, Tara and I returned and conducted the revival services. The response of the people was overwhelming as the church was full each night. God moved in power as many people were saved, healed, and delivered from demonic oppression.

Because the church was a national landmark, tourists would stop in to see the building and take pictures during the services. People who had walked in to take a picture were suddenly getting healed and receiving a witness of Christ. We were so full of joy to see what God was doing in this traditional, religious church. The people were hungrier for the Presence of God in their lives than ever before.

Because of the great things God was doing in the services, many people began to invite us to their homes. During the day we would do house visits, and at night we would hold the services. It was a great joy visiting the homes, drinking lots of chai, and ministering to the family members.

Mushtaq then invited me to return the following spring to minister at their Easter services. Easter is the high holy day of the year for the CNI, and it was a huge honor to minister there at that time. Even the local TV and newspaper people would attend Easter services and report on the grand event.

On Easter, the church would be overflowing with the most influential people of society, as their status dictated their attendance. They did not necessarily attend because they were believers, but because it was an opportunity to make a show of their importance. The Easter service was a great time for them to come to be seen.

Good Friday Service

On Good Friday, Mushtaq asked me to speak on the seven sayings of Jesus on the cross. I would speak on each one of the sayings for ten minutes and there would be five minutes of singing in between. As I spoke, the Holy Spirit moved gently yet powerfully across the congregation. Doctors, lawyers, professors, and government leaders were convicted of their sin and pride. The humility of seeing Jesus on the cross and understanding exactly what He had done for them cut them to the heart.

For nearly two hours they listened to the preaching and the powerful songs that were chosen for each of the sayings of the cross. Heads were lowered and tears flowed as God ministered to the deepest recesses of their hearts. Some actually groaned out loud as the truth of the cross was revealed to them.

The work God did that day was very strategic and powerful. I could have never gotten to these people by any other way than the way God provided that day. He was the one who set this day in place, and He was the one who gathered people from the highest places of society to make Himself known.

When I worked with the independent churches in India, we would minister to the lowest-caste people in society, but here, God was opening the door to minister to people of the highest caste in India. These were the people of power and influence who could bring Jesus into the highest places of government, education, and business. It was amazing to see the strategies of God unfold and, as always, do what man could never do on his own.

Over the following years, I became the best of friends with Mushtaq and Neera. We traveled thousands of miles across two states of North India conducting pastor conferences, organizing healing crusades, and speaking in local churches. Through them, God opened many doors for effective ministry where thousands were healed and delivered, and many became followers of Christ. One of the greatest friendships, and years of powerful and fruitful ministry, took place because God told me to go knock on the door of a priest.

Chapter 25

Focus on Jesus

Therefore God has highly exalted Him and given Him the name which is above every name, that at the name of Jesus every knee should bow, of those in heaven, and of those on earth, and of those under the earth, and that every tongue should confess that Jesus Christ is Lord, to the glory of God the Father.
Philippians 2:9–11, NKJV

In 2014, I was invited to go to Sri Lanka on a prayer journey. Sri Lanka had been devastated by the tsunami of 2004 and now, nearly ten years later, it was still recovering from the deep trauma that had ensued.

My friend David was Indian but had done years of wonderful ministry in this small island country off the southern tip of India. He took me all over the island, visiting different ministries and prayer walking spiritual high places.

One day, as we were driving in a city called Kandy, David pointed out a very large Buddhist temple. It is referred to as the Temple of the Sacred Tooth. As legend has it, one of the teeth from the Buddha is housed there.

"That is a very powerful temple," said David. "It controls everything in this region. Hundreds of thousands of people go there to worship the Buddha every year. It is very powerful!"

Hmmm, I thought. *It seems David has a very high regard for that place.* But I said nothing about it at the time.

A few days later we drove by the same temple, and again David said, "That is a very powerful temple. It controls everything in this region."

Maybe David had forgotten he had just said that a few days ago, but this time I decided to say something.

"So David, how long have you been worshiping demons?" I asked.

His head snapped around to look at me. "What? What are you talking about? I don't worship demons!" he said emphatically.

"Well, all I know is that every time we drive by that temple you tell that demon how powerful he is and exalt him. Why do you do that? Every time you tell that demon how powerful he is, he just says, 'Yes, I am! Thank you very much!'"

David looked at me sharply. He had never considered that what he had been doing was glorifying the Enemy. I could see his mind trying to adjust to what I was saying.

"The only reason that demon has any power is if you give it to him," I said. "The reason it has power over this region is because the people believe it is so. As a man of God, you set the example. Stop giving power to it by what you speak. He is not a powerful demon; he is a defeated demon. Through the cross, Jesus stripped him naked and marched him through the streets. How did he become powerful again? He can only be powerful if you believe his lies."

David continued to look at me strangely. All his life he had gone with the belief that Satan was powerful. David is very intellectual and highly educated. What I was saying was going against everything he had learned and believed. My words were registering in his spirit as true, but now his mind was trying to catch up with his spirit. He had to redefine his beliefs about spiritual warfare. I had presented a simple truth that radically changed his thinking.

Mark would have been proud.

Ravi's Village

I left Sri Lanka and went straight to North India. There I connected with Daniel, a local pastor, and our old friend and tour guide, Ravi. Ravi had invited us to come to his mountain village, where his family had lived for many generations. He had said that no foreigner or Christian had ever been there before. It was an honor for me to be invited as the first of both.

I reached out to Tara and asked her to join our team. I would need a good translator, and her ability to play the guitar and sing was an added bonus. Also, I was beginning to lean on her for her wisdom and helping me understand Indian culture.

On one of my first trips to India, I had met Pastor Daniel and his wife, Poonam, who had been working in the north of India for many years. They had suffered much working to see spiritual breakthrough in this region, referred to as the Pastors' Graveyard. Many people had come here to plant churches over the past decades, and most of them had left in defeat. But not Daniel and Poonam. Their prayers, faithfulness, and perseverance were establishing a spiritual stronghold in a place where it was said to be impossible.

Daniel had a team of five young men and women he had been training for some months. They were learning about intercessory prayer, the voice of God, and how to pray for healing and deliverance. It was a joy for me to meet them and spend time with them, and they were eager to get experience on the mission field.

Seven of us squeezed into a five-passenger car, and after several hours of traveling along the primitive mountain roads, we reached Ravi's village high in the Himalayas. It truly was one of the most beautiful places I had ever been. It was as if heaven was touching earth.

That evening, Ravi's cousin invited us to come to his house and meet his wife, his son, and his mother-in-law.

As we stood on the porch of his home, Kalpana, one of the young women on the team, came to me. "Dan, I can sense there are demons all over the place. I can see them on the roof, some there by the trees, one in the window. . . . I can see them everywhere!" Her eyes were very wide with concern as she relayed this information to me. I couldn't help but laugh, which didn't ease her fears a bit. She looked at me, wondering why I was not deeply concerned about this.

"Kalpana," I said, "this is a Hindu village that has been here for many generations. The Hindus worship millions of gods, and we are the very first Christians to ever be in this village. I'm not surprised there would be a few critters running around." I continued to laugh a little as she fidgeted with her eyes darting around, checking to see where the demons were. "Kalpana, it is wonderful that you are learning to see in the spiritual realms and I am very proud of you, but we did not come here to engage the Enemy, we came here to release and demonstrate the kingdom of God. Jesus has already defeated Satan through the cross. Let's look around a little more. Can you see Jesus anywhere?" I asked.

Her eyes moved from place to place until she stopped and smiled. "He is standing right here next to us."

"Well, let's just stay focused on Him and ignore those demons, and we will be just fine."

We gathered on the porch, and the night air carried our music and worship all through the village. After our worship time, I asked, "Is there anyone here who has pain? We would be happy to pray for you in the name of Jesus."

They had no idea who Jesus was, but they did know they had pain. In fact, the wife of Ravi's cousin had suffered from full body pain in her muscles and joints for years. We laid hands on her and she was completely delivered from the spirit of pain. We also prayed for the wife's mother who also was completely healed.

After being set free from the years of pain, the family asked, "Who is this Jesus who healed us? We have not heard of Him before."

I smiled. "I'm glad you asked."

We had come with a demonstration of the Spirit's power, and now we had permission to speak about Jesus.

I proceeded to tell them about the God who loved them and died as a sacrifice to pay for their sin so that they could be forgiven and have eternal life.

During that time, we had not focused on demons at all. We were aware of their presence, but we gave them no attention, and by doing so, we gave them no power. As we spoke about Jesus and healed those in pain, the demons could do nothing but watch and listen. They were powerless as God made Himself known in this small mountain village for the first time.

Praying in the Temples

All over North India, there are ancient Hindu and Buddhist temples. Many of these sites still have blood sacrifices offered on a daily basis, especially at the temples dedicated to Kali, the goddess of blood and war. I enjoy going into these temples and releasing the Presence of God. To me, this action puts the demonic strongholds of that region on notice that Jesus has come and their sham authority has been exposed.

Many times, people ask me, "When you enter those temples, doesn't it feel like you are walking into Satan's house? Don't you feel the presence of all those demons?"

"Well," I respond, "I could if that is what I wanted to focus on, but I have a different mindset when I enter the temple. You see, my body is the temple of the Holy Spirit. Scripture tells me that my body is the dwelling place of God. That means when I walk into the temples, those demons don't see me; they see Jesus, and that terrifies them. Jesus just walked into their living room, and they must bow before Him. So, with that in mind, it is kind of fun to go into those temples and know the demons have been put on notice that Jesus has come into their region to take His inheritance."

When I visit temples and spiritual power points, I focus on Jesus, and I use the Word of God as my weapon of warfare, which is "living and powerful, and sharper than any two-edged sword" (Hebrews 4:12, NKJV).

The key to spiritual warfare is to know what Jesus has accomplished through the cross, to know our authority as believers, and to give no place to the Enemy through sin, believing lies, or fear.

This is my confession as a believer: "I have no fear. I walk in the authority of Christ. I know who I am, and I know who my God is. There is no weapon formed against me that can prosper. I am a child of God." When that truth has solidified in our hearts and minds, what can the devil do to us?

Chapter 26

No Trespassing

It is my honor and constant passion to be a pioneer who preaches where no one has ever even heard of the Anointed One.
Romans 15:20, TPT

"How many villages are in these mountains, Joel?"

"There are thousands of villages in these mountains, Pastor," he responded.

"How many churches are in these villages?"

"There are no churches, Pastor."

"Are there any Christians in these mountains?

"No, Pastor, there are no Christians anywhere in these mountains."

Joel was a young pastor who had been working in the valley we were now overlooking. He had started a small church and loved Jesus with all his heart. His sincerity and humility of character stood out to me. In my heart, I knew this was the man God had given to me to connect with in this region. So now, it was time to stretch his faith a little.

"Thousands of villages and not a single Christian? How can this be possible?" I asked.

"The pastors in the valley are afraid to go there. They believe they will be rejected, beaten, or even killed. It is very dangerous to go into the mountains and talk about Jesus," Joel explained.

It was as if the devil had put up "No Trespassing" signs all over the mountains.

"Are you afraid to go into the mountains, Joel?"

"Yes, Pastor, I am afraid also. It is very dangerous."

"Have Christians tried to take Jesus into these mountains before?" I asked.

"No, Pastor, it is too dangerous."

I laughed. "How do you know it's dangerous if no one has ever gone?"

Joel laughed as well. "I don't know, Pastor. This is just what everyone says, so no one goes."

"Joel, I want to go into the mountains and visit the villages. Will you take me?"

He looked at me, his face showing great concern. "Are you serious, Pastor? You really want to go into the mountains?" He was hoping I was only joking.

"Yes, Joel. I want to go into the mountains. Please take me there. Let's see what Jesus will do if we go."

"But Pastor, what if something happens? What if it is not safe?"

"Well, if we die and go to heaven, that's not a bad day, right?" I said, laughing.

Joel didn't laugh. He put his head down, thinking hard. He wanted to be courageous and please the foreign missionary, so reluctantly he said, "Okay, Pastor, we will go."

I put my arm around his shoulder. "It's okay, Joel. I believe Jesus wants us to take Him into those mountains. He died for those people, and someone must be willing to share that good news with them. It is an honor that it gets to be us, right?"

Joel did not look convinced as he was thinking, *This American isn't quite right in the head.* But it was set. He would take me into the mountains.

Deliverance from the Spirit of Pain

The next day, Joel, Tara, and a few other young people from his church loaded into a Jeep and we began to make our way up into the mountains. After some time, we came to a village where there were about twenty-five to thirty homes. We unloaded and began to walk through the narrow streets of the village. Joel began to engage in conversation with a woman who had stopped him to inquire about the foreigner (me) in their group. After a few moments, she invited our entire group to come to her house for chai.

Tara had brought her guitar. It had been our experience that people in the mountain villages found music to be a special treat, and I enjoyed how her musical gift could change the atmosphere of a room.

As we sat cross-legged on the floor, Tara began to play and sing worship songs in Hindi. As some of the neighbors heard the music and discovered there was a foreigner present, they came over to see the novelty. Soon, the house began to fill with women, a few men, and some children. Tara sang, and the Presence of God began to fill the room.

After a while, I asked the question that I would always ask during our village visits.

"Is there anyone here who is in pain?"

All over the room, hands rose. Almost all of them had some type of pain they were living with.

Each person would step forward, and when I asked where they had pain in their body, each of them would respond with the same words: "I have full-body pain in my muscles and joints." Tara would stand next to me, translating and helping me pray.

Person after person was healed and set free from their pain. After we prayed for each one, they would stretch, squat, bend over, and move around. Then they would begin to laugh as they realized all their pain had gone.

As people were getting healed, they began to go get their family and friends and bring them to the house. Soon, the room was packed with people curious about who this foreigner was and what he was doing. They had never seen anyone who healed the sick before. They watched with delight and awe as God demonstrated His power.

Finally, the last person came forward for prayer. He was a small eight-year-old boy. When I asked him what he wanted prayer for, he said, "My entire body hurts all the time." Everyone in the room laughed, thinking the little boy was just imitating the grown-ups he had been watching.

But there was something else going on.

Breaking the Spirit of Witchcraft

I gently laid my hands on the boy's head and began to pray. As soon as I touched him, a demonic spirit began to manifest. His body became rigid, and his head began to violently shake from side to side. His eyes rolled back into his head and he fell to the floor as if dead. This got the attention of everyone in the room as their eyes grew large with fear. They knew this was a demonic presence that was manifesting, and they were terrified by it.

I knelt down next to the boy and noticed a silver amulet around his neck. By the Spirit, I knew this amulet had witchcraft attached to it. The boy's mother stepped through the crowded room and knelt opposite of me, next to her son, her eyes full of fear and anxiety. She was scared and deeply concerned for her son.

"Can I remove this amulet?" I asked.

She nodded an emphatic yes.

I reached down and snapped the chain with the amulet off of the boy's neck. Instantly, he raised up, screaming, "Bhai! Bhai! Bhai!" He was trying to get the amulet back from me. *Bhai* means "brother" in Hindi. The demon had convinced the boy he was his brother and had oppressed him for several years.

I looked at the mother and said, "This amulet is connected to a demonic power. May I destroy it?"

"Haan!" she said. "Yes!"

I handed the amulet to Joel and said, "Go destroy this and then bury it somewhere it cannot be found." As Joel left the room, we continued to pray for the boy until he received total freedom. I helped him up and he sat next to me, laying his head on my chest as I continued to pray and comfort him.

The mother asked me, "Who is this Jesus? How is it that He has power over our gods?"

"I'm glad you asked," I replied.

Once again, after a demonstration of the Spirit's power, we had gained permission to speak about Jesus.

Once Joel came back into the room, he and Tara told all of them in their own language about the God who loved them, had died for them, and wanted to heal them and give them eternal life.

A Church Is Planted

After some time, I stepped out of the house and stood on the porch. As I looked out over the beautiful horizon, I could see hundreds more villages scattered across the mountains. Some people came out of the house and began to gather around me. No one had been offended. No one had been threatened by our presence there. No one wanted to harm us or drive us away. Jesus had come to their village, and they were very glad He did.

"I must go now," I said.

"Why must you go?" they asked. "Why can't you stay here longer? We want you to stay with us." They were holding my hands and touching my arms. It was as if they wanted to cling to me, wanting more of Jesus.

"I must go," I said. "There are other villages I need to visit."

"When will you return?" they asked.

"I don't know, but I am sure Jesus will allow me to return and visit you again someday."

We left that day, but Joel and his team continued to go back to that village and began a house church. The entire family of the young boy and several of the neighbors became believers, and now Jesus is being preached throughout that region.

For years, the "No Trespassing" signs and fear had kept Christians from taking Jesus into the mountains. On that day, those signs were torn down and the mountain villages became open to the gospel of Jesus Christ. Joel had become my "man of peace" who fought his fear and joined me to go where no Christians had ever gone before.

There is no limit to what can be done for the kingdom of God when we have no fear.

FLASHBACK

"How is Ishan doing?" I asked Ashish, who had stayed throughout the surgery.

"He is doing the same. The blood clot has not moved or dissipated, but he is in stable condition and being well cared for. I have told Ms. Jan, and she has the entire network praying for him."

As long as Jan had that prayer network going, I knew we would be fine.

After a couple of days of recuperating in the hospital, I received a visitor. This man was the chief investigator from the district where the accident took place. He had come all the way down the mountain to interview me and give me a report on his investigation.

NO TRESPASSING

He asked me a few basic questions, but I was not able to tell him much. Being on the back of the bike, I wasn't really sure of what had happened to cause the accident.

"I have investigated many, many accidents on that road," said the man. "It is one of the most dangerous roads in the world, and many people have died there. In fact, the day before your accident, a man from England was on a motorcycle and went off the cliff just one kilometer from where you hit the truck. He fell sixteen hundred feet to his death."

Wow. A man had died on that same road just one day before my accident. As I tried to take that in, the investigator continued.

"What I have discovered in my investigation is that your driver lost control of the bike as he came around the curve. We are still not certain why he lost control, but he crossed the lane into oncoming traffic, and that's when you hit the truck. If the truck had not been there, you would have gone off the cliff and would have landed in the Sutlej River."

"What? Are you telling me the truck kept us from going over the cliff?"

"Yes, the truck saved your lives. If you had not hit the truck, you would be dead right now." The investigator was a devout Hindu, but even he recognized a miracle when he saw one. He threw his right hand into the air and said, "Nothing but the hand of God saved you! Nothing but the hand of God!"

Amen to that, brother.

Later on, the doctor came to my room to prepare me to check out of the hospital. He gave me instructions regarding my medicines and also set me up to receive physical therapy. There would be a strict regimen of exercises I would need to do every day to ensure proper healing.

"Also," he said, "I can't clear you for an international flight for at least six weeks. Flying at that altitude for that many hours could potentially cause a blood clot that could kill you. You will need to find a place here in India where you can recover during that time."

Six weeks. Where could I go for six weeks? I considered a hotel where I could order room service, but that would be expensive. I then considered finding a flat I could rent for that amount of time, but I knew I would not be able to cook and care for myself alone. Maybe I could hire someone to come by every couple of days and cook meals for me.

I said to Samson, who was always at my side, "Hey, can you do me a favor and try to find me a small flat I can rent for the next six weeks? Maybe there would be someone from the church I could hire to cook meals for me?"

Samson looked at me and laughed. "No, no, Pastor. You will not stay alone in a flat. We have already made arrangements. You will come home with me to my parents' house. They will give you a private room. My wife will cook for you, and I will give you therapy every day. You will stay with us for three weeks, and Pastor Daniel is very insistent that you stay with him and his family for the next three weeks. Everything has been arranged."

I was stunned. I had just met Samson and his family one year prior. I had become fast friends with him and his family. In fact, I had spoken at Samson's wedding six months earlier. But still, the thought of them doing this for me was overwhelming.

"Samson, I appreciate the offer, but this will be a huge inconvenience for you. I don't want to be a burden to you and your family," I said. I hated being in such a vulnerable situation where I could not care for myself. "Maybe it would be best for me to get a flat."

"No! It has been decided. You will come home with us!"

The fact that these people cared so much and were so generous, ready to make any sacrifice to take care of me, touched my heart deeply.

At that moment, my friend Ashish came into the room. He had been at the previous hospital, caring for Ishan while he remained in critical condition. I was surprised to see Ashish here.

"How is Ishan?" I asked.

"God has answered our prayers. The blood clot has completely dissolved, and the surgery on his leg has been completed. By God's grace, Ishan will be fine."

Chapter 27

Chai and a Nap

*How beautiful upon the mountains
Are the feet of him who brings good news,
Who proclaims peace,
Who brings glad tidings of good things,
Who proclaims salvation,
Who says to Zion,
"Your God reigns!"*
Isaiah 52:7, NKJV

"Do you see that mountain?"
My young pastor friend pointed to a grand peak far in the distance that towered above all the peaks around it.

"Yeah, it's beautiful," I said.

"We're going to climb over that mountain today," he responded. All of a sudden the mountain was no longer beautiful, but very intimidating. My first thought was, *You have to be kidding me!* My second thought was, *Help me, Jesus!*

After a few moments of trying to get up my courage, I hoisted my thirty-pound pack onto my back and set off, following my team of seven young Indian men and women. The incline became more and more steep as we followed the switchbacks along the narrow mountain trail. I was the old man of the group, and my age and the heavy pack kept trying to drag me back down the mountain.

Tara was walking close behind me, hoping I would not fall back down the mountain and smash my head against a boulder.

My pace became slower and slower as I would take a few steps up the steep incline, stop, and suck air, which was of short supply at this high altitude. Ten steps, bend over, suck air. Ten steps, bend over, suck air. It was a very slow and painful climb up that mountain, but eventually, we reached the summit and I was able to drop my pack and thank God I was still alive.

At eleven thousand feet, this was a great place to stop and pray over the valley below. From our vantage point, we could see hundreds of small villages scattered across the mountains.

"Are there any Christians in those villages?" I asked my pastor friend.

"No, Pastor. There are no Christians there."

We prayed for God to make Himself known in all of those villages, and I determined in my heart that someday I would return and visit as many of them as I could.

The Village Priest

After a short rest and some snacks, I once again hoisted the pack and we began our way down the other side of the mountain. After a couple of hours of trekking, we came to a small village. The young pastor, who was our guide, spoke to the village chief, who was also the head priest of the Hindu temple. The priest invited our team to come to his home and have chai.

A young woman, who was a daughter of the priest, brought us water and served us the hot chai. I settled back against some

CHAI AND A NAP

cushions on the floor and sipped the hot brew. The effects of the long hike began to settle in and I realized I was very tired. Everyone was speaking to each other in Hindi, so I was left to myself. I finished the chai, laid my head back on a cushion, and went to sleep.

After about forty-five minutes, I awoke and we began to prepare to leave. The young pastor approached me and asked, "Would you like to pray for the priest and his wife before we leave?"

"Certainly, with their permission, I would be happy to."

My friends also explained to me that this man was not only the priest for the village but for the entire region of mountain villages. Once a year a demon would possess him and he would prophesy over every person in the villages, telling them what would happen to them in the upcoming year. This man was very important, as well as highly respected and even feared by the people in the area.

I stood and approached them to pray. The man and his wife stood next to each other and lowered their heads respectfully as I laid my hands on them and began to softly pray in the Spirit.

The seventeen-year-old daughter who had served us chai was sitting on the floor behind us with her back against the wall. Suddenly, demons began to manifest in her body. Her head began to snap back and forth so hard her hair came loose and was whipping through the air. Her eyes rolled into the back of her head and her body began to shake and vibrate uncontrollably, like she was being electrocuted.

The demons had been quiet until I began to pray, but now they were responding to the Presence of God that was being released.

I stepped back, looked at the girl, and addressed the parents: "I worship Jesus, the Son of the Most High. If you would like for me to pray for your daughter, Jesus will set her free from these demons."

"Haan! Haan! Yes! Yes! Please pray!" they cried.

They had no idea who Jesus was, but they were desperate to see their daughter set free. They were willing to try anything.

The Battle

My friends and I knelt next to the girl and began to pray. Normally, it only takes a few moments of prayer before the demon is expelled and the person is set free, but this one was being stubborn. Even after several minutes of prayer, the demons continued to manifest. I tried to get the girl to become cognizant and communicate with us, but the demons had full control.

Fifteen minutes passed, then thirty. My team and I were growing weary and feeling a little frustrated. I knew we were making no progress at all as we continued to pray and tell the demons to leave.

"Nikal! Nikal! Get out! Get out!" we said. But to no avail.

I stepped away and went out to stand on the porch for a few moments, asking God what to do. All I knew was there was no way I was going to leave this house until the young woman had been set free.

The girl's father and Tara stepped out on the porch with me, and Tara translated for him as he began to explain, "The demons that come to me to prophesy entered my daughter three years ago and have been tormenting her ever since. I have taken her to many doctors and gurus; we have done many rituals and pujas and made offerings to the gods, but nothing has helped her. I have spent all my money and we have nothing left. It is my fault that this is happening to my daughter, and I do not know what to do." The man looked at me with desperation in his eyes.

I stepped back into the room and saw my team had grown weary and had stopped praying. I sat on the floor next to the girl and put my arm around her shoulders. Her head was down and her hair covered her face. Suddenly, she raised her face and looked at her father.

With a man's voice that sounded more like a growl, the demons said, "We are Panchveer (Five Spirits), and we control this region. Why have you brought these people here? Get them out! They don't belong here!"

A Lion's Roar

The demons were speaking in Hindi and Tara translated so I could understand. As I listened to the demons speak, I began to get angry. The anger in me quickly rose to a boiling point. I spun around on my knees, kneeling in front of the girl, my nose touching her nose.

"That's enough! No more! Shut up and come out in the name of Jesus!"

As I yelled, I pounded my fists into the wall behind her. I yelled so loud I felt like a blast of the Holy Spirit was being released right into that young lady. I then stood up and was feeling such a spirit of war on me, I roared like a lion, as loud as I could.

Suddenly, the young woman's body relaxed. She raised her head and her eyes were clear and she was fully cognizant. She looked at her father and jumped to her feet and ran to him, holding him tightly. Jesus had set her free!

For the next two days, the father trekked with us, asking questions and learning about Jesus.

"From now on I will never pray to the Hindu gods," he said. "Now I know Jesus is the only true God, and I will only pray to Him."

I had the opportunity to visit this man about eighteen months later. He, his wife, daughter, and son, had all become followers of Jesus. He had given up the position of being the temple priest and was training to be a pastor. A house church was now meeting in his home. Many of the people who had once gone to him as the temple priest were now coming to him to learn about Jesus.

What began with a cup of chai and a nap had become a church full of new believers worshiping the one true God.

Before we began this trekking journey, my pastor friend had asked me, "Why do you want to walk to all these villages? It is very difficult to walk through the mountains, and there are roads now. We can get to the villages by car instead of walking."

"Yes," I said. "But there is something different that happens when you get your boots on the ground. When you walk through the mountain villages, you are allowing your presence to change the atmosphere. You get to experience the surroundings in a way you could never do in a car, and you become available to connect with people along the way. Just driving through, you may miss what God wants to do."

Chapter 28

Dirty Cups

Eat whatever is set before you, asking no question.
1 Corinthians 10:27, NKJV

I was once again ministering with Pastor Daniel. Over the years, Daniel, Poonam, and their two sons became dear friends and ministry partners.

Daniel had set up house visits for me for several days while I was visiting his city. We never knew what would happen during these visits, so it was hard to plan a set time to be at each one. We could go to a home with four or five people and think, *It shouldn't take too long to pray for these people.* But then, God would move and there would be a dramatic healing or deliverance and all of a sudden the people were calling their friends and family to come for prayer. What started as four or five could turn into ten or fifteen. Because of this, we never knew what time we would arrive at the next house.

Since the people had no idea what time we were coming, they would take off work all day and wait in anticipation for us to arrive. They would spend their hard-earned money buying chai, cookies, sodas, and food to serve us. Each one wanted to give us their very best and made every effort to do so. Indian hospitality is very important, and the people took it very seriously.

Sometimes we would go into a home where it was obvious the people were very poor. They had taken off work to host us and had lost their pay for that day. Because of this, I was very aware as a foreigner that they were offering me their very best, sometimes at great cost to themselves. It did not matter if I'd had five cups of chai during my earlier visits. When they offered chai, cookies, food, or whatever else, I would always receive it graciously and thankfully. To reject their offering was the same as rejecting them. I would sip the chai and tell them how delicious it was, and their faces would light up with satisfaction. The foreigner was pleased with their hospitality. All was well.

Whenever I was offered food, especially in the villages, I would sit on the floor cross-legged and eat with my fingers. It never ceased to amaze me how this simple gesture would bring down walls of suspicion and open their hearts to receive me. It was my goal to never do anything that would make me look prideful or place myself above them. I never wanted to do or say anything that would make these beautiful, humble people feel that they were below me. I always tried my best to show as much honor as possible, no matter how base the circumstances.

Because these precious people gave me their very best, I wanted to do the same in return. I never thought about how tired I was or how many more visits I had to do. Every house and every person was the most important house or person, and I gave them my fullest attention.

I would pray with all the faith and power God would give me. Every person had a need that only God could meet, and it was my job to connect them to the God who could help them.

Pastor Daniel would take me from place to place. I never knew what kind of situation I would be walking into, who was there, or what needs I would encounter. One time it would be a homeless woman living in an old abandoned building, the next, a man with his family who lived in a small shack behind a tea stall, another time, a wealthy doctor in the middle of the night. I would never know what the next visit would be like or what would happen. But God would always show up and miracles would take place.

A Sick Child

On one of these visits, Daniel took me with a small team from his church to visit a husband and wife who had a small baby just a few months old. The father was a day laborer who worked breaking rocks to make gravel. This was done with sledgehammers and was hard, back-breaking work. He would make the equivalent of about two dollars a day, and that was barely enough to provide a little food for his family to exist. His job was only a step away from being slave labor.

They had brought me to pray for their baby girl who was gravely ill. Because of their extreme poverty, taking her to a hospital was completely out of the question.

We stepped out of the sunlight into a one-room brick shack, and it was dark inside. There was no electricity, no lights of any kind. As our eyes began to adjust to the darkness, we could see empty rice sacks scattered around like rugs trying to cover the dirt floor. There were no chairs, just a bed in the corner to sit on.

A woman sat on the floor clutching a small baby girl to her chest, rocking her back and forth as the little one coughed and wheezed. Her husband scurried about the room looking for some cups as he prepared chai over a small mound of hot coals. He reached his hands, covered with dirt and calluses, into a tub of dirty brown water and retrieved some cups. He wiped his dirty hands around in the cups in a gesture of trying to clean them for us and then poured the hot liquid that had been steaming on the coals.

My team of young Indians watched me with their eyes growing wide. They knew my standards about receiving anything offered to me and never rejecting it. But this? Surely the American would graciously decline. I smiled and sipped the chai. There would be no walls between me and this dear family.

The woman's dark-skinned face was etched with worry as she told me of her child's illness and showed me the medicine bottles that had taken their last rupees. Despite their efforts the child was not getting better. I told them about the God who loved them, who died for them, and who answered prayer. After a few moments the woman stepped across the small room and laid her little girl in my arms.

The gravity of the moment hit me. This woman was entrusting her child to me without reservation. I felt the responsibility of whether she lived or died was in my hands.

As the mother looked at me, I could see sparks of hope trying to flicker in her eyes, hope that this God I spoke of would help her baby live.

The little girl had been crying and coughing, but as I held her in my arms and began to gently pray, the crying stopped. Her big brown eyes were filled with wonder as she looked at me intently. I was the first white person she had ever seen. I continued to softly pray in the Spirit. As I did so, she began to smile, and then the smile turned into a laugh. Her laughter changed the atmosphere. The darkness turned to light. Hope and faith were being stirred.

I sat holding the baby for some time, continuing to pray softly, and then handed her back to her mother. The little girl once again nestled against her chest, this time without wheezing, coughing, or crying, as she slipped into a peaceful sleep. The mother looked up at me, smiling broadly, with tears running down her face.

"Danyavaad, Danyavaad. Thank you, thank you," she repeated again and again as she rocked her baby in her arms.

Pastor Daniel then prayed with both parents as they received Jesus into their lives and became His followers.

DIRTY CUPS

Their gods could not help them. Their offerings and rituals only made their poverty and hopelessness worse. But this Jesus, whom they had never heard of, came into their home and did for them what no man could do.

That day Jesus knew of a desperate mother and a sick child, and He took me to them. He then healed the little girl and changed the lives of that family forever. That is who Jesus is; that is what Jesus does.

Chapter 29

Give Him Room

I am convinced that when I come to you, I will come packed full and loaded with the blessings of the Anointed One!
Romans 15:29, TPT

Over the years, God continued to open doors to minister in the Anglican churches of North India. During one of my early visits to a northern state, I met Sunny, another Anglican priest. We became dear friends as we worked together on many prayer journeys across Jammu and Kashmir.

Pastor Sunny was very bold in his faith and desired to see revival in the traditional churches. Therefore, he invited my team and me to come and hold revival services in his hometown. As usual, Tara accompanied us. By this time, we had been on several prayer journeys together and she had become the coleader of the teams. I was to the point that I did not want to travel anywhere in India without her. Her spiritual strength and wisdom was invaluable.

Two Anglican churches from nearby towns, along with a Catholic church, had invited us to come for three days of revival services.

What had been considered dead and dry religious institutions were now hungry for a move of God in their region.

I had come to this area over a year earlier. We had prayer walked two towns where we knew no one. We simply prayed. Now, it was these same two towns that had joined for revival and asked us to come release God's Presence. We knew this was not a coincidence. Repeatedly, places where we had previously prayer walked later invited us to return and proclaim the gospel of Christ.

Pastor Sunny introduced me to the Catholic priest, Father Joseph. I was almost amused at the father's appearance. He looked like a monk who just stepped off Ferdinand Magellan's boat in the 1500s. He was a slender man with long black-and-gray hair, which looked like a wiry bush and flowed down to his shoulders. He wore a brown, ankle-length cassock with a hood that was akin to sackcloth, and he had a wide brown sash tied around his waist. He had a long beard that matched the hair on his head.

I shook his hand politely, but to be honest, I was judging him by his appearance, thinking there was absolutely no common ground for us to have a relationship. This man had been a part of a religious institution filled with rituals and traditions all his life. I was just an uneducated Pentecostal country boy. *What could we possibly have in common?* I thought.

Again, God smiled.

Holy Spirit Came

The old Anglican church was packed. The old wooden pews were filled, and young people were on the floor, knee to knee across the front, leaving just enough space for Tara and me to stand and preach. Dozens of people sat on the grass outside under the moonlight, straining to hear every word.

That night Tara and I spoke about God's grace, and the Holy Spirit began to fill the room. His Presence seemed to grow stronger and stronger as we preached. Suddenly, I could preach no more. I could only stand in awe of the intense Presence of God we all were sensing. It was as if God Himself had come into the room. So we let Him.

We stopped speaking and waited. For nearly one hour no one sang. No one prayed. There was no music. We simply stood and made room for His glory. There were times of silence. Times of intense weeping. Other times, there was shouting and crying out to God. Wave after wave of His Presence swept through the room.

He had come, convicting, cleansing, forgiving, restoring, encouraging, transforming, loving.

I looked over and saw Father Joseph on his knees with his face buried in the floor. The nuns from the Catholic church were doing likewise. There was nothing we could do but bow before the holiness of His Presence. Here, in what I considered an uncomfortable religious setting, God had come. All pretense of religious rituals were gone. There was no order of service or regimen to follow. There was nothing here but the purity of His holiness.

The hour slipped by like it was only a few moments. We then released healing, and over one hundred people stood and proclaimed that their pain and sickness were gone and they had been set free.

Following the last service of the three-day revival, Father Joseph approached me. With the greatest humility, he said, "I have witnessed the Holy Spirit in a dimension I have never experienced before. I did not know it was possible to experience Him in this manner." Then, with tears in his eyes, he asked, "My brother, will you pray for me to receive the Holy Spirit?"

It was a great joy to lay hands on my new friend and ask God to fill him with His holy Presence.

There is a time for preaching, worship, and prayer, but there is also a time to just let God come and have His way.

Chapter 30

No One Wants to Come Here

> *But I promise you this—the Holy Spirit will come upon you, and you will be seized with power. You will be my messengers to Jerusalem, throughout Judea, the distant provinces—even to the remotest places on earth!*
> Acts 1:8, TPT

From my first trip to Tibet, it was my deepest desire to take Jesus to the most remote places in the world. As I prayed over a map of India, the Holy Spirit highlighted a place called Leh, Ladakh, in northeastern Kashmir.

Leh is located in a remote mountainous region. At nearly twelve thousand feet above sea level, Leh is completely isolated for six to eight months each year as the two mountain passes fill with snow, blocking off all supplies and trade goods coming in or out. The population is two hundred thousand, mostly Buddhist, with fewer than three hundred Christians. I decided this was the place God wanted me to take a prayer team.

In the town of Leh was a small Moravian church that had been established in the late 1850s. The Moravian missionaries had come to this remote place and planted the first church despite much difficulty and opposition from the Buddhist people. The Moravians had a rich and glorious history of planting strong churches all over the world. There were stories of how some of them actually sold themselves into slavery so they could become missionaries to the slaves. The motto of the Moravians was, "May the Lamb of God receive the reward for His suffering."

As my team and I bounced along in our Jeep over the rough roads toward Leh, we received a phone call.

"This is my brother on the phone," said Tara. "He knows someone in Leh and told them we are coming. They spoke with the pastor at the Moravian church, and they want us to preach there this Sunday morning." We laughed and again shook our heads. God was opening doors for us before we even arrived.

We had a wonderful time with Pastor Elijah and his wife, Meena, while visiting the church. They were humble and wise, and being in their seventies, they were nearing retirement. Pastor Elijah was very knowledgeable of the Moravian history and told us many stories of the early years, when the first missionaries had entered that part of India.

A special treat was that Pastor Elijah's grandfather had been the one who had first translated the Bible into the Tibetan language. We sat in awe as he pulled out a special case that contained his grandfather's original handwritten translation of Scripture. It was a special glimpse into the Christian history of the region.

Isolated and Lonely

While we were in Ladakh, we met a young couple who had moved there from another part of India as independent missionaries. Ajit, Jayanti, and their two sons lived in an old schoolhouse on the edge of town, and we were taken to visit them.

NO ONE WANTS TO COME HERE

We sat in a classroom that had become their home. Ajit spoke softly, sharing his story.

"We came here as missionaries two years ago. For years I asked my pastor for his blessing to come here, but he always refused. After seven years, he finally gave his blessing. When I arrived here, I met with a motorcycle accident. I broke both my wrists and my shoulder. I was in great pain and required surgery, but I was not able to go to the hospital in Delhi. It was four months before I had surgery. My shoulder is still not healed and is in constant pain.

"This is a very difficult place to live and minister. If the Buddhists knew we were here to convert people to Christ, they would do great harm to us. We minister by becoming friends with them, and one at a time, we share Christ. It has been two years and no one has responded yet. We have suffered much, but this is what God has called us to. We will be faithful. No matter how lonely we get or what we suffer, we will not leave this place."

Then Ajit looked at me closely. "Why have you come here? No one wants to come to this place." Jayanti echoed the same words as she choked back tears.

The electricity had gone out and we sat in the warm glow of a small kerosene lamp. I looked at this beautiful family that had given so much. The love of God for them filled my heart.

"Jesus wants to come here," I said. "Jesus sent us here to let you know you are not forgotten. You are not isolated. You are not alone. And as a sign of His faithful love, He will heal your shoulder."

Tara began to play her guitar and sing. As we worshiped, His Presence filled the room. Tara and I then laid hands on Ajit's shoulder and prayed.

"The pain is gone!" Ajit exclaimed as he started swinging his arm in a windmill motion. "This is the first time in two years that there has been no pain."

We laughed. We wept. We rejoiced at the love of the Father being demonstrated. As we left, Ajit held us close and again spoke.

"No one wants to come here, but you came. Thank you for coming."

Jesus commanded us to go. That command has never been rescinded. It has been my greatest joy to go to the most remote places on earth to bring the love of the Father and release His Presence.

Chapter 31

A Lifesaving Drug

You therefore must endure hardship as a good soldier of Jesus Christ.
2 Timothy 2:3, NKJV

It was October 2015 when I returned to India and went with my team high into the Himalayas to minister in remote mountain villages.

This time, the team consisted of Pastor Daniel, Ashish, his wife Kalpana, Tara, and me. We connected with a young pastor who had started a small church in his village. Desraj was the first believer in his family, and the first believer in his village. He was zealous to see God move in this region and had invited us to come and pray.

Prior to this trip, while I was still in America, I began to have problems with my lungs. Ever since the Valley Fever years ago, my lungs were damaged and prone to asthma-like symptoms. Most often it was nothing serious, and I always had access to medications that would bring relief. But now, with the passing of each day, it became more difficult to breathe. My condition worsened as we traveled higher into the mountains, and I began to have coughing fits that would last fifteen to twenty minutes.

All I had for medicine was an emergency inhaler that I had bought in Delhi. In fact, I bought several of them, but now, no matter how many puffs I took, it was doing nothing to help.

My team grew very concerned for me as they watched me get worse with each passing day. Ashish even came into my room at night to massage my feet, trying to calm me.

But now, after several days of not sleeping, and the coughing fits increasing to the point that they were virtually nonstop, I realized I would have to get to a hospital to get the help I needed.

I told my team I needed them to take me down the mountain to a hospital. I felt terrible asking them to do this, as it was early Sunday morning and people had come from all over the mountains to hear us speak at the church service. Many of them had walked more than three hours along the mountain trails just to come to church.

While I felt terrible about letting them down, I could also sense that if I didn't get medical attention, I could possibly die. I knew I had no choice but to go to the hospital.

Ashish and Desraj loaded me into the car, and we began the two-hour journey down the mountain.

The Remote Indian Hospital

We arrived at the hospital, and as we entered the dimly lit corridor, I could see how dirty and primitive the place was. My first thought was, *People don't come here to get better, they come here to die!*

As we walked down the corridor, we met a doctor and got his attention. At this time, I could barely stand and was having another intense coughing fit. The doctor became very alarmed at my condition. He saw the inhaler I had in my hand and asked, "How many puffs of that have you taken?"

"A couple hundred," I replied. "Each inhaler has 250 puffs, and I have been going through about one each day for the past several days."

A LIFESAVING DRUG

His eyes opened wide in shock as he took me by the arm and began to lead me to a room. "We must get you to the intensive care unit right now!"

He led me into a room that had six beds, all of them filled with people except for one in the far corner. The sheet on the bed was dirty and covered with black hairs. There was a red blanket wadded up in the corner to be used as a pillow.

The doctor began to give orders, and several nurses began to attend to me. "I am very concerned that your lungs are near collapsing. You are in very serious condition. Why did you wait so long to get medical attention? If you waited any longer you would have died!"

A nurse took my arm to give me an injection.

"What are you giving to me?" I asked. Her head snapped around to look at me. I could see that she was not only concerned, but I also could see fear in her eyes.

It suddenly dawned on me that she actually thought I could die.

"This is a lifesaving drug, sir!" she said sternly. I smiled, stuck out my arm and said, "Well, you just go ahead and save my life!"

I looked at the doctor and asked, "How long will I be here?"

"You will need to be here at least four days. It will take time to get your lungs to the place where you are no longer in danger."

Four days? There is no way I'm going to stay in this place for four days, I thought.

The nurse gave me a breathing treatment using a nebulizer, and I was supposed to have another one every two hours. But there was only one nebulizer for the entire hospital, so when it was time for my next treatment, the nebulizer was not available.

Ashish went into the city, found a medical store, and purchased a nebulizer for me. After two breathing treatments and the other medicines that were taking effect, I could feel my lungs opening. The coughing slowed down considerably.

About that time Tara called to check on me and I gave her an update. While she was deeply concerned for me, she also knew how dangerous it was to be in a very primitive, unsanitary hospital.

"Dan, you need to get out of that hospital as soon as possible. Just get all the meds you need and we will care for you back here." I could hear the urgency in her voice and I was going to do everything I could to follow her advice.

The doctor came back to check on me and I said, "I'm feeling much better. I have my own nebulizer now, and I have all the other meds you gave to me, so it is time for me to leave."

"No! You cannot leave! You are still in danger, and you need to have an injection each day. I must keep you here under observation for at least four days."

"Doctor, just give me the medicine and the needles for the injections and I will take care of doing them myself. It is time for me to go."

He looked at me like I was insane, but very reluctantly he signed the papers releasing me from the hospital.

Instead of four days, I was there for four hours.

The Shot

Ashish and Desraj took me back up the mountain to the village where we had been staying.

"Dan, get some rest today, and then tomorrow we will pack up and go home," Ashish said.

"Go home? Why would we go home? We have promised to do ministry here for several more days. I'm not going home until our work is done here."

Ashish looked at me like I had lost my mind. "Dan, you almost died, and the doctor said you are still not out of danger yet. Don't you think it is best to go home where you can rest and be properly cared for?"

"Look, Ashish, I'm not dead yet, and God brought us here to pray for people. I'm not going home until we fulfill the assignment given to us."

I then looked at Desraj. "I understand that people walked for hours to come to church, and I was not there to minister to them. Tomorrow, please take me to each of their homes so I can visit them and pray for them."

The next morning it was time for my injection. Tara, who had been deeply concerned for me, did the honors. None of us really knew what we were doing, but Ashish and Daniel held my arm tightly, trying to expose a vein. Tara, full of confidence and totally unafraid, stuck the needle into a vein and released the medicine into my arm. Then it was time to get back to work.

Mountain Ministry

Later that day, we were able to visit the homes of each person who had come to church. At one of the homes, about fifteen people had gathered for me to pray for their healing. I still felt very weak, and I coughed a lot as I prayed for them, but God was faithful to heal each one of them.

At one point, I thought, "God, as You move through me to heal these people, could You pause for a moment and heal *me*?"

God did not instantly heal me that day, but He did show me that in my weakness, He becomes strong.

"I know it seems strange to have a sick man pray for your healing," I told the people, "but I am not the one who heals you. Jesus is the one who heals you, and He is not sick."

For the next several days we continued to make visits and watch God do the miraculous as person after person was healed or received deliverance from demonic oppression. None of this would have happened if I had just quit and gone home.

Over the years of international ministry, I have spent hundreds of hours on planes, trains, buses, cars, and horses, going to some of the most remote places on the planet. I have slept on many airport floors because of canceled or delayed flights, eaten food and drunk water that has made me sick, and even came home once with double pneumonia and sepsis in my blood. (Thank God for the doctors at Mayo Clinic who saved my life that time.)

For me, being uncomfortable, tired, inconvenienced, or even sick is just part of the job description of following Jesus, "who for the joy that was set before Him endured the cross" (Hebrews 12:2, NKJV).

For me, the joy of someday hearing Jesus say, "Well done" will make anything I have ever endured more than worth it. Everything else is trivial compared to that. I would gladly do it all over again to have the privilege of walking with Jesus and watching Him make Himself known to those who have never heard. To me, it is not a sacrifice at all. In fact, there is nothing that could be more rewarding than to partner with Jesus. Does it ever get any better than that?

PART VII
SOUTHEAST ASIA

Chapter 32

There Are No Closed Doors

*The key of the house of David
I will lay on his shoulder;
So he shall open, and no one shall shut;
And he shall shut, and no one shall open.*
Isaiah 22:22, NKJV

Tara, a friend of hers from Delhi, and I were invited to go to Kathmandu, Nepal, for a prayer journey. Our guide, Man Dai, was a wonderful man of God who took us all over the region to pray at historical and spiritual high places.

Man Dai was a small man who was disabled from a serious accident when he was young. Because of this, it caused him to walk with a limp. In spite of this handicap, he was full of joy and had a constant smile on his face.

On one of our outings, Man Dai took us to a very famous Buddhist temple. We approached the entrance and removed our shoes as was customary. There was an iron accordion gate at the doorway. We could see inside there were two monks dressed in their ochre-yellow robes. One of the monks approached the gate and spoke to Man

Dai, explaining the temple was closed and they were not allowing any visitors at that time.

I thought, *Well, I already have my shoes off. I will just stand here at this gate and pray.* I placed my hands together, held them chest high in the traditional Buddhist prayer position, and began praying in tongues, mimicking a Buddhist chant. The two monks could hear and see me clearly through the iron gate. I could feel the Presence of God as I prayed, and it seemed the two monks could feel something as well.

One of them stood and came to the gate, pulled out a key, and unlocked it. He slid the gate open and motioned, inviting me to come in. He led me to the front of the temple to where the Buddha statue was placed. We smiled at each other, and once again, I placed my hands together and prayed in tongues.

After a few moments, the other priest approached us, and together, they placed a white silk scarf around my neck as a token of respect. I placed my hands on the priests and prayed for them as they respectfully bowed their heads. We smiled again, and I bowed slightly with my hands together showing them respect in return.

It was just a small moment in time, but it felt very significant. What were they feeling as I prayed? Why did they open the gate and invite me in? Why did they honor me with the silk scarf? Why did they allow me to pray for them?

As I left the temple, I heard the Lord say, "Do you understand what just happened?

"No, Lord, what was that all about?"

"You stood in front of a closed door. You prayed. The door was opened. You were invited to come in and release My Presence. Because of My Presence in you, they received you and honored you. When they received you, they were receiving Me. This is the anointing I have given to you for the nations. There are no doors closed to My Presence."

This has been the hallmark of our ministry to the nations. Everywhere we go, ancient doors that have been closed for generations are opened as we pray.

We go, we pray, God moves.

Egypt

Another example of this happened in Egypt. Tara and I were invited to join a team taking a prayer journey across this ancient land. The team was led by Chrissy and Krista—two wonderful women who had been working in Egypt for nearly ten years—as well as Pat, Chrissy's mom from the United States.

We began in the cities along the Suez Canal, then went to the Nile Delta and down along the Nile River all the way to Aswan, near the southern border. We stopped in cities along the way to pray with the local believers or at spiritual and historical locations.

We prayed inside the Great Pyramid of Giza, rode camels in the desert, prayed at the ancient gates of Cairo, and prayerwalked through Luxor and several other ancient cities along the Nile. I rode a white Arabian horse in the Sahara Desert, danced with a group of boys in the city streets of Cairo, and stood in King Tut's burial chambers in the Valley of the Kings. It was an amazing journey in an ancient land full of history and mystery.

One such location was a cave where it was said Mary and Joseph had hidden with the baby Jesus when they fled to Egypt. A Coptic church and monastery had been built around this location, and it is a major tourist destination for many Christians. Because of recent terrorism in this part of Egypt, we were required to have two policemen escort us everywhere we went.

Our team went into the caverns, which were wide open and spacious. There were many religious relics and icons to be seen. A priest greeted us, and then asked one of the Coptic nuns to give us a tour and show us around. We had not asked for this but were happy to have someone lead us and explain the history of this religious site.

The nun was a pleasant woman and dressed in the traditional robes and *qalansuwa*, a black headpiece that covered her hair. She was a little shy about speaking English, but we found we could communicate with no problem.

As we walked around the premises, she stopped and asked us, "Would you like to see the room where we do baptisms?"

We responded affirmatively and she began to lead us farther back into the cavern. Shortly, we came to a large iron accordion gate that was locked. Behind the gate we could see a large dark room. The sister opened the lock and grunted softly as she strained to push the heavy iron gate open. She turned on the lights to reveal a large, ornate baptistry with carved wooden tables and a baptismal font.

Our security escorts entered the room with us and stood in the back of the room, waiting for us. The atmosphere of this room felt spiritual to me. I could tell the Coptic Christians considered this a very holy place and we felt honored that the sister would bring us here.

I asked the sister, "Would it be okay for us to pray here for a few moments?"

"Certainly," she replied.

Our team gathered in a circle near the front of the room. I thought the sister would stand to the side and simply wait for us to pray for a bit, but instead she stepped into our circle to pray with us. She stood between Pat and me, and the Holy Spirit prompted us to focus our prayers on her.

Our prayers became prophetic as God began to show us things about this dear woman. By the Spirit, we knew she loved Jesus very much and had served Him faithfully for many years. As we continued to pray, it became very personal for her and the tears began to roll down her cheeks. The Holy Spirit was ministering to her at a very deep level.

THERE ARE NO CLOSED DOORS

The Presence of God came and filled the room. Our two security guards were watching closely and sensing the Presence of God. As we finished praying, they both approached me for prayer.

After a few moments of praying for our security detail, we began to exit the room with the sister leading the way. At the door, she stopped and began to speak with a few people who had seen the lights on. Suddenly, the sister turned to me, motioned to one of the people, and said, "This man has a heart condition, will you pray for him?"

"Certainly," I responded. As I prayed for him, others began to come down the narrow corridor of the cavern and ask for prayer. Our team began laying hands on person after person, praying healing prayers for them. As we prayed, the sister went down the corridors of the cave telling the visitors to come receive healing prayer. In a short time, a small crowd had gathered around us.

Our security detail was becoming slightly alarmed at the crowd that was forming and told us we needed to leave and get back to the car. We obeyed, even as we continued to pray for people who were following us out of the caverns. By the time we reached our car, another larger crowd had formed. We were praying for the people as fast as we could. The Presence of God was strong on us as we felt healing power flow through us with each person we touched. Jesus was there to heal.

As the crowd continued to grow, our security team was even more alarmed and told us to get in the car. Our team members were becoming alarmed as well. This was Egypt. The reason we had a security detail in the first place was because of concerns about religiously motivated terrorism. It was not a safe place for Christians to be doing mass healings in broad daylight.

Tearing ourselves away from the people trying to touch us, we jumped into the car and began to drive away. Even as we did so, people were running next to the car, trying to reach through the window to touch us and receive healing.

As we finally distanced ourselves, we took a moment to meditate on what had just happened. It truly felt like another story from the book of Acts. How could something like that possibly take place? We had gone to a religious site to pray. Our spirits were alert and ready to see what God would do. We were invited to have a tour of the monastery. We were invited to go into a place that had been closed. We prayed and God moved. It was God who orchestrated every step. We were simply willing participants and then became spectators of His glory. Once again, He opened doors we could never have opened on our own.

COVID-19

One of the best examples of "no closed doors" took place in March 2020. I was finishing a prayer journey in India with Jacob and Deborah. We had been out for ten days, doing a prayer drive across a northern state.

As we were nearing the end of our journey, we were ready to visit our last location before going back to Delhi. That afternoon I received a phone call from my tour guide, Ravi.

"Don't go to the next city on your itinerary. There is a bad sickness going around, and the hotels are putting all the foreigners in quarantine for at least two weeks."

We had no idea that the COVID-19 pandemic had just begun.

Unsure of what to do, we decided to get a train and go back to Delhi. By the time we reached the city we were hearing about large gatherings being shut down and that some hotels were not allowing foreigners to stay. I still had three weeks of travel planned, and a lot of what we were hearing was rumor. I was not sure what to believe or how seriously to take the news.

When we reached Delhi, I stayed at Jacob and Deborah's house. We had a short time of prayer and as soon as we finished, I heard God say, "Go home!" in my spirit. It was strong and commanding.

THERE ARE NO CLOSED DOORS

Instantly, I picked up my phone and texted my wife. I told her about what was going on with the sickness spreading, and that I felt I was to cut the trip short and come home.

At that same time, my daughter, Jenni, who was a missionary in Cambodia, called Jan and said the same thing. She felt the urgency to get out of the country. Jan and God went to work. She was able to find flights for us and we both left our respective countries the next day. In fact, our flights landed in Los Angeles one hour apart, and then we connected to take the same flight home to Phoenix.

I later found out the airports in Delhi and in Cambodia were shut down the next morning. If we had not been on those flights we would have been stuck in the country for months. God kept the door open just long enough for us to get out and make it home safe.

On the flight home I began to think about the idea that there are no closed doors. All of these years, God had opened impossible doors. Everywhere we went, what had been shut became open. But now, with the onset of this new disease, everything seemed to change.

"Well, God, I guess this time the door to India has been slammed shut."

God smiled.

By the time Jenni and I reached home, India was on complete lockdown. Every shop, every business, all trains, flights, churches, temples . . . everything had been shut down, and the people were required to stay in their homes. No one was prepared for this. No one had time to collect supplies of food, so very quickly things began to become dire for the people. The government was in a panic, not knowing what to do. Every decision was motivated by fear, and that fear swept through the nation. Every door in India was shut.

Because of the lockdown, people were not able to get food and it did not take too many days for children to begin to grow hungry. Many parents went without food for days giving their last rations to their children. But it was only a matter of time before they would starve.

The feelings of hopelessness and desperation were pervasive all over the nation, but especially in the rural and poorer areas of the country. Fear was the giant that controlled everything.

In desperation, people would leave their homes to go out to look for food, but the police patrolled the streets. They carried long, heavy sticks and were ordered to beat anyone who broke curfew.

It was at this time God spoke to my friend Ashish to take food to a family that was in great distress.

"But God, if I go out into the streets the police will beat me," he informed God.

But the prompting of the Holy Spirit only became more intense. He had to go, no matter the consequences. He gathered what little groceries he had and headed out the door.

He barely got a few feet from his house when two policemen confronted him, yelling at him to get back into his house, brandishing their sticks at him. Ashish remained calm and in a gentle voice, with wisdom and patience, explained to the policemen the severe plight of the family he wanted to help.

"Please, please come with me and I will show you this family," Ashish begged the officers.

Finally, one of them agreed to accompany him to visit the family. Upon reaching the house a young mother opened the door, completely shocked to see Ashish holding bags of groceries and accompanied by the policeman. Looking through the doorway, the officer could see three small children.

The young mother began to cry as she received the bags of food from Ashish. She had become hopeless and feared her children would die from lack of food, but now, suddenly, in the middle of the night, this man stood at her door and her situation was instantly changed.

THERE ARE NO CLOSED DOORS

Ashish spoke encouragement and hope to the mother and told her Jesus had directed him to bring her food. "He is the God who sees you and loves you," said Ashish. The officer watched as Ashish ministered to her and then prayed for her.

Greatly touched by what he had just witnessed, the officer said, "I must bring you to meet my supervisor."

The officer took Ashish to the police headquarters of the city and introduced him to his captain.

"This is a good man, and he is doing good work to help the people. We should do what we can to help him," the officer said, and then he explained to the captain how he had just watched Ashish minister to a desperate family.

The captain looked at Ashish. "Do you have a car?" he asked.

"Yes, I do," Ashish replied.

"We have bulk supplies of rice and beans that we can make available to you at a discounted price. You can come here to pick up the large bags and then divide them into smaller parcels to deliver to the people. I will give you a permit so you can go anywhere in the district to deliver food at any time of day."

Ashish stood, staring at the captain in disbelief. Every door in the nation was shut, but for Ashish, every door in the state was open.

During the next weeks, we were able to send donations to Ashish to purchase thousands of pounds of rice, beans, and other emergency supplies that he and his team distributed to starving families all over his district.

At each home, the people would receive the lifesaving gifts with great gratitude and thankfulness. Each time, Ashish and his team would pray for the people, many times seeing healings and deliverances take place. Homes that never would have been open for him to share Christ were now open by the thousands. Ashish was able to minister to many more people during the lockdown than we had when the country was open. For God, there are no closed doors!

FLASHBACK

After checking out of the hospital, Samson and my friends took me to the home of his parents.

I had met Pastor Vijay and his lovely wife about one year prior. After being with him for only a short time, I was impressed with his spiritual maturity and knowledge of the Word of God. He told me how he built his church on discipleship and teaching the word. During that first visit, I began to tell him about the International School of Ministry (ISOM), which we were using to train Christian leaders. He smiled broadly and asked Samson to go into his office to get something for him. Samson returned holding a large case of DVDs. Pastor Vijay opened it, and to my shock, it was the entire curriculum of ISOM on DVD!

"I have been using this training for the past fifteen years in my church. That is why my people are so well grounded and mature." We all laughed as I shook my head in bewilderment. God used this moment to quickly form a strong bond between Pastor Vijay and me.

Every morning during my convalescence, Priyanka brought me chai and served me breakfast. Each day Pastor Vijay came and spent time with me to keep me from getting bored and lonely. We would talk and pray for several hours each day.

Every evening Samson would enter the room and say, "Okay, Pastor Dan, it is time for therapy!" Samson would help me bend my leg. He would push against it, slowly bending it back until I yelled in pain.

"Adhik! Adhik! More! Push it more!" I would yell through the pain. I wanted him to push me hard so I could make as much progress as quickly as I could.

These therapy sessions were the highlight of my day, as Samson would make me laugh and yell so much that his wife, Priyanka, would run to the door to see if he was abusing me. Each day the swelling would go down a little more until it was time to return to the hospital to have the staples removed from my leg.

We reached the hospital, and they laid me on a gurney and removed the bandages from my wounds. The doctor, who was the same man who had done the surgery, took a small pair of pliers and began to remove each staple, one at a time. As he would pull them from my skin I would slightly flinch. The doctor stopped and looked at me.

"Are you all right?" he asked. "Does it hurt?"

I laughed. "Well, it doesn't hurt as much as when you put them in!" I had to give him one last jab for the pain I had endured during the surgery.

Three weeks after my surgery, there was to be an ISOM graduation at Pastor Vijay's church. I had originally been scheduled to speak at this graduation and was determined to follow through with that commitment.

The service was held in the lower level of the building, so Samson and two other strong men sat me in a chair and carried me down the long, steep steps. They had arranged a chair for me near the pulpit so I would be comfortable speaking to the graduates. But there was no way I was going to sit while I preached. I stood, and putting most of the weight on my good leg, I spoke for nearly forty minutes while Samson translated for me.

My text was from Philippians: "I want to know Christ—yes, to know the power of his resurrection and participation in his sufferings" (Philippians 3:10, NIV).

The fact that I had narrowly escaped death and suffered the broken leg, along with the knowledge that many of these graduates could also experience some type of persecution, made it seem like an appropriate subject.

Yes, we all want to experience the power of His resurrection, but I can testify that there is nothing sweeter than the intimate fellowship of sharing in His sufferings.

Chapter 33

Prayer That Affects a Nation

During the night Paul had a vision of a man of Macedonia standing and begging him, "Come over to Macedonia and help us."
Acts 16:9, NKJV

After leaving India, Tara and I, along with Jacob and Deborah, went to Malaysia to attend a conference hosted by Mark Geppert. During our time there, we told of our prayer journeys throughout North India and how God was making Himself known to the unreached people groups located there.

While in the lobby of the hotel, a man—also named Dan—approached me.

"I heard about your prayer journeys and how God is using them to bring breakthrough," he said. Suddenly tears filled his eyes. "My wife and I have been ministering in Thailand for more than twenty years. There have been hundreds of missionaries in Thailand for more than one hundred years. Yet after all of our labors, I don't know of a single place in Thailand that has had spiritual breakthrough."

I could see the burden Dan was carrying for this land. He and his wife had given years of hard labor and prayer to see the

Thai people come to Christ. As the tears rolled down his cheeks he asked, "Is it possible you could bring a team to Thailand and pray like you do in India? We desperately need your help to bring breakthrough there."

Dan's desperate and passionate plea affected me deeply. As the tears began to fill my eyes, I knew it was not just Dan who was inviting me to come, but also God. God wanted to do something powerful in Thailand, and He was inviting me to participate with Him to see that accomplished.

"Yes, yes, of course we will come," I responded. I had met Dan briefly a couple of times before, but at that moment, I felt I was making a covenant with him. We were committing ourselves to each other and to see the kingdom of God released in Thailand.

A few months later, God assembled a wonderful team consisting of twelve people from India, Egypt, Cambodia, and America. These people were full of faith and ready to contend for spiritual breakthrough in Thailand.

Upon arrival, we connected with Dan, his wife, Debbie, and several Thai believers. One of those Thai believers was Joanna, a powerful woman of God, who was a pastor on the southern coast of the country. She and her husband also operated a coffee shop, which they used to build relationships with the locals and do street ministry.

Dan and Debbie decided to divide our team and do prayer journeys across the nation. Dan took half of the team and headed north into the mountainous jungle regions. Joanne and I took the other half of the team to the south. Our mission was to take a train all the way to the southern tip of Thailand, where Buddhism had entered the country nearly two thousand years ago.

Train Ride

Our team boarded the train in Bangkok and we spent the next seventeen hours praying, talking, and thoroughly enjoying our time together. The sweet fellowship with kindred spirits on an assignment from God is a beautiful thing. I was especially thrilled to have my daughter, Jenni, with me on this prayer journey.

I always enjoyed being with the teams God brought to me. One of the hallmarks of our teams was that we loved to laugh. We were always cracking jokes, teasing each other, or playing pranks. (Sometimes, I actually think they prayed to God to get ideas to prank me!)

I always endeavored to do my best to be attentive to the needs of my team, watching closely to see how they were doing emotionally, spiritually, and physically. It was always my desire to protect them, minister to them as needed, and have them know how valuable they were to the mission. But at the heart of every prayer journey was joy.

We reached our destination, and connected with a local church and prayed through most of the night and part of the next day. We visited an ancient fort that was the original gateway to the nation and had a wonderful time of prophetic intercession. The local pastor and I quickly bonded, and we had powerful times of prayer together.

We were there for less than twenty-four hours before we again boarded the train and began the seventeen-hour journey back to Bangkok. We had hit what we felt God directed us to, finished our assignment, and headed back.

Some people may think it was foolish for us to travel thirty-four hours round trip, just to pray in a certain location for a few hours. But when we are on an assignment from God, we feel like we are the tip of the spear. We go, we hit the target, and we move on.

Simple obedience can bring the greatest of breakthroughs.

We reached Bangkok and joined with the team that had gone north. They too had gone to many spiritual high places and significant historical locations to pray.

The Upper Room

The next day, we gathered in an upper room above Joanna's coffee shop to begin our prayer vigil. We had decided we would pray for thirty-six hours nonstop. We had no agenda or schedule. We simply asked the Holy Spirit to lead us and pray the will of the Father through us.

The first portion of our time was gathering information about the history of Thailand. Our missionary friends Dan and Debbie were able to give us many insights into the history, culture, and religion of the country. Each one of these nuggets of information became prayer points to help direct us. A small group of Thai believers also joined us and were able to provide pertinent information to direct our prayers.

We began with worship, as several members of the team could play guitar and piano. We worshiped for about two hours and then began to pray.

Throughout the night the Holy Spirit led us, and as we prayed, we would be given prophetic revelation to pray with deeper insight. Again and again, we felt God say, "Look at this, pray this, I want you to understand this." In this manner, we were able to pray things we could have never known about on our own.

As we prayed, wave after wave of God's Presence would come, sometimes leading us back into worship, sometimes focusing on a certain prayer point. When He did this, we would stay on that one prayer point until we felt breakthrough. Then the Holy Spirit would lead us to the next point.

As people grew tired, they found places to go rest for a bit and then rejoin the group when they felt refreshed enough to do so. There was no schedule of who would rest and who would pray. It was all completely controlled by the Holy Spirit. He was faithful to move from person to person, giving energy and anointing to one and then another so the flow was continuous.

Conducting a thirty-six-hour prayer vigil above a coffee shop turned out to be a fantastic idea. The hot black coffee kept the anointing flowing very nicely!

At about three o'clock in the morning, Dan looked over at me. "I have been through some of the best training in the world, and I have been a missionary for more than twenty-five years. I have never prayed at this level before in my life. What you are doing, and how you are doing it, is taking me to a place in prayer that I have never been to before."

I looked at him, somewhat surprised. I began to realize what I had been doing intuitively, without much forethought, had spiritual principles that could be taught to others.

About one year later, while I was visiting Jenni in Cambodia, I met with Matt Geppert, Mark's son, who was now leading the ministry his father had founded. He had just been with our friends in Thailand and had come over to Cambodia. We sat and had a coffee, and he began to tell me about what was happening there.

"Ever since the prayer team came, there have been pockets of breakthrough all over the nation. Churches that have been stagnant for years are beginning to see supernatural growth. Ministries are working in unity, doing major street outreaches with hundreds of people coming to Christ. Prayer meetings are taking place in many sections of the country now."

"Wait," I said. "What prayer team are you talking about? Was there a team that went there recently?"

"No, I'm talking about your prayer team! All of this has happened after your team traveled through the country and did that prayer vigil one year ago."

I sat back in wonder at the goodness of God. Yes, targeted, informed, prophetic, Spirit-led prayer can actually affect a nation.

Chapter 34

Blood Moon

In fact, the law requires that nearly everything be cleansed with blood, and without the shedding of blood there is no forgiveness.
Hebrews 9:22, NIV

My daughter, Jenni, is a force of nature. She stands less than five feet tall and is very petite, but she is a walking explosion of personality and energy. She is crazy smart, hilariously funny, and completely fearless. I have never seen such a huge spirit stuffed into such a small body.

In high school, she made her first trip to Peru to work with my friends in the Amazon jungle. After graduating, she returned for another two years to teach at the school they had opened. After Peru, she moved to China to work as a teacher, developing a new curriculum for an international school.

In January 2018, my friend Mark Geppert invited Jenni to move to Cambodia to develop a Christian curriculum to teach English in the public school system.

Mark started prayer walking Cambodia many years ago, when Pol Pot and the Khmer Rouge were still in power. Between 1975 and

1979, this evil regime murdered more than two million people. The places where these executions took place are known as the Killing Fields. Mark walked through those Killing Fields while the war was still ongoing, crying out to God to redeem that blood-soaked land.

Over time, Mark helped establish twelve orphanages to care for many of the children whose parents had been killed in the war. At each of these orphanages, schools were established to educate the children.

Soon, the government of Cambodia took notice that the schools at the orphanages were far superior to the government-run schools. The Cambodian government invited Mark to come into their schools and establish excellence in education.

Cambodia is 99.5 percent Buddhist. For the Cambodian government to invite an American Christian into their schools and impose no restrictions teaching about Jesus or praying with the students and faculty was a huge miracle.

This is what Mark invited Jenni to come help with.

Water Drop

Jenni was given responsibility to develop a Christ-focused language program to teach English to the Cambodian teachers in the province of Banteay Meanchey, one of the poorest and most broken provinces in Cambodia.

Using a children's Bible that had been produced by Every Home for Christ and translated into Khmer, she began to form a program called Water Drop.

Jenni was given the responsibility to mentor and train fourteen young men and women who had grown up in Banteay Meanchey. These trainees would then take the program into all the schools throughout the district.

Jenni arrived in Cambodia and immediately went to work creating the curriculum, producing videos, and hosting large gatherings for the teachers to come and learn about the program.

Starting a large Christian program in a very poor, neglected area of Cambodia had its challenges. Over time, the hardships and spiritual oppression began to take their toll on her, emotionally and physically.

Sickness and Discouragement

In November of 2018, Jenni was stricken with dengue fever. This sickness is extremely painful, and in some cases fatal. She struggled with a 104-degree temperature and other symptoms that put her in the hospital for five days. Sometimes, being in a poor hospital in a foreign country can be more dangerous than the sickness itself. Day after day, alone and twelve thousand miles from home, she did her best to fight and recover enough to finally leave the hospital.

By the time Jenni came home for Christmas break, she was a shadow of her old self. Her joy and energy were gone, and she was struggling emotionally as her body was still trying to recover from dengue. Just the thought of returning to the mission field in a few short weeks brought anxiety and depression.

My little girl was in very bad shape and needed a breakthrough.

I would sit, pray with her, and listen as she shared the stories of hardship she had been suffering for the past twelve months. Tears rolled down her face as she recounted story after story of the difficulties she had encountered.

"Jenni," I said, "I believe God wants me to bring a prayer team to Cambodia to help bring spiritual breakthrough."

Suddenly, a glimmer of hope appeared in Jenni's eyes. "Oh, Dad, would you? That would be so wonderful if you would do that!"

Within just a few days, God assembled a team of prayer warriors from four different countries. Each one of them responded with an immediate yes when they heard that Jenni needed our help.

Our team reached Cambodia in February 2019, and we hit the ground running.

Set Free from Cancer

We spent much time praying and prophesying over Jenni's team of fourteen young locals, who were all first-generation Christians in their families. Jenni then took us to the villages to meet each of their parents and pray with them. None of the parents were believers, so the students were very excited that we would go pray with them and speak with them about Jesus.

One day, as we were in the villages praying for one of the parents, a demon manifested, and I cast it out. At that same moment, our Thai friend Joanna became very sick.

When I had reached out to Joanna to come, she had told me she had just gone to two different doctors and had been diagnosed with cancer.

"Joanna, if that is the case, please stay home and get treatment and rest! Please don't feel obligated to come."

"No!" she replied adamantly. "I know God wants me to come on this trip with you. I know I am supposed to be there. I will come and trust God to care for me."

Joanna is one of the bravest people I know, and her faith in God knows no bounds.

Joanna had been doing just fine all through the trip, but now, suddenly, her body was in great pain and she could barely stand.

I looked at the man I had just cast a demon out of, then at Joanna. Suddenly, by the Spirit, I realized this was not just her feeling sick. When I had released the Presence of God to minister to the man, that spirit of sickness in Joanna began to manifest.

We immediately began to pray for her and cast out the spirit of infirmity. Instantly, all pain and discomfort were gone, and she was totally fine. In fact, when she returned to Thailand and went back to her doctor, they could find no trace of cancer at all.

Joanna had honored God with her obedience to come to Cambodia, and God honored her by setting her free from cancer.

The Blood

Day after day, Jenni would take us to her schools, where they were doing the Water Drop program, and we would pray at each location. She would also take us to various spiritual high places, where we would pray and release the Presence of God. We ended the trip with twenty-four hours of nonstop prayer and worship.

We gathered on the flat rooftop of a large home and watched as the sun set and the moon began to rise.

"Look at the full moon tonight," said Kenda. "Doesn't it look a little pink in color?"

Kenda had traveled with me on several prayer journeys. Her compassion, gentle spirit, and ability to adapt to any situation made her invaluable to every mission.

I glanced at it and said, "Yeah, it does a little," and really didn't give it a second thought.

The primary focus of our prayer time was the fact that so much blood had been shed in this small South Asian country. All the way back to the ancient city of Angkor Wat in the twelfth century, innocent blood had been shed. It was as if Cambodia had been cursed with the shedding of blood for generations.

To counter this, we prayed for a new covenant to be made with God through the blood of Jesus Christ. All that night we sang songs about the blood of Jesus and prayed for God to forgive the sins of shedding innocent blood. We prayed for ancient curses to be broken and for Jesus to redeem Cambodia from her bloody past.

We then had communion together, asking God to establish His blood covenant with the people of Cambodia.

Suddenly, at two o'clock in the morning, Kenda looked up into the sky and said, "Look!"

We all looked up and were shocked to see the full moon had turned a solid blood red.

"This must be a sign from God that He has heard our prayers," Kenda declared.

We stood and stared in awe, and each of us could feel the Presence of God sweep over us. Yes, God had given us a sign that He had heard our prayers.

Jenni stepped over and wrapped her arms around my neck and hugged me tight. With tears in her eyes, she said, "Thanks, Dad. I needed this more than you can know."

A few days after our team left Cambodia, Jenni called me.

"Dad, it's like Cambodia was covered in a dark cloud, and now it's gone and the sun is shining. The entire atmosphere here has changed. My joy is back and I feel full of energy again. I can't believe the transformation since you were here with the prayer team!"

Over the next months, what had been difficult or impossible became easy, and Jenni had wonderful, fruitful ministry until she left just prior to the COVID-19 shutdown.

It is amazing what God can do with a small team of devoted men and women who gather in unity of mission and purpose, believe Him for the impossible, and pray.

PART VIII
KASHMIR

Chapter 35

Praying in a War Zone

Yea, though I walk through the valley of the shadow of death,
I will fear no evil;
For You are with me;
Your rod and Your staff, they comfort me.
You prepare a table before me in the presence of my enemies.
Psalm 23:4–5, NKJV

"The riots have continued nonstop for more than two months now. The city has been on lockdown that entire time."

I was speaking to Pastor Sunny in Kashmir, India. Kashmir is one of the most unreached places in the world with a population of more than twelve million, less than 0.02 percent of which is Christian. We had planned to take a prayer team there, but he was telling me the city was in great distress.

"Everything is closed—all the stores, schools, and businesses have been closed for more than sixty days. If you come, we can get you to the church, but you will not be able to go anywhere off of the property. There is very little food—maybe a little rice; that is all we have."

"Well, Pastor Sunny, do you still want us to come?" I asked.

"Yes, yes, we need prayer more than ever, but I want you to know the situation here is very dangerous."

Unfortunately, this was normal for Kashmir. Ever since the partitioning that separated Pakistan from India in 1947, there had been conflict along the border. Insurgents from Pakistan would cross over and try to recruit the Kashmiri youth to instigate riots and create conflict for the Indian army stationed there.

The Indian army occupied Kashmir to keep Pakistan from moving in and possessing the land. The Kashmiri people were caught in the middle with atrocities happening from both the Pakistan and India side. It was a constant war zone and the United Nations never established a recognized border between the two nations. They are divided by what is called the Line of Control. Along this line there is constant conflict as the two nations fight over the land.

Now, Pakistani insurgents had churned up trouble among the Kashmiri youth. These latest riots were some of the worst they had ever experienced. This is what my team would be walking into.

I had already assembled a group of ten people for this journey. Now I would need to speak to them and let them know the situation on the ground.

A few days later we gathered and I explained the situation in Kashmir. After relaying the information from Pastor Sunny, I looked around the room.

"All right, guys, there is no pressure at all. I can understand if you don't feel comfortable doing this. So, how many of you still want to go?"

Without hesitation, every hand shot up.

I looked at my team, feeling love and pride in my heart for them. There was no one I would rather go into a war zone with than these dear friends.

I contacted Jacob, Deborah, and Tara in India, whom I had also invited. After hearing the report and knowing the dangers, they also responded, "They need prayer. Let's go!"

We reached the airport in Srinagar and went through layers of security before finding our bags and stepping outside. Our friends were there waiting with two large vehicles. As fast as we could, we loaded our bags and ourselves into the vehicles and took off for the church compound.

Normally, it is a twenty-minute drive to the church from the airport, but this day the vehicles were driving as fast as they could through the abandoned city streets.

"Why are we driving so fast?" I asked the driver.

"Because the young men have been gathering and pelting cars with rocks. If we drive fast they have less of a chance of hitting us. Some of them attacked us on the way to get you at the airport."

As we drove, we saw thousands of Indian army personnel patrolling the streets, wearing full riot gear and carrying machine guns. There were tanks and armored vehicles on every block. Many of the streets had been blocked off with razor wire. The air was thick with the smoke of tear gas that had been used to disperse rioters.

We had just landed in a war zone.

Forty-Hour Prayer Vigil

We reached the church compound, which was next to a military base. It was actually the safest place to be in Kashmir. By the time my team reached Srinagar, the city had been shut down for seventy-five days.

Pastor Sunny greeted us, and we unloaded our bags in the church. By seven o'clock that evening, we were ready to begin our prayer and worship vigil.

Hour after hour went by as we worshiped and prayed for Kashmir. There was no set agenda. It was all led by the Spirit. People rested, prayed, and worshiped as they felt led.

At about 3:30 a.m., I was getting tired and my eyes were growing heavy. *I'm going to take a break for an hour or so*, I thought. Just as I was preparing to go lie down, Tara caught fire in the Spirit and began to pray with fervent passion. All of a sudden, there was a fresh wind of the Presence of God, and we all joined her intense praying. Tara kept praying about the Lion of the tribe of Judah walking along the border of Pakistan and India, shaking His mane and roaring loudly. It was a powerful picture of the will of God being released between these two nations.

Praying for the Man of Peace

A major key to doing ministry among unreached people groups is to find the "man of peace," whom the Holy Spirit will lead you to (see Luke 10:6). In every place I have gone, God has been faithful to give me that one person of influence who is able to take me to places I could never go to on my own.

During this prayer time, I began crying out to God to connect me with a Muslim man I could build a relationship with—a man of influence who could open doors in Kashmir. This was my fourth trip to Kashmir and I had yet to meet a man that I could connect with. For some reason, I felt compelled to pray passionately for God to connect me with a Muslim man in particular. I prayed long and hard for this as the rest of the team agreed with me. I was knocking on the door, and I was asking God to do what I could never do on my own.

God would answer that prayer beyond my wildest imagination.

At seven o'clock in the morning, I finally decided to go lie down. Just as I spread my blanket on the floor and my head touched the pillow, Pastor Sunny shook my arm.

"Things were very quiet in the city last night. I'm going to take a drive and look around to see what the conditions are. Would you like to come with me?"

Drive around in a war zone? Absolutely! It would be much better to pray on the streets of the city anyway.

As we drove, the sun was just beginning to rise and we could see the streets were quiet and mostly abandoned. As I looked out over the war-torn city, I prayed, asking for the Prince of Peace to come and bring revival. The people of this region had suffered so much for many years, and only Jesus could ever be their answer for peace and safety.

Suddenly, Pastor Sunny slammed on the breaks, and the vehicle came to an abrupt stop.

"Look!" he said.

"Look at what?"

"They are selling chickens on the street! This is the first time the sellers have been out in seventy-five days! We can have chicken for dinner tonight!" In Srinagar, the merchants would be on the side of the streets with live chickens. You could go up to them, choose which one you wanted, and they would kill it and pluck it for you, right there on the spot. You can't get fresher poultry than that!

By the time we returned to the church, there were a few people from Sunny's congregation brave enough to venture out. They had heard we came to pray, and they were desperate to join us and receive any encouragement we could offer.

At about two in the afternoon, I again made my way to a back room to lie down for a short rest. Once more, just as my head hit the floor, someone shook my arm.

"Dan, my wife and I have come. Will you please pray for us?" the man asked humbly. I looked up; it was Pastor Vino.

I had met this man of God on my previous trips to Kashmir. This man had been beaten viciously and barely escaped with his life for preaching the gospel in Kashmir. *The Voice of the Martyrs* had written magazine articles about this man. Pastor Vino was a true hero of the faith. I jumped up as quickly as I could. To be asked to pray for such a man was both an honor and humbling at the same time.

"Of course!" I said. "And then, I ask you to pray for me!"

Our team prayed and worshiped nonstop for forty hours. Forty hours of crying out to God to come visit Kashmir and show His glory . . . and I never did get that nap.

Reconciliation

At the end of our prayer time, we had communion together, as well as a reconciliation service where Indians and Kashmiris asked forgiveness of each other and washed each other's feet. It was a powerful time of God's Presence as we all humbled ourselves at the feet of Jesus.

The day after we left, our friends in Kashmir sent us a newspaper headline: "After 78 Days the City Has Reopened"!

For us, that headline was evidence that our time of prayer was honored by God and helped bring peace into a war zone.

Chapter 36

The Man of Peace

Whatever village or town you enter, search for an honorable man who will let you into his home until you leave for the next town. Once you enter a house, speak to the family there and say, "God's blessing of peace be upon this house!"
MATTHEW 10:11–12, TPT

"Today's agenda is to make snow angels," I teasingly texted Tara as I looked out the window of our guesthouse and saw the snow piling up.

It was January and we had returned to Kashmir. It had only been a few months since we conducted the prayer vigil, and I wanted to return for a short, two-day visit. My team included Tara, her mother Deborah, and two friends from America.

The snow began to fall shortly after we reached Srinagar, and it kept falling until the airport and all the roads were closed. The irony was that the city was once again completely shut down—this time not because of riots, but snow.

Originally, my team and I were to be in Kashmir for two days, then fly to another state of India to minister at a pastors' conference.

But now, our two-day trip had become five days of sitting in a room drinking kahwa (a Kashmiri tea) and trying to stay warm around a wood-burning stove.

Hour after hour, day after day, we sat with nothing to do and nowhere to go. Tara and I were in perfect peace, completely unfazed by our situation. We had been on many of these journeys together and we knew God always had a plan. Besides, we were totally out of control. There was absolutely nothing we could do to get out. We may as well relax and enjoy the kahwa and the wonderful hospitality of Pastor Sunny and his family.

The rest of the team, on the other hand, were not quite as content. Tara's mom had huge responsibilities back home and was feeling the pressure of not being where she felt she was needed the most. My American friend, Greg, was stir crazy. Cabin fever was setting in as he expressed his frustration at being stuck in this room day after day.

"I can't believe I spent all that money to just come here and sit in a room doing nothing all day!" he said.

I smiled. It was interesting to watch how people handled feeling powerless. For Tara and me, it simply came down to whether we trusted God or not. We were completely content to wait, trust, and see what God would do. We had learned long ago that when we didn't understand, it was our job to trust Him fully without complaining.

Each day, we would check for flights, but the airport was shut down, as well as all the roads leading out of the city. Each day, we would drink our kahwa and play with Pastor Sunny's one-year-old daughter, who thankfully brought some distraction to the boredom.

Sheep Project Proposal

On the fifth day, Pastor Sunny received a visitor. He was a Muslim businessman named Amir, whose mother was Christian. This dear sister attended Pastor Sunny's church and had mentioned to her son that a group of Americans was staying at his guesthouse.

Amir's presence was a pleasant diversion for us, and after some time of small talk, he got to the purpose of his visit. Amir was a man of small stature in his mid-forties who carried an air of authority. It was easy to see he was accustomed to being in charge.

"I raise sheep in the mountains of Kashmir. I have hired some men from a mountain village to care for them. They are from the Gujjar tribe. These people have been shepherds for generations, but this village is very poor and none of them own their own sheep." Amir spoke slowly and distinctly. "I would like to do something to help these people and I want to propose a business plan."

"What do you have in mind?" I replied.

Amir pulled a sheet of paper from a notebook he had been holding and handed it to me.

"I would like to start a sheep project for the economic development of the village. There are about two hundred people in the village. Most of the people are illiterate and cannot afford school for their children. They cannot afford medical care. This sheep project could provide continual income for them and change their lives."

I listened to Amir speak and looked into his eyes, trying to get a read on this man. What manner of man was he? Was he an honest man? What were his motives for wanting to do this? Could I trust him?

He drew my attention to the paper. "We will purchase 125 sheep. We will divide them into five flocks of twenty-five. At the end of each year, as sheep are being born, each shepherd will pay back five sheep. This will start another flock of twenty-five sheep, and we can give them to another shepherd to begin his herd. This will continue with each shepherd, multiplying flocks as they pay back the sheep. As the shepherds take charge of their flocks, they gain dignity by being sheep owners, providing for their families. In time, I believe this project will change the entire village."

I sat in deep thought. This seemed to be a brilliant plan. Could it be possible that God would use this plan to open doors for me to share Christ with an unreached people group? Would this Muslim businessman allow me to go to the village to pray and to tell people about Jesus? That thought sounded absurd, even to me. What were the chances of a Kashmiri Muslim taking a Christian into a mountain village to share Christ?

"How much would this project cost?" I asked.

"Twenty-five thousand US dollars," he replied. "One hundred twenty-five sheep at two hundred dollars each. That includes the cost for winter shelters and the first winter's feed."

I gulped. Twenty-five thousand dollars! That was a huge number for me. I had no agency behind me, and I had promised God I would not ask for money. I was going to need time to pray and hear from God on this before I could make such a commitment.

"Give me time. I will pray to Jesus and ask if He wants me to do this," I said. "I will let you know when I return this summer."

When I reached the States, I called Mark and told him about the opportunity to do the sheep project in Kashmir.

"Well, God has just opened the door for you to take Jesus where He has never been before. What are you going to tell Him? That it costs too much? I'm glad Jesus didn't say that when He died for them."

Ouch! Mark had a wonderful gift of exposing my foolish concerns.

"Okay, God. Let's do this!" I prayed.

Making a Covenant

That summer, I returned to Kashmir and asked to meet with Amir. It happened to be Eid, the holiday Muslims celebrate at the conclusion of Ramadan, the month of fasting. Eid is observed to commemorate the story of God providing a ram in the bush when Abraham was told to sacrifice his son.

Amir invited my team and me to his house to celebrate with his family. After an incredible feast of traditional Kashmiri dishes, we sat in his living room to talk. My team gathered around us, full of anticipation of what this encounter would be like. Amir sat close to me, face-to-face. There was something about this man that I liked. I knew he was not a follower of Jesus, but I still saw something in him that made me want to trust him.

Amir spoke perfect English, so there was no need for Tara to translate, but she sat close, listening to every word, praying softly under her breath. She sensed the next few moments would be very significant.

"Amir, I went home and considered your proposal. I have prayed to Jesus about this and asked Him what He wants to do. You see, I am not a rich American. I do not have the money for such a project. The only way I can get this money is if I ask Jesus for it. I do not do fundraising. I do not ask people for money. I can only get this money if Jesus wants to give it to me."

Amir looked at me intently. He was asking himself the same questions about me that I had asked myself about him: *Is this man honorable? Can I trust him?*

"So, I asked Jesus about your proposal, and He said yes. He wants to do this, and He will give me the money for it. I trust Him to do that." I spoke softly, as if it was only he and I in the room.

Amir nodded, trying to take in this information. He was not accustomed to someone talking about Jesus in this manner. I was letting him know I had a relationship with Him and that He spoke to me. He had been around Christians in the local Anglican church, but he sensed I was different and he had no reference point to know how to receive me.

"Also, I am not just a nice guy who is going to give you twenty-five thousand dollars and then walk away," I said, smiling. "You know I am a follower of Jesus and that I have come here to pray for the Kashmiri people."

Once again, he nodded, his eyes fixed on me intently.

"So, if I do this, I want to have access to the village. I want to be able to meet the shepherds and their families. I want to be able to pray for people and talk about Jesus. I want to pray for the sick and see them healed. I will not try to convert anyone—only God can convert someone's heart—but I do want freedom to do what I do and to be who I am."

I paused as we both looked at each other intently. The Presence of God was in the room. I felt like we were on holy ground as a heavenly transaction was taking place. We both knew that if we did this, we would be making a covenant with each other, and neither of us knew where that would take us. We could feel the weight and importance of this moment. It would change both of our lives forever.

Amir lowered his head for a moment in deep thought. For him, there was much to consider. Would it be safe to take an American into that area? ISIS and Al Qaeda roamed those mountains. While he could assure my safety in the village, what about other nearby villages that might harbor Muslim insurgents from Pakistan? After all, the village was barely ten kilometers from the Line of Control, and sixty kilometers from where Osama bin Laden was killed. And what about this man wanting to talk about Jesus and pray for people? There could be great conflict in a Muslim village over such a thing.

While all these thoughts went through his mind, I am sure he wanted to say no to my requests. But as he lifted his head and looked into my eyes it seemed something rose up within him and prompted him. He could not say no.

After a long silence, Amir said, "Yes, we will do this." We continued to look at each other and both of us saw that the other's eyes were getting misty.

It was a historic moment for the kingdom of God in Kashmir. An American Christian and a Muslim Kashmiri had made a covenant with each other.

Not far from Amir's house is Lal Chowk. In English, this means "Red Square." This is where the Muslims have anti-American protests, burn the American flag, and shout, "Death to America." But here, a short distance away, in this man's home, God did the impossible and knitted us together to become not just friends, but the closest of family.

Then I remembered the forty-hour prayer vigil we had done eight months earlier. I remembered how I had cried out to God, "Connect me with a Muslim man who has influence and can open doors for ministry! Please reveal to me my man of peace!" God had abundantly answered that prayer. God would use Amir in a tremendous way to open the mountains of Kashmir for Jesus.

Chapter 37

The Good Shepherd

I am the good shepherd. The good shepherd gives His life for the sheep.
JOHN 10:11, NKJV

The day after celebrating Eid with Amir, he took us into the mountains to meet the shepherds and the village chief. They were from a tribe that in the past had been nomadic for hundreds of years. Now they had settled in villages and built permanent homes. Their people had been shepherds since the beginning of time. But now, in their poverty, they did not own any sheep of their own but cared for the sheep of other wealthy owners.

We were there to change that.

We stood on a hill, surrounded by twelve-thousand-foot mountain peaks and lush green forest, and looked out over the village. Kashmir is known as a paradise on earth, and we were truly looking at a piece of that paradise right here. About forty to fifty homes were scattered across the small valley. Most of them had smoke rising from their brick chimneys as their cookfires burned in the kitchen hearths. The azure sky was filled with puffs of white clouds behind the foreground of dark-green pine trees. A few cattle grazed in the fields, and a beautiful mountain stream cascaded through the valley.

Meeting the Shepherds

Amir led Tara and me, along with our small team, to a house on a hilltop overlooking the valley below. There was no furniture in the room of any kind. We sat on the thinly carpeted floor and leaned against pillows strewn around the room. As we sipped our salt tea (a Kashmiri delicacy that requires much time to acquire a taste for), the chief of the village and about fifteen shepherds entered the room. They were all curious about meeting the white American and stared at me with great interest.

These shepherds were hardworking, down to earth, and humble. They were honest men who dreamed of a better life for their families. They sat on the floor as Amir introduced me and translated as I spoke.

I told the shepherds the same thing that I had told Amir: that I was a follower of Jesus Christ, the Son of God. I told them Jesus wanted to help them and I would pray to Him to give me the money to purchase the sheep. I also told them I wanted freedom to visit their village often, pray for people, and tell them about Jesus.

"If someone is sick, I will ask Jesus to heal them," I said. "If someone is tormented by demons, I will ask Jesus to set them free. I am a servant of Jesus, and I know He will answer my prayer for you, because He loves you and wants you to know Him."

The shepherds and the village chief sat, listening intently, as Amir translated. These men had never met a Christian or an American before. What were they to think of this white man saying he wanted to pray for them and tell them about Jesus? Amir continued to speak to them in their language for quite some time as I sat and sipped my tea, waiting for the final verdict. The village chief and the shepherds began speaking to each other as they discussed my proposal. Again, I waited.

The fact that an American Christian was sitting in this Muslim village high in the mountains of Kashmir was a miracle. If they decided to allow me to do what I was asking, it would be an even greater miracle. I looked around the room at these men, their dark skin weathered and hardened by the outdoors. They looked at me intently, wondering if they could trust this American Christian. Finally, Amir looked at me.

"It has been decided," he said. "They are in full agreement. You can begin by praying for us and the success of this project right now."

I lowered my head and for the first time in the history of that Muslim village, an American Christian prayed in the name of Jesus Christ, the Son of God.

Over the next several years, I would return to my adopted village many times. I became dear friends with many of the shepherds and their families. Sometimes, we would go on horseback to the top of the mountain, where they would graze the sheep in the summers. There were thousands of acres of green grass across the mountain meadows where the sheep would feed and grow fat.

It was always a great joy for me to ride the small mountain ponies up the steep slopes of the mountain. They would struggle slowly up the steep, rough incline, but when we reached the flat meadows, they wanted to run. Riding a Kashmiri pony at full gallop across the mountain landscape is a special piece of heaven for me.

Story Time

Many times, I would sit with my shepherd friends telling Bible stories. Almost all of the adults in the village were illiterate, so the tradition of telling stories was very important to them. All of their traditions were passed down orally to the next generations. Stories are a wonderful way to express the truths of Jesus. We would sit on the floor, sipping salt tea, and I would tell my stories, trying to make them as dramatic and meaningful as I could.

One evening, I shared the story of David, the shepherd boy who had killed the mighty warrior giant, Goliath. I shared about how David had told the king he had killed the lion and the bear with his bare hands and that he would do the same to this giant. When I made that point of the story, the shepherds laughed and they all looked at one of the shepherds named Mehboob, who sat against the wall. I asked, through my translator, "What is so funny?" Obviously, there was an inside joke I had missed.

Mehboob smiled sheepishly; he was a very humble man and did not want to attract attention to himself. He raised his hand and pulled back the sleeve of his coat. His hand and wrist were deeply scarred.

"A lion tried to attack my sheep one night and I had to fight him off. He got a good piece of me before I was able to kill him."

I stared at him in awe. These men were very brave and were willing to lay down their lives for their sheep. Fighting off bears, wolves, and lions was very common for them. They were understanding my story at a deep level, as they could relate to it personally. I was talking about something that was a common occurrence, and they could picture exactly what I was trying to describe.

This opened the door for me to talk about Jesus, who had said He was the Good Shepherd and would lay down His life for His sheep. I explained that we were the sheep Jesus was talking about, that He had given His life as a sacrifice to pay for our sin, and that through the cross He had laid down His life for us.

Jesus, the Good Shepherd

One afternoon, Amir took me to the home of one of our shepherds. Each time I came to the village, Amir was faithful to make sure I could visit all of them, tell them about Jesus, and pray for them and their families.

A few of the shepherds had gathered at this home and I began to tell them the story about Jesus saying that His sheep knew His voice (see John 10:27).

I asked them, "Do your sheep recognize your voice?"

"Oh, yes," they said.

"Will your sheep follow another shepherd's voice or just yours?"

"The sheep will not follow the other shepherds, only the one they know."

"Well, this is how it is with Jesus. He wants you to know His voice, to trust Him and only follow Him. He is the one who loves you and died for you, and He wants to lead you into eternal life."

Amir, who was translating for me, paused and looked at me. "It seems shepherds are very important in your religion," he stated.

"Yes," I said. "Shepherds are very important to God. In fact, when Jesus was born, shepherds were the first people God sent angels to tell about it."

For the next several minutes I told the story of how the angel appeared to Mary, a young virgin, and told her the Holy Spirit would come upon her and place the seed of the Son of God in her, and that she would give birth to the Savior of the world. I told of Joseph being visited by an angel to tell him to stay with Mary and that the baby was sent from God. I told them how they had to travel to their hometown and they could not find a place to stay. The only place they could find was a barn, and the Son of God was born in the presence of cows, goats, and donkeys.

The shepherds listened intently as I continued to tell them how the shepherds were on the hills watching their flocks at night, and the angels of God appeared to them in bright glory and told them that the Son of God, the Savior of the world, had been born in a barn. I emphasized to them that the first people to hear this good news were not the rich people, the king, or the government leaders. The first people God wanted to tell about the birth of His Son were shepherds.

And now, two thousand years later, I had the privilege of sitting with shepherds in the mountains of Kashmir telling them this same good news. Jesus Christ, the Son of God, the Savior of the world has been born!

"Yes," I told them. "Shepherds are very important to God, and that is why He has sent me to tell you of His great love for you."

As I ended the story, the shepherds began to chat among themselves, discussing what I had just told them. Then they asked me to pray for each of them. Mehboob would always go stand against the wall to brace himself whenever I would pray for him. Each time I prayed, he would feel God's Presence so strong it was hard for him to stand. Tears would fill his eyes as he experienced the love of God enveloping him. We all laughed as he ran to the wall and stood firmly against it, smiling broadly, waiting for me to come to him.

It is always a great honor for me to sit with my Kashmiri friends and tell stories about Jesus. The miracle of an American Christian being welcomed into a Muslim village in the mountains of Kashmir, to share Christ and to pray, never gets old for me.

I have always said that I am the donkey that Jesus rides into the villages.

I will never lose the wonder and the deep gratitude of Him allowing me to be that donkey.

Chapter 38

There Is No Explanation for This

You have kept track of all my wandering and my weeping. You have stored my many tears in your bottle—not one will be lost. For they are all recorded in your book of remembrance.
PSALM 56:8, TPT

"Amir, do you know anything about grace? Have you heard of this word before?" I asked.

We were sitting in Pastor Sunny's home having chai and discussing the sheep project. Jesus had answered our prayers, and the twenty-five thousand dollars had been given in less than two weeks' time. As we discussed the business side of the project, I had suddenly stopped and asked my question.

"No, I have not heard this word before," he responded. "What does it mean?"

"I'm glad you asked," I said, smiling.

I proceeded to tell Amir that grace was God's supernatural power to do what we could never do and to be what we could never be on our own. I told him the story about Cain and Abel.

"No matter how hard Cain worked, no matter how good he was, or how hard he tried, he could never earn God's love and favor," I said. "This is what religion is—always working as hard as you can to please God, but no matter how hard you try, it is never enough."

As I spoke, the Presence of God gently came. Amir was fixated, listening intently to what I was saying.

"Amir, there is nothing you can do to make God love you more than He loves you right now. And there is nothing you can do to make Him love you less than He does right now. He is a good, good Father, and He loves you intensely."

The Presence of God swept over us even stronger as tears began to run down Amir's face. God was letting him know that what I was saying was true, and it was hitting home. All his life he had been trained to serve a god that would never love him back, no matter how good he was or how hard he tried.

Amir was a strong man and did not often show his emotions. He had lived in the war zone of Kashmir all his life. He was—and is—a tough, no-nonsense man who immediately takes control of any situation. He is a man of action, always ready to solve any problem with wisdom and insight. He is extremely intelligent and intuitive at the same time. He is a rare person of strength, wisdom, and integrity.

But now, he was being confronted with truth he had never heard before, and it was affecting him deeply. Tears ran down his face as he quickly wiped them away.

Sharing My Testimony

Throughout our times together, I would gently find ways to talk about Jesus and His love. Each time I would come to Srinagar, Amir would not allow me to stay in a hotel, but would have me stay in his home. His wonderful wife, Inaya, and their two boys received me as part of their family. We would sit in their home, drinking kahwa and talking for hours.

One night as we were together, Inaya asked me how I was raised as a boy. I was able to tell them of the pain and abuse of my father and the love of my mother. I told them how I became an orphan and was hated by my stepmother. I confessed how I had been a drug addict and an alcoholic. But best of all, I was able to tell them how, through a sister's prayers, Jesus came to me, loved me, delivered me, and made me His own.

I looked across the room at Amir, and the tears were rolling down his cheeks. He tried his best to brush them off until he finally rose and left the room. His pride would not allow him to be seen crying in front of his family.

The Lamb of God Who Was Slain

Months later, I happened to be in their home as they again celebrated Eid. The day before this we had been in the mountains, and I watched as the shepherds selected a group of sheep that they would sacrifice for the occasion.

Amir and I sat on the front porch of his house. It was a beautiful day full of sunshine and warmth with the grand mountain peaks in the background.

"I don't like the day of sacrifice," he said. "It saddens me to know they are killing the sheep because I have spent much time with them and I know them."

"I understand," I responded. "This day has great significance for me as well. This day reminds me of Jesus and the sacrifice He made for me. Jesus is called 'the Lamb of God who was slain.' Eid reminds me of Jesus dying on a cross as the payment for my sins. You see, the place Abraham laid his son on an altar to sacrifice him was the exact same mountain Jesus was crucified on eighteen hundred years later. What Abraham was willing to do, God actually did to His only Son. So yes, this day of remembrance has a deep effect on me."

I glanced over at Amir, and again, he was wiping away the tears.

Life was very difficult in Kashmir. Amir had tried to build a business but not long after he opened, there was a massive flood that destroyed much of the city, including his shop. He worked hard to reopen, and shortly after that, there was an earthquake that devastated the valley and once again destroyed his business.

He decided to work from his home and began to rebuild, but suddenly the Indian government invaded and took over the government of Kashmir. The city was shut down for months and Amir's business was closed.

As time passed and things began to settle down, he tried again to reopen the business, but then COVID-19 came and shut everything down. No matter how hard he tried, he was met with defeat after defeat, none of which were his own making.

The discouragement and depression were settling in. He was becoming weary, feeling powerless and hopeless. He was a good man, trying to make a living for his family, but it seemed the world was against him.

Amir was preparing to go to the local mosque when he stopped in the living room and sat down next to me. He reached over and took my hand in his.

"Please pray for me, my friend. I desperately need God's help."

I held his hand tightly and wept with my friend as I prayed and God ministered to his heart.

Later that day, as Amir drove me to the airport, he suddenly hit the steering wheel with his fist. I looked over at him, not sure of what to expect.

"There is no explanation for this!" he said with anger in his voice. "There is no explanation! All my life I have never cried. I keep my emotions bottled up. My wife has never seen me cry. My sons have never seen me cry. But, when I am around you, all I do is cry! There is no explanation for this!"

While Amir seemed to be very upset about this, I found it to be quite humorous. I laughed and said, "There is an explanation for this, Amir. His name is Jesus, and He loves you very much. That is why you cry; you are feeling the love of Jesus. And you know what? I think you love Him too."

Amir sat quietly, in deep thought. My dear Muslim friend was being encountered by Jesus, and it was too much for him to process.

I still continue to pray for Amir, his family, and my Kashmiri shepherds. It is my prayer that someday they will come to fully know the God who loves them, died for them, and wants to give them eternal life.

PART IX
MATURING MINISTRY

Chapter 39

Be Fruitful and Multiply

Be diligent to present yourself approved to God, a worker who does not need to be ashamed, rightly dividing the word of truth.
2 Timothy 2:15 NKJV

Back in 2012, on that first mission to North India with Mark, I'd had the joy of meeting Richard and Linda. They were in their early seventies and full of faith. We connected and enjoyed being with each other and became quick friends. The thing I liked most about them was their heart for prayer and unreached people groups. This couple carried the heart of God for the nations in a very special way.

After that journey, we stayed connected over the years, with visits in each other's homes from time to time. Richard and Linda have an incredible ministry of connecting people to make a difference in the kingdom of God and introduced us to several missionaries during our visits.

Introduced to ISOM

For years, Richard and Linda would talk about a ministry project they were involved with called The International School of Ministry (ISOM). ISOM is a Bible college on video. Dr. Berin Gilfillan, the founder of ISOM, traveled around the world finding the most gifted and anointed teachers and then videotaped their teachings. There are 160 video teachings that cover every topic necessary to train and equip men and women to be church planters. This "Bible college on a flash drive" has been used all over the world, training millions of people to have powerful and effective ministries.

Richard and Linda tried to get me involved with ISOM for years, but it just wasn't something I was interested in. I was always going into new territory where people had never heard of Jesus. Thinking of doing a Bible college just didn't seem to fit in with what I was doing.

In 2017 and 2018, they invited me to the international conferences for ISOM held in California, but I politely declined. I still had no interest in a Bible college.

Finally, in 2019, they once again invited me to the international conference, but this time they purchased a ticket for me.

Hmm, no pressure here, I thought.

The conference started on the day I was coming home from a prayer journey in Cambodia. Since I was landing in California anyway, I decided to attend the conference and make Richard and Linda happy.

As I sat, trying to stay awake from the jet lag, I listened to the speakers tell of the wonderful miracles that were taking place through the ISOM training. The more I listened, the more I thought, *Maybe this is something I could use*. A number of churches had been planted by this time, so maybe this training could be useful.

Then Richard and Linda introduced me to Dr. Berin.

"I have been working on translating ISOM into different Indian languages for almost twenty years, and to this day we have only had a handful of people use those translations," he told me.

"Well, I am not sure what I can do, but I am willing to take it and see if we can get it into the hands of the right people," I said, a little hesitantly.

"Good!" said Richard. "Because I just paid the fee for you to have the rights to use the training in Hindi."

I laughed and again thought, *No pressure here.*

Taking ISOM to India

That summer I returned to India and met with my friends Ashish and Kalpana. I spoke at length about ISOM and the video teachings. With this tool, Bible colleges could be started anywhere. No buildings were needed. Class time could be anytime the people could gather. The class size could be large or small. And the best part was that it was perfect for the underground churches that needed to do this in secret to avoid persecution. India had become one of the top ten most persecuted countries in the world. ISOM would be a perfect way to continue Bible training in secrecy.

As I spoke, Ashish and Kalpana smiled.

"Dan, we know all about ISOM," Kalpana said. "We both took the courses and graduated from the program in Delhi seven years ago. We love ISOM, but the person who was directing it left several years ago, and no one is providing the courses anymore."

I just shook my head and laughed. I had no idea that my friends had graduated from ISOM training or even knew anything about it. Now here I was trying to sell them on an idea that they already embraced.

"Are you saying we could use ISOM to train our leaders here?" Ashish asked.

"Yes, but more than that: I am asking you both to become the national directors of ISOM for India. I want you to lead this initiative so we can see thousands of leaders trained all over the country."

Ashish's eyes grew large as he looked at me, wondering if I really meant what I said.

"I am serious. Dr. Berin has given me this assignment to plant ISOM in India, and I believe you and Kalpana are the ones to make it happen."

Ashish and Kalpana received their new initiative and began to implement ISOM training. Today, there are thousands of Christian leaders being trained and equipped to have powerful and effective ministries. Even in the face of persecution, the churches are growing and multiplying.

Empowering Women

Women especially have found dignity as they become leaders in training others. Even men are now coming to their classes to be trained, which is very uncommon in India.

I had the privilege of meeting one of these remarkable women and hearing her story of how God used ISOM to not only change her life, but also to help change a culture.

She stood under five feet tall and probably didn't weigh a hundred pounds. She was quiet, almost shy. At first glance one would almost overlook her, but as I looked closer, I could see the fire in her eyes and a determined look on her face. My first thought was, *This woman is a warrior!*

She stood in front of a group of thirty-seven pastors who represented fifteen thousand house churches in North and Central India. All of them were leaders of at least one hundred to one thousand churches. Of these thirty-seven leaders, six of them were women.

She began to speak, and in her soft voice she told a powerful story.

BE FRUITFUL AND MULTIPLY

She and her family were very poor. Her home was a hut with a dirt floor. In India, a woman is considered a second-class citizen, especially if she is a poor village woman from a very low caste.

Over the course of one year, she had made the twenty-three-hour train ride to Delhi five times to finish all five levels of ISOM's training, and the anointed teaching of the Word of God changed her life. She went back home and began to share the ISOM training with pastors in her network.

She said that through ISOM, women are gaining dignity and purpose. Women are now looked at as being important and valuable, and they are gaining honor by becoming powerful leaders.

"When I first began," she said, "I was despised, and very few people wanted to come to the classes. They would gossip and spread lies about me, but there were a few women who wanted the training, so I began with them. When others saw the difference in their lives, they began to come to me and ask for the training.

"The women who have received the training have become better wives and mothers. Some have started small businesses and are beginning to prosper. They walk differently; they carry their heads high and are not ashamed or downtrodden. The Word of God has changed their identity forever. This training is changing our lives and our culture. For the first time in our history, women are being looked at as important and valuable."

Suddenly, her voice became firmer, and she raised her chin a little higher. "Now I have 390 leaders who have finished three levels of the training, and many of them are men. Men are now coming to a woman to receive training. In our culture, this is a great miracle."

This determined woman is only one of many who are actively beginning thousands of small groups that are being trained in the Word of God. The Bible training is still changing lives. It is changing culture, and it is equipping people to advance the kingdom of God. Strong spiritual leaders are being multiplied by the thousands in North India.

People tell us that because of the training, the believers in a region no longer argue over false doctrine. ISOM has brought them together in unity. Now they are all teaching the same solid Bible doctrines of the faith.

Because of this training that is multiplying leaders, I have found that I am working myself out of a job. The indigenous leaders are now doing for the thousands what I was doing for only a few. Because of the ISOM training, the foreign missionary is needed less and less.

Thank God for an elderly couple in California that, through their persistence, finally helped me see what they could see. I am only the donkey that carried a flash drive to India. It is Richard and Linda who are responsible for thousands of lives being changed for the kingdom of God.

Chapter 40

To Be Found Worthy

For to you it has been granted on behalf of Christ, not only to believe in Him, but also to suffer for His sake.
PHILIPPIANS 1:29, NKJV

When I first began to visit India, I was aware that there was persecution against Christians, especially in the northern states. But over the years, the persecution has intensified dramatically.

It used to be that I could conduct open-air meetings and have large gatherings, but now that is no longer possible. The Indian government and fanatical Hindu groups have been opposing Christians more and more. It is a common occurrence to hear of churches being burned, homes of Christians being torn down, and Christians being beaten. Some are even killed.

In one northern state, a law has been passed that if someone leads a person to Christ, the punishment is life in prison. Recently, in the middle of the night, the police in that state went house to house arresting pastors. At three o'clock in the morning, they banged on the doors of the homes, waking the families from deep sleep. Wives and children watched in horror as their husbands and fathers were slapped, beaten, and then dragged away to jail.

In 2023, in the northeastern state of Manipur, hundreds of churches and thousands of Christians' homes were burned down. Hundreds of believers were killed with no repercussions at all.

Many times, militants will enter a church during services and begin throwing acid on the believers or beating them with sticks, driving them out of the church.

In the face of this persecution, my friends say, "Don't pray for it to stop. The persecution is purifying the church. It brings greater unity and righteousness. Pray that we will be fearless and never stop preaching the gospel."

It has been a great honor for me to know so many of these brave Christians who love Jesus so much that they are willing to lay their lives down rather than deny Christ.

One of these brave men is Pastor Ajay.

A Promise Made

I met Pastor Ajay when I was speaking at a pastors' conference in 2015. I always enjoyed doing these conferences, as I would share my story of failure and then my experience of finding God's grace. It always seemed that the pastors could relate to my journey and were deeply ministered to. After finishing my message, Pastor Ajay introduced himself to me. He was slender, wiry, and had a very determined look in his eyes. He held my hand and tears began to fill his eyes as he spoke.

"I have been ministering in my area for more than ten years and we only have a few converts. It has been very difficult, and many times I have considered quitting. Today, your message has given me the determination to seek God and find His grace for my life. Please, I need you to come and minister at my church. We need you to come and help bring breakthrough. How much will you charge to come?"

I looked into his eyes filled with desperate hope.

"No, no, no," I said. "I will never charge money to do ministry. I will come for free, but I am not sure when that will be. Let's pray and see what God will put together for us. Perhaps I can come on one of my next trips to India."

Over time, I must admit I forgot about Pastor Ajay and returned to India several times without contacting him. There were always many people pulling at me to come here, or go there, to minister. In the business of it all, Ajay had slipped from my mind. But he had not forgotten me or his request.

After several years, he met my friend Ashish and found out about our relationship.

"Please, please! You must bring Dan to my place to do ministry!" he told Ashish. Pastor Ajay was very determined and would not take "no" for an answer.

Ashish said to me, "Do you remember meeting a pastor at the conference you did several years ago? He was begging you to come to his place and had asked you how much your ministry would cost?"

"Oh yes, of course. I always wanted to go be with that man," I replied. "Please set up a time for us to go and spend at least four days with him."

Ashish set up the dates and made all the arrangements. I asked Tara to join Ashish and me.

Signs and Wonders

I felt God wanted to honor this man for all the years of fruitless sacrifice he had made. He had been serving God faithfully with little results for so long, but now, God wanted to show up and bring breakthrough.

During our time there, we witnessed some radical miracles. One woman whose neck and shoulder had been broken and not healed correctly was instantly healed. A blind man regained his sight. A man who was dying of AIDS was completely delivered. Miracle after miracle took place as we ministered and prayed those four days. God was validating this man's calling to be the pastor in this village with signs and wonders.

As the miracles manifested, the people who were healed became living witnesses to the love and healing power of Jesus Christ. In a short time, the church began to grow, as many people became followers of Jesus because of the miracles they had witnessed—or had even experienced for themselves.

But with the wonderful news of the church growing, opposition began to come as well. So many people were getting saved that the militant Hindu faction was taking notice and wanted to put a stop to it.

Persecution

The militants began to threaten Pastor Ajay, his family, and members of his church. Pastor Ajay ignored their threats and continued his ministry as normal. Finally, after a few months of threats, a group of men met Pastor Ajay in front of his church.

"We told you to stop preaching here!" they said. "We will not allow you to keep converting Hindus! We warned you again and again. Now we will not warn you anymore!"

The large group of men began to rain down blows on Pastor Ajay with sticks, knocking him to the ground. For nearly a half hour, they slapped, kicked, and beat him as he lay on the ground in a pool of his own blood. Finally, they walked away, thinking they had made their point.

It took Ajay several weeks to recover from his injuries, but the beating did not dissuade him in the least. In fact, the people of his congregation grew even bolder in their faith and surrounded their pastor with more support and encouragement. People continued to become followers of Jesus, and the ministry grew even more.

Ajay continued to fearlessly preach the gospel, and God continued to back it up with signs and wonders, drawing more and more people to Himself.

This only made the Hindu militants angrier, and they were determined to stop this man from converting Hindus to Christianity.

Again, Ajay was confronted by a large group of men, and once more, they beat him mercilessly with their sticks, pounding his face with their fists, and kicking him as he lay in the dirt.

Fearless Determination

Ajay and his wife became more determined than ever not to leave or be silenced. Every night and every morning, they would pray for the souls of the men who were beating him. Every day, he would try to minister to those who despised and hated him.

Then one day, Ajay heard a loud commotion outside his church. He jumped up, concerned because his wife had just left a few moments before. As he came out of the church, he saw a large group of men and women gathered around his wife and threatening her. This time, it was not just a small group of men; this was a mob of more than two hundred people.

Ajay ran to his wife to protect her, but when he entered the fray, the mob immediately became violent and began to beat both Ajay and his wife. It was as if the people had lost all sense of reason and become wild beasts—kicking, hitting, and screaming until Ajay and his wife lay motionless in the middle of the street.

Church members ran to them, picked them up, and placed them in cars to rush them to the hospital. Ajay's wife was beaten badly but had no broken bones. Ajay was unconscious and in critical condition. Day after day, the church members would gather and pray for their pastor. Days turned into weeks as Ajay fought for his life in the hospital.

After nearly two months, Ajay was finally released from the hospital, but the beating had done permanent damage. The right side of his body was paralyzed, and his throat had been so badly damaged that he could not speak.

For the next year, Ajay struggled to recover from the beating, all the while encouraging the church members to remain faithful and to be fearless in the face of opposition. His wife took over the services and preached the Word of God boldly.

Ajay continued to grow worse, and finally, with his family gathered around his bed, holding the hand of his wife, he breathed his last, went to be with Jesus, and joined the great cloud of witnesses that had gone before.

Today, his wife continues to lead the ministry, boldly proclaiming the name of Jesus in that region.

Counting the Cost

Once, many years ago, I heard a man say, "God, why haven't You opened the countries in Asia and the Middle East for missionaries?"

He said he heard the Lord respond, "I am protecting them from Western Christianity."

In the West, many people come to Christ believing He will make things better, that they will be blessed in every area of their lives, and that they will live a life full of joy and prosperity. They believe that if you love God and do what is right, He will protect you and bless you.

In the persecuted countries of the world, this teaching is unthinkable. When they come to Christ, they know they could lose everything. In many countries, people who have become followers of Jesus have had their own families disown or even try to kill them. Some had once been prosperous, and suddenly, they were stripped of everything and on the run for their lives. Sometimes they literally hide in mountain or desert caves.

Some of them, whom I have personally met and interviewed, have been forever separated from their wives and children. Their loss is unfathomable and all due to their decision to become a follower of Christ.

What about my friend Amir in Kashmir? Now, he is a highly respected businessman with connections in the highest places of government. What would happen if he publicly professed his devotion to Christ? He would probably lose everything. His brothers would turn against him. All of his relationships and connections would instantly be gone. His entire network of support that he has built over so many years would be completely lost. He would be an outcast at best, and killed at worst.

And I, as a missionary, how can I casually think Amir would become a follower of Jesus without counting the cost? I think that is the biggest difference between American Christianity and Christianity in the persecuted world. They do not ask, "What's in it for me?" They say, "The truth of Jesus Christ has been revealed to me, and I cannot deny Him."

Americans come to Jesus to receive and be blessed. In India and other persecuted countries, they cannot come to Jesus without counting the cost of what they will lose.

This is why, when I go to these remote places of the earth and bring Jesus for the first time, I do my best not to bring an American Jesus. I do not offer them a Jesus who says, "Come to me and be blessed." I offer them a Jesus who says, "If anyone desires to come after Me, let him deny himself, and take up his cross daily, and follow me" (Luke 9:23, NKJV).

Dietrich Bonhoeffer, a German pastor who was martyred by the Hitler regime in World War II, once said, "When Christ calls a man, He bids him to come and die." This is the Jesus we present to the unreached people of the world. A Jesus who is worthy of our love and devotion, even unto death.

Once, I was with two Indian men who both had been in ministry for many years. Jacob and David had not seen each other since their Bible college days, and rejoiced to meet once again. They chatted excitedly for several moments when, suddenly, they grew quiet, and Jacob looked at David intently.

"I'm surprised you are still alive, brother. I thought you would have been killed by now."

David nodded his head and quietly responded, "God has not found me worthy to die for Him yet."

God found Pastor Ajay worthy to die for Him.

May I also, someday, be found worthy.

FLASHBACK

After three weeks, I moved to Pastor Daniel and Poonam's house. It was long overdue for Samson and Priyanka to get their bedroom back.

Daniel and Poonam's concern for me was overwhelming. This was the couple who, with many of their church members, met my ambulance at the hospital at four in the morning. They had gone the extra mile for me over and over again.

Throughout my stay there, Daniel would bring his neighbors to me to pray for them. There were also several pastors who came to visit and receive prayer. It was a joy to still be able to minister to people even in my weakness.

During that time, to my surprise, Amir flew in from Kashmir to spend a couple of days with me. He had been so concerned that he just had to see me face-to-face. This was the man who had gotten me out of the hospital where the head surgeon wanted to have me arrested. And he was the man who found the best hospital and doctor to do my surgery.

It was a great joy to see Amir. His friendship and love did much to comfort me.

"You came within inches of being killed," he said, looking at me with much compassion.

"Yes," I replied, "but now, because of what I have experienced, I can honestly say I have absolutely no fear of death. I know my God loves me, and I know exactly where I will be when I die. Not only do I not fear death, I almost welcome it."

Amir looked at me strangely. *How could someone say they did not fear death?* "Amir, I came so close to heaven I could almost touch it. I long to go there and be with Jesus someday."

My heart overflowed with love for my friend. I wished he could have the same assurance of heaven as I did.

My daughter Jenni had come from the States to be with me and help me travel. It was a great comfort having her. We had been on many mission trips together over the years, and now it was her honor to come get her wounded dad and help bring him home. It had been almost seven weeks since the accident, and I was anxious to be with Jan again.

After two days of travel, we finally reached the Phoenix airport and went through customs. As they wheeled me to baggage claim, I caught sight of my wife. I stood, leaning on a walker, wrapped my arms around her, and held her tight. With that hug, all the weeks of trauma and pain disappeared. Everything I had gone through was just a distant memory.

God had brought me home.

Chapter 41

Cliff-Jumping Faith

And without faith living within us it would be impossible to please God. For we come to God in faith knowing that he is real and that he rewards the faith of those who passionately seek him.
Hebrews 11:6, TPT

"Joel, I want to jump off a cliff," I stated boldly.

Once again, Joel looked at me like I was crazy. Tara and I were in a part of North India that was famous for paragliding. The high mountains and open valleys, along with the wind currents, made this area very popular for the sport. I would watch with wonder as people jumped off mountaintops with an open parachute behind them, then glide down to the valley floor thousands of feet below. Each time I saw someone do it, I would think, *I want to do that!*

"Pastor, you should not do this. It is very dangerous. Many people have broken their legs, and some have been killed. It is too dangerous, Pastor."

"Joel, have you ever done it before?" I asked.

"No, Pastor, it is too dangerous."

I laughed. "How about you, Tara? Do you want to go jump off a cliff with me?"

"Sure, let's go!" she responded enthusiastically. I loved having Tara as a ministry partner. Her fearless spirit, great faith, and deep relationship with God always made our times in the field so much more enjoyable and productive. Whether it was going into the war zone in Kashmir, doing deliverance in the mountain villages, eating fried tarantulas in Cambodia, riding camels in the Sahara Desert, driving a boat on the Red Sea, climbing Mt. Sinai in the middle of the night to catch the sunrise, or jumping off cliffs, she was always right there, ready to go.

"Come on, Joel, let's do this!"

Joel looked at me, wondering why I was always wanting to do something that could get him killed. Finally, against his better judgment, he agreed, and we headed for the mountains.

After signing the forms promising we would not sue anyone if we died, we jumped into the truck and the driver began our journey up the mountain. He sped around the twists and turns of the dirt road so fast we were all hanging on for dear life. Later, we decided that the ride up the mountain was much more dangerous than jumping off of it!

Finally, we reached the top and stood on the edge of the cliff, looking at the valley floor, thousands of feet below. We knew we were at a very high altitude when we could see the eagles flying below us instead of above us.

Tara got strapped into the harness with the parachute spread out on the ground behind her. The guide strapped in and shouted, "Run, run, run!"

With a yelp of delight, Tara ran headlong and took the leap of faith off the cliff. The brightly colored parachute deployed and she began to slowly glide through the air, catching the mountain breeze.

Joel was next. He was doing his best not to throw up, but he overcame his fear and ran off the cliff with his guide behind him.

It was now my turn. I was strapped into the harness, and my guide shouted, "Run!"

I took a deep breath and laughed as I ran and jumped off the cliff.

As the parachute quickly filled with air, we began to gently float, making a switchback pattern as we slowly descended. The views were breathtaking as my pilot manipulated the parachute to catch the airstream and glide effortlessly like the eagles we had seen earlier. For the next several minutes, I had the best seat in the house with a priceless view, praying over the region until we safely landed.

I think jumping off a cliff has been the story of my life, and really what this book is about.

What If?

Once, a man asked me if I ever wondered, "What if?" What if the parachute was tangled? What if you stumbled and fell off the cliff? What if you landed wrong and broke your legs?

I guess I could have asked a lot of "what ifs" in my life. What if my mom had married a better man? (Then I would not be here.) What if I had been shot in the projects of Chicago? What if I had been arrested for preaching the gospel where it was forbidden? What if the demons attacked me when I went into their high places? What if someone betrayed me and turned me in to the authorities? What if I had died in the mountains when my lungs were collapsing? What if I'd been killed when I hit that truck?

Asking "what if" may seem like sound reasoning; after all, shouldn't a contingency plan be common sense?

The truth is that faith does not have a contingency plan. Trust does not need a contingency plan.

Thinking of the "what ifs" robs me of my faith. It robs me of my courage. Can you imagine David running toward Goliath thinking, "What if. . ."? It would have robbed him of his authority to fulfill the assignment God gave him.

A Faith to Die For

I believe a hallmark of my life is that I know who I am, I know who my God is, and I trust Him with every ounce of my being. This is the foundation that gives me courage, gives me authority, and brings me into my purpose and destiny. Without this foundation, all else is just sinking sand.

Yes, bold, audacious faith can be dangerous, and one can pay a heavy price for it. Every year, thousands of people worldwide die for their faith. Every time a person in a persecuted region becomes a follower of Christ, they jump off the cliff and take a leap of faith.

Playing it safe does not mix with pure, radical faith.

It is one thing to have faith to overcome. It is another to have faith to suffer and not deny the one we are suffering for.

It is one thing to have a Jesus worth living for. It is quite another to have a Jesus who is worth dying for. Paul said, "I want to know Christ—yes, to know the power of his resurrection and participation in his sufferings" (Philippians 3:10, NIV).

This is the faith I long for.

Some people have told me that my motorcycle accident happened because I was not in the will of God. Somehow I had missed Him and opened myself to an attack of the Enemy.

"The devil tried to kill you," they say.

I am not convinced of that.

In 2 Corinthians 12, Paul gives a list of his sufferings: floggings, beatings with rods, imprisonment, shipwrecks . . . on and on the list goes. Interestingly, Paul does not bring up these sufferings to point to his failures in following Christ, but as badges of honor to prove his apostolic authority.

I believe that during every one of Paul's beatings, sufferings, and imprisonments, he was in the perfect will of God.

I still believed—even as I lay in the middle of that road, looking at my broken leg—I was in the perfect will of God.

Being in pain, a time of waiting, or a place of not understanding does not automatically mean you are not in the will of God.

I don't understand why God allows His servants to go through pain. But I do know He uses that pain to create weakness that drives us into His Presence to receive His strength. As Jesus told Paul, "My grace is sufficient for you, for My strength is made perfect in weakness" (2 Corinthians 12:9, NKJV). And because of this, I choose to trust Him fully in every aspect of my life.

He has proven to me again and again that He is faithful and will never leave me or forsake me. He is the God who loves me, died for me, and forgave me. He will never let go of me.

Paul says, "For to you it has been granted on behalf of Christ, not only to believe in Him, but also to suffer for his sake" (Philippians 1:29, NKJV).

My eyes are fixed on Him. My life's verse is: "I have been crucified with Christ; it is no longer I who live, but Christ lives in me; and the life which I now live in the flesh I live by faith in the Son of God, who loved me and gave Himself for me" (Galatians 2:20, NKJV).

I have had the amazing honor of walking with God for more than forty years. That walk has taken me places and given me experiences I could never possibly have imagined. Truly, as I surrendered my life to God and gave up the desire for my own ambitions and glory, I became a spectator of *His* glory. I wouldn't trade that for anything in the world.

The purpose of this book is to challenge you to have radical faith, radical love, and radical abandonment to the God who loves you. It is my prayer that what has been written will prompt you to pursue God with an intensity that will change you and change the world.

I cannot promise you it will be easy or safe, but I can promise that you will live a life of great adventure and purpose. You will also see the will of God manifested in your life and in the lives of those He takes you to.

CLIFF-JUMPING FAITH

The Book of Acts has never stopped being written, so look to see where God is working, go join Him, and start the adventure of writing your very own chapter.

Go! Pray! Jump off cliffs, and pursue God until there's nothing left of yourself. Only then do you truly begin to live.

ABOUT THE AUTHOR

Dan Taylor is the founder and director of 5 Rivers International, a ministry with a passion for unreached people groups. He has traveled throughout Southeast Asia leading prayer journeys since 2011. Dan and his wife, Jan, also minister together with BridgeBuilders International, taking prayer teams throughout their state, training and mobilizing people to pray and contend for revival. They currently live in Phoenix, Arizona, and have three children and two grandchildren.

www.5riversinternational.org

www.ingramcontent.com/pod-product-compliance
Lightning Source LLC
Chambersburg PA
CBHW070127080526
44586CB00015B/1590